THE INFORMATION SYSTEMS SECURITY OFFICER'S GUIDE

THE INFORMATION SYSTEMS SECURITY OFFICER'S GUIDE

Establishing and Managing a Cyber Security Program

THIRD EDITION

DR. GERALD L. KOVACICH

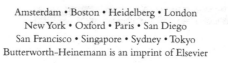

Amsterdam • Boston • Heidelberg • London
New York • Oxford • Paris • San Diego
San Francisco • Singapore • Sydney • Tokyo
Butterworth-Heinemann is an imprint of Elsevier

Butterworth-Heinemann is an imprint of Elsevier
The Boulevard, Langford Lane, Kidlington, Oxford OX5 1GB, UK
225 Wyman Street, Waltham, MA 02451, USA

Notices
Knowledge and best practice in this field are constantly changing. As new research and
experience broaden our understanding, changes in research methods, professional practices,
or medical treatment may become necessary.

Practitioners and researchers must always rely on their own experience and knowledge in
evaluating and using any information, methods, compounds, or experiments described
herein. In using such information or methods they should be mindful of their own safety
and the safety of others, including parties for whom they have a professional responsibility.

To the fullest extent of the law, neither the Publisher nor the authors, contributors, or
editors, assume any liability for any injury and/or damage to persons or property as a
matter of products liability, negligence or otherwise, or from any use or operation of any
methods, products, instructions, or ideas contained in the material herein.

ISBN: 978-0-12-802190-3

British Library Cataloguing in Publication Data
A catalogue record for this book is available from the British Library

Library of Congress Cataloging-in-Publication Data
A catalog record for this book is available from the Library of Congress

For information on all Butterworth-Heinemann publications
visit our website at http://store.elsevier.com/

Working together
to grow libraries in
developing countries

www.elsevier.com • www.bookaid.org

DEDICATION

To all the cyber security officers and information warriors fighting the good fight against all odds.

CONTENTS

Section II: The Duties and Responsibilities of a Cyber Security Officer

Section III: The Global, Professional, and Personal Challenges of a Cyber Security Officer

ABOUT THE AUTHOR

Dr. Gerald L. Kovacich graduated from the University of Maryland with a bachelor's degree in history and politics with emphasis in Asia, the University of Northern Colorado with a master's degree in social science with emphasis in public administration, Golden Gate University with a master's degree in telecommunications management, the DOD Language Institute (Chinese Mandarin), and August Vollmer University with a doctorate degree in criminology. He was also a Certified Fraud Examiner, Certified Protection Professional, and a Certified Information Systems Security Professional.[1]

Dr. Gerald L. Kovacich has more than 40 years of experience in industrial security, investigations, information systems security, and information warfare as a special agent in the U.S. government; a technologist and manager for numerous technology-based international corporations; and an information systems security officer, security, audit, and investigations manager, and consultant to U.S. and foreign government agencies and corporations. He has also developed and managed several internationally based information systems security programs for Fortune 500 corporations and managed several information systems security organizations, including providing service and support for their information warfare products and services.

Dr. Gerald L. Kovacich has taught both graduate and undergraduate courses in criminal justice, technology crimes investigations, and security for Los Angeles City College, DeAnza College, Golden Gate University, and August Vollmer University. He has also lectured internationally and presented workshops on these topics for national and international conferences, as well as writing numerous published articles on high-tech crime investigations, information systems security, and information warfare, both nationally and internationally. He has written more than 100 security-related articles that have been published in various international magazines.

[1] Now retired from all three.

Dr. Gerald L. Kovacich currently spends his time on Whidbey Island, Washington. He continues to conduct research, write, consult, and lecture internationally on such topics as:

- Global and nation-state information systems security;
- Corporate information systems security;
- Corporate and government fraud;
- Corporate security;
- High-tech crime investigations;
- Information assurance;
- Proprietary information protection;
- Espionage—including "Netspionage," economic, and industrial; and
- Information warfare—offensive and defensive.

He is also the founder of ShockwaveWriters, an informal association of trusted cyber security and global information warfare professionals, writers, researchers, and lecturers who concentrate on these topics. He can also be found on LinkedIn.

Dr. Gerald L. Kovacich has begun to expand his writings into the world of poetry and fiction. I guess this is what happens when one "matures" in age and longs for writing genres other than that of the security realm. All his writings can be found on the usual Web sites, for example, amazon.com.

OTHER BOOKS AUTHORED OR COAUTHORED BY DR. GERALD L. KOVACICH

1. *Information Systems Security Officer's Guide: Establishing and Managing an Information Protection Program* (Elsevier; 1998; ISBN: 0-7506-9896-9), Kovacich
2. *Information Systems Security Officer's Guide: Establishing and Managing an Information Protection Program* (second edition; Elsevier; 2003; ISBN: 0-7506-7656-6), Kovacich
3. *High-Technology Crime Investigator's Handbook: Working in the Global Information Environment* (Elsevier; 2000; ISBN: 13: 978-0-7506-7086-9; 10: 0-7506-7086-X), Kovacich/Boni
4. *High-Technology Crime Investigator's Handbook: Establishing and Managing a High-Technology Crime Prevention Program* (Elsevier; 2006; ISBN: 13: 978-0-7506-7929-9; 10: 0-7506-7929-8), Kovacich/Jones
5. *The Manager's Handbook for Corporate Security: Establishing and Managing a Successful Assets Protection Program* (Elsevier; 2003; ISBN: 0-7506-7487-3), Kovacich/Halibozek

6. *The Manager's Handbook for Corporate Security: Establishing and Managing a Successful Assets Protection Program* (Instructor's Manual) (Elsevier; 2005; ISBN: 13: 978-0-750-67038-1; 10: 0-750-67938-7), Kovacich/Halibozek

7. *I-Way Robbery: Crime on the Internet* (Elsevier; 1999; ISBN: 0-7506-7029-0), Kovacich/Boni

8. *Netspionage: The Global Threat to Information* (Elsevier; 2000; ISBN: 0-7506-7257-9), Kovacich/Boni

9. *Information Assurance: Surviving in the Information Environment* (Springer-Verlag; 2001; ISBN: 1-85233-326-X), Kovacich/Blyth

10. *Information Assurance: Security in the Information Environment* (second edition; Springer-Verlag; 2006; ISBN: 10: 1-84628-266-7; 13: 978-1-84628-266-9), Kovacich/Blyth

11. *Global Information Warfare: How Businesses, Governments and Others Achieve Global Objectives and Attain a Competitive Advantage* (Auerbach/CRC Press; 2002; ISBN: 0-8493-1114-4), Kovacich/Jones/Luzwick

12. *Global Information Warfare: How Businesses, Governments and Others Achieve Global Objectives and Attain a Competitive Advantage* (second edition; Auerbach/CRC Press; 2015; 9781498703253), Kovacich/Jones

13. *The Corporate Security Professional's Handbook on Terrorism* (Elsevier; 2008; ISBN: 978-0-7506-8257-2), Kovacich/Halibozek

14. *Mergers and Acquisitions Security: Corporate Restructuring and Security Management* (Elsevier; 2005; ISBN: 0-7506-7805-4), Kovacich/Halibozek

15. *Fighting Fraud: How to Establish and Manage an Anti-Fraud Program* (Elsevier; 2008; ISBN: 978-0-12-370868-7), Kovacich

16. *Poems of Life: Thoughts of Human Experiences* (AuthorHouse; 2012; ISBN: 978-1-4772-9634-9; 978-1-4772-9633-2; 978-1-4772-9632-5), Kovacich

17. *I-Way Robbery: Crime on the Internet* (2000; Japanese Translation; http://www.horei.com; ISBN: 4-89346-698-4), Kovacich/Boni

18. *High-Technology Crime Investigation* (2009; Chinese Translation; http://www.sciencep.com), Kovacich/Jones

19. *Fighting Fraud* (2010; Russian Translation; Ernst & Young; ISBN: 978-5-903271-31-30), Kovacich

20. *The Corporate Security Professional's Handbook on Terrorism: Protect Your Employees and Other Assets against Acts of Terrorism* (Elsevier; 2007; ISBN 978-0-7506-8257-2), Jones A, Kovacich G, Halibozek E.

PREFACE

The purpose of this book is to provide information systems security officers—today often called cyber security officers, professors, students, other security professionals, information warfare specialists, related managers, auditors, and general management an awareness and basic approach to establishing and managing what had been known as an information systems protection program, but is now commonly called a "cyber security" program, for a government agency or international or national corporation. It can also be used by any group wanting to protect its networks and information. It reportedly has been, and can always be, used as a textbook by university professors to teach a basic course on this and related topics, as well as recommended reading for related courses.

It provides, I hope, an easy-to-read, understandable implementation plan for establishing a basis—a foundation—for a cyber security program, especially for those who have little or no knowledge on the topic or how to proceed. It also provides information that can be used by intermediate and advanced professionals, students, and other types of professionals in this and related topics of business security and information warfare, for example, defensive measures.

There are many books on the market related to computer security, information systems protection, cyber security, and the like; however, this is one of the first and best approaching the topic in the manner that it does and is now considered a "classic" since first published in 1998. If not, there wouldn't have been a second and now a third edition.

This book has been updated where deemed appropriate and new chapters have been added, with little or no major change in format, as why mess with a well-selling, popular "classic"?

Just so there is no misunderstanding, this a *basic* book on building a cyber security program and a primer on being a cyber security officer. There is much in this edition that is as true today as it was in the first edition back in 1998. Therefore, the basics of it all are still the same, with new stuff added to keep this "classic" up to date.

This third edition, as with the past two editions, will provide the reader with the information to help meet the twenty-first century cyber security and related management challenges.

Key words, as a minimum, that the reader should know are:
1. Security
2. Cyber security
3. Cyber security officer
4. Computer security
5. Information systems security
6. Information warfare
7. Auditing
8. Managing assets protection
9. Managing information systems organization
10. Managing computer security organization
11. Assets security
12. Audit trails
13. Information protection
14. Privacy
15. Malware
16. Hacker
17. Phishing

As with any book, sometimes the readers are critical. That's fine. Variety is the spice of life, as they say, and everyone is entitled to their own opinion. If one can sit down and discuss cyber security and cyber security officers' responsibilities with the critics it would be great to share information. After all, they may have important points that could be considered when updating the book. However, that is usually not possible.

So, with all that said, let me state for the record what this book is not:

- It is *not* a book that is the "end all and be all" of a cyber security officer's functions, duties, and responsibilities. The rapid changes in cyber environments, high technology, etc., make such a book impossible to remain current.

  Note: In this environment, beware of anyone considering themselves "experts." I, for one, confess I have never considered myself one (although working in the field since 1980) and correct anyone who introduces me as such. Nor will I ever consider myself to be one. Too much to know and all rapidly changing.

- It is *not* a technical book and does not purport to be—it will not tell you how to install a firewall, for example. The rationale is that there are many good books on the market that cover specific aspects of cyber security, narrowly focused and technical. It is expected that the cyber security officer will read and understand these books as needed based on specific cyber security needs.

In short, this book's goal is to provide a basic overview of the cyber security officer's world, duties, responsibilities, and challenges in the twenty-first century. It is a primer. It is also about the cyber security officer who must establish and manage a cyber security program for an international corporation, although all of the material is applicable to various work environments, such as government agencies or charitable organizations.

This is the third edition of this book and has been updated where appropriate, and where the baseline still fits the current environment, it has only been "tweaked," as what has been provided from the beginning is still valid today. This is primarily relevant to Section II, which is the heart of the book, and the establishment and management of a cyber security (formerly known as InfoSec) program. What was written in the first and second edition is still valid in this third edition. Therefore, it has been modified, but the basics of what is covered have not changed. What has changed is the environment of the world of the cyber security officer. Therefore, that was the focus of the changes in this third edition.

It was written because over the years many associates and I had to establish and manage such organizations and found no primer to guide us. So, over the many years that I have been involved in various aspects of security, eventually focusing on cyber security—and its related functions since about 1980—I think I have developed a basic approach that has been successful. Others who have read this book, who have listened to my lectures based on what became this book, and whom I have mentored over the years have agreed with me. It also successfully worked for me when I had to establish a basic program for a corporation or government agency, from aerospace to Wall Street to the Pentagon, as well as being a consultant.

So, if you are a cyber security "techie," "engineer," or the like and looking for the Holy Grail of information assets protection or cyber security, that is not what this book is about. However, if you want a cyber security officer career, want to know what the cyber security officer's profession is all about—especially from a management perspective—and want to be able to build a foundation for a successful cyber security program and organization, then yes, this book is for you.

This book was also written for non-cyber security professionals in management positions who are responsible overall for a government agency or business and therefore its assets protection–cyber security program. These professionals should also know what the cyber security profession is all about and the basics of information-related computers and networks processing, transmitting, and storing information, data, knowledge, or whatever term suits them. Why? Because they manage a business, and today a successful business must include a cyber security program if it is to avoid disasters, since technology, for example, networked computers, is an integral part of a business these days.

This book can also be used as a textbook or "recommended reading" for university courses related to general security, assets protection, cyber security, information systems security, or information warfare (although my coauthored book on *Global Information Warfare,* first and second editions, may better serve the reader's purpose).

I hope you enjoy it. After reading it, please drop me an e-mail through my publisher and let me know:

- Any questions you may have;
- What you liked about it;
- More importantly, what you didn't like;
- Why you liked or disliked it;
- What ideas presented were most important to you;
- Your implementation of some of the ideas presented, and your result; and
- What I should include or cover differently in a fourth edition.

After all, I want you to be able to use this book in the real world of global information sharing, cyber warfare, and cyber security battles. All feedback is welcome.

Thanks!

Jerry
Dr. Gerald L. Kovacich, ShockwaveWriter
Whidbey Island, Washington, USA

ACKNOWLEDGMENTS

Writing a book is only part of bringing a book to you, the reader. As with any book project of this magnitude, to carry out a project such as this, it takes more than just the author. It takes friends, professional associates, and others who unselfishly give of their time and effort to help make the author's writing life easier and his or her books worth publishing.

I am also very grateful to a special group who over the years have supported, encouraged, and assisted me time and again with such projects as this, including the following friends, associates, and colleagues:

- Motomu Akashi, my mentor and a great sage; rest in peace my dear friend.
- Ed Halibozek, security professional, professor, writer and consultant, former fellow aerospace colleague, and longtime friend.
- Dr. Andy Jones, cyber security and InfoWar professional, professor, writer and consultant, and also a great friend.
- William Boni, vice president and corporate security information officer, T-Mobile Corporate, a friend for almost longer than the Internet has been around.
- Winn Schwartau, The Security Awareness Company, a good friend.
- Steve Lutz, CEO, WaySecure, fellow professional and longtime friend.
- To the staff and ISSO-3 project team of Elsevier Butterworth–Heinemann, led by Tom Stover and including Hilary Carr and Mohanapriyan Rajendran thanks for the time, effort, and support in making ISSO-3, and my other BH books, a reality and success. Without your support and guidance this book truly could not have been written.

INTRODUCTION

Much has happened and yet, little has changed![1]

There are many debates as to where the information and information systems security (InfoSec), now generally referred to as cyber security, and the information systems security officer (ISSO), now commonly referred to as the cyber security officer, position fit in a company or government entity. Some believe they belong in the information technology (IT) department, others say they belong in the security department. Others believe the position should report to the corporate executive officer (CEO), corporate information officer (CIO), or some level of executive management other than the two mentioned.

The IT people may want control of the cyber security function so that they can ensure that it does not hamper their IT functions—in other words, dilute its authority—and over the years have been successful, and we all know how well that has been working.

A corporate security manager may want the function to be sure these valuable assets, like other assets whose protection is the responsibility of the security department, are properly protected.

Some of my friends and fellow cyber security and business/government security professionals, with different backgrounds and cyber security responsibilities over the many years they have been in the business, share their views on cyber security and the cyber security profession, environment, and functions. They are:

- Ed Halibozek, security professional, professor, writer, and consultant;
- Dr. Andy Jones, cyber security and InfoWar professional, professor, writer, and consultant;
- William C. Boni, Vice President and Corporate Security Information Officer, T-Mobile Corporate;
- Steve Lutz, CEO, WaySecure, fellow professional and long-time friend.

---

[1] Author's thoughts but feel free to quote me. :)

WHAT OTHER CYBER SECURITY PROFESSIONALS HAVE TO SAY

William C. Boni

Information security is one of the fastest growing professions at this time. The combination of the terrorist attacks of September 11, 2001, and the increasingly critical role of information systems and technology in global business have contributed to that increase. As this book was being written, the Internet was subjected to an attack against the core infrastructure, terrorists and nation-states are reported to be honing their skills for future cyber attacks, and criminals are siphoning off profits from electronic commerce systems around the globe. There has never been a greater need nor greater appreciation of the need for capable, skilled information security professionals to guard the frontiers of businesses and nations.

Yet, as the importance of information security has increased, the field has become crowded with "instant experts." Many of those who now call themselves "experts" owe their current notoriety to some specific technical skill or to short periods of time in consulting or vendor organizations. Most who publish books and articles on information security have never been accountable for protecting major organizations against the dizzying array of risks nor dealt with the harsh realities of doing so in the context of corporate cultures, politics, and the grind of daily operations.

In contrast, you hold in your hands a book containing the distilled wisdom of 40 years of practical experience from one of the original leaders in information security. Dr. Gerald L. Kovacich, "Jerry" to his many friends and admirers, has spent a lifetime developing and perfecting the materials that are the core content of this book. The original has held up over the years precisely because it is "technology independent." The assumption is that the reader has either attained already or can obtain, from other books, courses, and seminars, the technical skills to work in the information security field.

Therefore, if you are looking for technical solutions to the current or latest set of acronym challenges, then this is not the book you want to buy. However, if you are an information security professional seeking to understand what it takes to be successful as a manager and to become a leader in your organization and ultimately in the profession, then you have the right book.

Students considering their career options, as well as professionals in other but related fields such as IT, physical security, or IT audit, will also find the information presented so artfully by Dr. Gerald L. Kovacich to be of great value. Readers from all these backgrounds will find this book expands their knowledge of the many activities involved in establishing and sustaining an organization's information security program.

This updated and expanded edition builds upon the content that made the original volume one of the best-selling security books ever published. What the *Guide* does that is different, perhaps unique in the information security field, is coach, mentor, and tutor the reader in the various managerial and operational skills that will ensure a more successful and ultimately more satisfying career.

From my personal experience I can testify to the practical wisdom that is captured in these pages. I owe a significant part of my professional success and achievement to actually applying many of the methods and techniques described in the original *Guide*. Over the past six years I have recommended the previous edition to countless aspiring information security professionals, and note with satisfaction that many found the content to be key to their successful participation in the rapidly burgeoning information security profession.

Understand that a keen appreciation and lifelong commitment to information technology will be required for success as an information security practitioner. However, much as that background is necessary, it alone is not sufficient for professional success and personal satisfaction. Those who aspire to leadership and seek to become the managers, directors, and vice presidents of information security in the future will enjoy and learn much in the *Guide* that will support their success. I believe they will find, as I have, that Dr. Gerald L. Kovacich has provided them with knowledge that better prepares them for the challenges of managing these important responsibilities.

Ed Halibozek

Make no mistake about it. Information security is critical to the success of a business. Whether the enterprise is for profit or not for profit, protecting information is an essential part of managing information and information systems. Modern companies, corporations, and governments, for their success and survival, are dependent upon information: information that is created, processed, stored, and shared. Yet the act of creating, processing, storing, and sharing information makes that same information vulnerable to loss, manipulation, theft, or destruction.

Whether information concerns a new product or technology, a proprietary process, a business plan, a customer or donor list, or military operations, information has value to its owner. That same information may also have value to competitors, criminals, or enemies. Some will take bold measures to obtain information. Others will rely on the failure of organizations to adequately protect their own sensitive and proprietary information, making it easy for unauthorized collection and use. A few will seek to obtain information any way that they can, using legitimate or illegitimate means.

The very information that contributes to the viability and success of an enterprise, if unprotected and found in the possession of competitors or enemies, may cause the loss of a competitive edge or the embarrassment of exposure or, in the event of military operations, may place war fighters in "harm's way." Thus, protecting the availability, confidentiality, and integrity of information is an essential task.

In this book, Dr. Gerald L. Kovacich addresses the question, "Is the position of an ISSO necessary?" Bluntly, unless your goal is failure, the answer is clearly "Yes." Protecting information is not an easy task. So much information resides on sophisticated and complicated information systems linked in local and wide area networks. To effectively and efficiently protect information and information systems requires the skills and dedication of a security professional: an ISSO.

The ISSO must be skilled in the disciplines of management, security, and information systems; must be capable of convincing others of the need to protect information; and must understand that protecting information is more about risk management than it is about risk avoidance. The ISSO needs to understand how information is used in the context of the world and business environment in which we operate. This includes understanding threats and where they come from, such as competitors, detractors, enemies, opportunists, and "bad guys."

A skilled ISSO is essential to any enterprise. However, an ISSO is not the only answer or solution. Understand that the ISSO is not an übermensch. The ISSO alone cannot do everything that needs to be done to protect information. The ISSO must be capable of bringing together diverse persons with divergent interests in an effort to develop a protection profile for the enterprise. In this book, Dr. Gerald L. Kovacich provides the architecture to do just that. He provides a framework for establishing an effective information protection program.

Regarding the debate as to where an ISSO should report in the organization hierarchy...stop! Now is not the time for debate. Now is the time to act. Information security is serious business. The protection of information is just as serious as the management of information. In today's organizations most company information is processed, stored, displayed, and transmitted on and over information systems. CIOs are skilled executives employed to ensure that information systems are effectively managed, meeting the needs of the enterprise and making information available to all users. Protecting this information and its availability, integrity, and confidentiality is just as important. A skilled executive is needed to accomplish this—a corporate security officer (CSO). The CSO is someone knowledgeable in matters of security, information protection, information systems, and business management. The CSO should be independent of the CIO and report directly to the CEO or corporate operations officer. Separating the CIO function from the CSO function is important, as the need to protect information is often in conflict with the need to share and disseminate information. The ISSO should either report to the CSO or be the CSO.

Let's end the discussion on the need for information protection and the need for an ISSO. One would have to be a resident of Plato's cave to not realize that information is critical to a business and requires protection. Let's shift our focus to understanding just what requires protection, how it should be protected, and from whom. Using this book by Dr. Gerald L. Kovacich is a very good beginning.

Dr. Andy Jones

The role of the ISSO has never been of greater importance than in the environment in which we currently find ourselves and which we anticipate for the future.

As organizations and companies continue to become more dependent on information systems and connect to an ever wider group of partners that they have to rely on and "trust," the probability that they will encounter problems increases on an almost daily basis. In addition to this increasing reliance on systems that are increasingly interconnected, it is now an unfortunate reality that those people who would seek to do us harm increasingly have the knowledge and capability to do so.

For a number of years, the governments of a number of countries have been aware that there are some industries and systems that are essential to the well-being and maintenance of normal life within a country. These may include power production, telecommunications, water supply, food distribution, banking and the financial sector, and a whole range of other industries and have, together, been tagged the critical national infrastructure. It is unfortunate for the ISSOs of these industries that in addition to all of the other risks that they must deal with, they now have to be concerned that they will be a target of attack by terrorists and others who wish to affect not their organization, but the government. This makes life a whole lot more difficult in a number of ways.

Some organizations are starting to better appreciate the implications of these developments and are recognizing that the role of the ISSO is not only increasingly important, but also increasingly difficult. Unfortunately, others have not taken the situation on board for an often repeated, endless set of reasons that have caused them to ignore it in the past. These include a lack of understanding of the underlying problems, a lack of skill to address them, insufficient resources, the "it won't happen to me" attitude, a lack of education and training, and a lack of direction from government.

The last of these has changed significantly in the recent past, and there is now a will by the governments of most developed countries to improve the security of information systems. This is particularly true of the United States, and huge investment has been made in "Homeland defense," with an apparently genuine drive by government to make information-dependent countries a safe place to live and trade.

One of the major problems that an organization faces in recognizing the need for an ISSO is based on the undeniable truth that in most cases, security is a costly drain on resources, in both financial and staff terms, that delivers no tangible return on the investment. If you are a member of the board of a company and have to make the choice between investing in a new plant that will reduce production costs and improve profitability and investing in information security, which is likely to get your vote? This is often the decision that must be made, especially when the argument for "spend on information security" is based largely on the intangible and the unprovable. How do you prove that you are likely to be attacked or have security problems, when the evidence from past experience is that it has not been a problem before? How does the person presenting the argument for the information security investment convince a group of people who have probably never suffered the consequences of an information security breach that this is good value for money? If the members of the corporate board have been involved in a previous breach of information security, the investment argument will be received in a very different manner and by people who understand the value of it.

What is different about an ISSO from other types of security officers? Well, the short answer is that the ISSO is a hybrid that did not need to exist in the past. Security officers have traditionally gained their experience in the military or in government or public service (police or three-letter agencies) and they can tell you all about protecting tangible "things," whether they are objects or people. They are normally very good at it and the methods, tools, and techniques that they use have all been tested and refined over a long period of time.

Because the security of information systems cannot and must not be treated in isolation, the ISSO needs to have all of this knowledge and then, in addition, needs to be able to understand information systems and computers and the implications of their use. In this area, there is no collective pool of knowledge that has been gained over centuries by a large group of people. Information systems are, in historical terms, very young, and their maturity has taken them through so many evolutions in such a short time that there are very few computer professionals, let alone security specialists, who are able to keep pace with the changes and the diversity that have occurred. So the ISSO needs to have a wealth of knowledge and experience in security and in information technologies and has to be able to develop, implement, and manage policies that will protect the information resources of the organization in a dynamic environment.

A complication now arises. Where people will complain about physical security and will subvert it if it becomes too inconvenient and complain about the delays that the checking of passes and locked doors will cause, when you apply security to the information environment, a whole new set of problems is exposed.

The users of information systems have been exposed to and suffered from years of badly conceived and implemented information security that has caused inconvenience and prevented them from getting on with their job. It is a sad comment that, in the field of information security, the user of the system has often had more knowledge of the information technology than has the "security expert."

The bright side of the situation is that things are improving—the "information security experts" within organizations are gaining experience and the technologies that can help them to provide coherent security for systems are becoming available. The whole issue of threat and risk assessment is gaining credibility as methods are developed that give traceable routes to support the decisions that are made.

In the global context, while things proceed at a very slow pace, there are at least discussions on ways to harmonize the laws in different countries and groups of countries and the exchange of information between those who need it to maintain security.

It is easy for information security officers to become very insular and to look at the problems that they are facing in terms of only their organization—after all, these are busy, overworked people who are struggling just to keep pace with events and developments. This is a huge mistake and can lead only to disaster in the long term. We can no longer, for the most part, "conduct our business in isolation." The organizations that we work in have an ever-increasing need to communicate and to interconnect with other systems and organizations and in doing so, we have to be aware of the problems that such connections expose us to.

Learning from the best practice that has been developed in other organizations provides two benefits: The first is that it allows the knowledge of many to be applied to the problem of one; and the second is that it is one step down the line toward common standards and practices, which engenders confidence in others that the security that is being applied to your systems is of an acceptable standard (they can understand what you have done to make your systems secure and why you have done it!).

When the larger picture is examined, the responsibility that is placed on an information security officer is immense. The ISSO has a responsibility and a duty to the organization that the ISSO works for, but also has responsibility to partner organizations and others that may rely on the product of the organization. An example of this might be a power company, in which the effect of a security breach might be the loss of availability of their systems. Unfortunately, the power supply company is networked to a number of other power suppliers to facilitate the balancing of power production to meet the customer needs. If one is affected, it may prove to be the weak link in the chain and allow the attacker to gain access to other power suppliers. There is also the issue of the customers—what impact will the loss of power supply have on their businesses? In turn, will it have an effect on their customers?

From the ISSO's point of view, life can only get worse. In some countries, laws are being introduced that place a legal obligation on organizations and their employees to take what is referred to as "reasonable" (or in some cases "appropriate") care of information that they have in their possession and also to take "effective measures" to protect the business, sometimes referred to as "due diligence."

How can ISSOs cope with doing the job of developing, implementing, and managing the security of the information while at the same time making sure that they understand the current risks and threats to their organization and the current technologies and techniques and the laws and best practice and standards? Well, no one ever said it would be easy...

Gone forever are the good old days when we could operate with an island mentality and rely on the perimeter security of our organization to provide the first and main line of defense. The security perimeter is now almost meaningless with regard to our information, although it still has some benefits for the protection of physical assets. Now the routes into our organization are as much about the wires and fibers as they are about the roads and sidewalks. We can monitor physical access to our environment with a variety of technologies (CCTV, access control, pass entry systems) and we can also, fairly effectively, monitor what our staff is doing on our information systems (as long as we have the monitoring systems turned on and are watching them). We can put our security barriers up on the information systems (firewalls), but unless we deploy methods and tools to allow us to see what activity is taking place in our environment through systems such as intruder detection systems, we cannot see what is happening in the area around our "virtual office." The nearest equivalent would be having the external doors locked, but not having any windows or cameras to let you see what is happening on the sidewalk outside the door (a potentially dangerous situation for when the door is opened, given that our door on an information system opens onto a sidewalk anywhere in the world).

It is also reasonable to suppose that, after the World Trade Center attacks, there is increased consciousness of the impact that a terrorist attack can have. It is a sad fact that in addition to the lives that were lost as a result of the outrage, a number of organizations that could and should have survived the incident did not, as they could not reinstate their business within the necessary period of time. Who was responsible for their demise? You could argue that it was the terrorists, but the reality is that it was actually their own lack of foresight and resilience and, in some cases, just plain bad luck. If the organizations had all carried out risk assessments for their businesses in the environment in which they were operating, more would have taken steps to ensure that they had taken action on very old advice—have backups and store them in a safe place in another location, have contingency plans and practice them. As the ISSO, part of this is your responsibility—how are you going to ensure that your information is stored securely elsewhere and that you can recover it when you need to?

The life of an ISSO can never be an easy one—you are the voice of doom and authority within an organization that says "No" to users who want to do things that to their mind are quite reasonable. You are the one who acts as their conscience and highlights or investigates their sins, and you are the bearer of bad tidings to the board (you need more investment to keep the systems secure, or you have just had a security incident and are reporting the damage). You are the one who is responsible for the security of the "crown jewels" of the company. So why would you want to take on this role? Well, the answer is that it is one of the most satisfying and rewarding roles that you can imagine. It should never be boring, and there will usually not be the same problems to tax your intellect twice. It also allows you to use and develop skills in an area where you can make a difference and to contribute to a struggle that is becoming increasingly fast-moving and ruthless. It can be a hugely satisfying role, for those who can survive the apprenticeship and can accept the responsibility while maintaining a balanced view of the world.

Steve Lutz

The demand for information security consulting has been steadily increasing since 2005, and for good reason. As everyone got on the technology bandwagon in the 1990s, the pressure increased to find innovative ways to deploy technology and increase productivity. The business community "discovered" the Internet and grand proclamations were made about the obsolescence of "brick and mortar" to be replaced by "e-commerce." While much of this was overhyped, the race was on and "time to market" became one of the anthems of the new economy.

So in the frantic race to beat the competition, technology was deployed with little thought to security. Indeed, people had just enough time to get whatever it was working, let alone secure it in any meaningful fashion. And then *pow*, some security breach was discovered and it had to be fixed fast. In the rush to put the Web site or whatever together, no one budgeted for security, and there's nobody in-house with the expertise to handle it. Enter the information security consultant. Since it wasn't budgeted for in the first place, it's an out-of-cycle approval from management, and there you are trying to secure a system that has deep design flaws from a security perspective with an obscenely small budget. You explain that to really do it right, a complete redesign is in order. Yes, we understand, and no, we can't do that. "It's a production system," "Our competition will kill us," "We don't have that kind of budget for security," and so on. With a sigh, you do the best you can to place some security Band-Aids on it and advise them to call you before the next design meeting for version 2.0. Guess what happens when v2.0 is released? Same thing.

This cycle repeated itself for pretty much the entire "dot-com" era, with some exceptions. Some of the more forward-thinking companies hired consultants for security architecture and design work and saved themselves a whole lot of money and headaches. Still, the InfoSec consultants had more work than they could handle. (The same was probably true in the 1920s for radio engineers.) One good thing that came out of the 1990s was raised awareness of the role that information systems security plays in a successful technology deployment. Oh, and there are now hundreds (thousands?) of companies offering security products for every conceivable problem.

Now that the party is over and technology has fallen back to being just another business tool, what will this mean for information systems security consultants? Virtually all companies have cut back on their IT spending and are focusing on using what they've already overbought. Part of the hangover is that companies have had to lay off significant numbers of people across the board, including IT. Lean and mean, baby. Now it's time to take stock of what we did during the frenzy and see if there's anything we missed. Did we buy enough servers? Yes, we've got plenty. Networking? Yup, plenty of that. Web sites? Got 'em. There was something we missed, though…What was it? Something critical…Oh, yeah! That security thing. OK, get somebody on it. Oops, we laid them off. Hmm, can we hire someone? No way, there's a hiring freeze on. Well, we better call a consultant then.

And that's where we're at now. Information systems security consulting is doing quite well in these times and mainly for those reasons. A lot of what we're seeing is going back over everything and locking it down. That's great, but where is it going? I think that this will continue for some time during the economic downturn. At just about the time the retrofitting work is done, the economy will probably heat up again and companies will start buying IT again. When that happens, we InfoSec folks will be there to secure the next generation of information technology. Let's just hope everyone does it right the next time around, rather than rushing into every project just to get it out there fast.

The Working Environment of the Cyber Security Officer

Section I (Chapters 1–5) provides an introduction, an overview, of the ever-changing world in which today's cyber security officer must work. This section is composed of five chapters, titled as follows:

- Chapter 1: Understanding the Past and Present Cyber-Information World Environment
- Chapter 2: Understanding the Past and Present Global Business and Management Environment
- Chapter 3: An Overview of Related World Views of Cyber Security
- Chapter 4: A Glimpse at the History of Technology
- Chapter 5: Understanding Today's Threats in the Cyber Vapor—"War Stories" from the Front Lines

CHAPTER 1

Understanding the Past and Present Cyber-Information World Environment

This is a terrible time of unwanted liberties

Sandy Nichol[1]

Contents

Chapter Objective

The objective of this chapter is to provide a general overview of the cyber-information-dominated and information-technology-dependent and constantly changing global environment in which the cyber security officer must work.

---

[1] Sandy Nichol is a freelance editor based in the United Kingdom.

The Information Systems Security Officer's Guide

AH, THE GOOD OL' DAYS!

Yes, much has happened and yet, little has changed.

What has not changed are the threats, vulnerabilities, and risks to information and information systems. What has changed is the level of sophistication of the threats—the attacks and the threat agents—as well as the exponentially growing number of them all over the world and from various sources.

Information[2]:
1. Facts provided or learned about something or someone.
2. What is conveyed or represented by a particular arrangement or sequence of things.
   2.1. *Computing* Data as processed, stored, or transmitted by a computer.

[2] Oxford Dictionary.

We have gone from an environment of young hackers with a 300-baud external modem, writing hacker programs in BASIC, looking for dial-up tones, to a world of extremely sophisticated attackers, from government agents to organized crime groups to terrorists. Yes, the teenage hacker and "computer enthusiast" is still out there among the threat agents a cyber security officer must face; however, compared to the others out there now, one only wishes for some of the good ol' days when such hackers were the greatest threat to information and systems.

Even so, it is important to understand the environment in which today's cyber security officer must do battle—and yes, it is a battle, and yes, we are at war and should be on a war footing. However, we are not, and thus, we are losing to those threat agents who are attacking our systems and destroying our information, or stealing our information, 24/7.

We live in a world of information, known these days as cyber information, computer information, the information environment, or the like. More than ever, the world wants to talk to the world about anything and everything. In fact, the world now demands it at an unprecedented scale and is doing it at a level never seen before. Thus, vulnerability types and numbers have also continued to increase.

Furthermore, the users that the cyber security professional must support and defend do not want to be tied down to any physical location. Today's users, which basically means pretty much all of the technology-driven world and increasingly those in the Third World, who may not have running water but do have a cell phone and increasingly Internet and other network connections, want—demand—it all, with mobile capabilities!

Information is pulled, pushed, dragged around the world through wireless, cable, optical fiber, satellite, and other assorted physical and increasingly more than ever mobile devices—and all of us along with it. We are dependent on information as individuals, companies, and government agencies. In fact, has that not always been the case? It's just that now, it is in a cyber form more than ever.

In days gone by, information was communicated by word of mouth, by drums, by smoke signals, in writing carried by couriers on horseback, by telegraph, by telephone, and now through the use of high technology.

The difference today is that in the "modern" countries of the world, we are more dependent on information and the high technology that allows us to communicate and do business, globally, at the speed of light. Today, more than ever, information—accurate information, and more of it, delivered faster—allows one an advantage. More than ever, this applies not only to companies—especially the increasing number of them going or trying to go global to take advantage of opportunities for new customers—and to governments of nations, but also to groups and individuals. We have all been sucked into the quicksand of technology dependency.

Fast, accurate, and complete information that is secured and protects privacy—yeah, good luck with that one—is what is demanded; however, it is seldom realized these days as our identity, networks, and information are hacked, sold, and misused. The old saying "information is power" is probably more true today than ever before.

> Information of greatest value must be:
>   Accurate, acted upon correctly, and acted upon before it is used by the adversary, e.g., a competitor, another government, etc.

Remember that if the information you need is on an information system that is a victim, for example, of a successful denial-of-service attack, important information could not get to you or others at the right time so that you or they could use that information to your advantage; this may have serious consequences in terms of lives, money, or other negative factors.

Understanding Your Information-Driven Environment

As a cyber security officer, it is very easy to get caught up in high technology and view that as "your world." After all, in today's high-technology-driven and high-technology-dependent world, and one can also say cyber world, it is very easy to look at information and high technology as your working environment, as what causes your problems, and as where the solutions to your problems lie. However, the truth is that high technology is just a tool like any other tool. And as with any tool, it can be used as intended, abused, or used for illegal purposes—by people.

It seems that we are so focused on the information and technology for answers to cyber security and mitigating risks, we forget our first priority should be the people who are using and abusing these systems and information. It is especially necessary to focus not only on the outside threat agents but also on those people who have authorized access to those systems and information.

In today's information world environment that a cyber security officer must work in, it is much more than just high technology. You, as a cyber security officer, must understand this world and also us humans, as all these topics have a direct bearing on the protection of information and information systems—cyber security. They include such things as:
- Global and national marketplaces;
- Global and nation-states' economies;
- International politics;
- World cultures and societies;
- International and national laws and treaties;
- Major languages of the world;
- Major religions;
- Business;
- Human relations and psychology; and
- Governments of nation-states.

To be successful, the cyber security officer should have a varied background not only in such things as computer sciences but also in psychology, criminology, social science, geopolitical matters, international business, world history, economics, accounting, and finance. Also, the more foreign languages the cyber security officer knows, the better. Volumes have been written about each of these topics. It would behoove the cyber security officer to have a working understanding of each of these topics, as they all affect the cyber security officer's ability to successfully establish and manage a successful cyber security program. There are few professions today that offer the challenges that face the cyber security officer, whether that person is in a government agency or business—no matter what country or business that person works for.

Cyber security officers must understand the world in which they will work in order to be successful. In the past, this understanding was generally limited to the company or government agency in which that person worked, and to its computer systems, which were isolated within the company or government agency or even just in one's home. The cyber security officers generally were once concerned only with the events that took place within their respective working environment or living environment or even just within their country, as what happened outside of that limited world usually did not affect their work or life. However, that was in the past.

> If you know the enemy and know yourself, you need not fear the result of a hundred battles. If you know yourself but not the enemy, for every victory gained you will also suffer a defeat. If you know neither the enemy nor yourself, you will succumb in every battle.
>
> **Sun Tzu**

The environment of the cyber security officer that may affect the protection of information and information systems is now global in scope, and high technology and global networking are changing more rapidly with each passing year. This new global environment and its associated high technology must be clearly understood. This is because it is all integrated into a driving force that will dictate what must be done to protect the information systems and the information that they store, process, display, and transmit. It will also determine how successful the cyber security officer's information systems security program, now generally referred to as cyber security program, will be in providing protection at the lowest cost to the business or government agency.

Today's computer system environments—networks that span the globe—are all based on the microprocessor. Microprocessors have become cheaper and more powerful at the same time. This is the primary cause for their proliferation throughout the world. Some say that today's cell phone has more computer power than the computer systems in the vehicle that landed on the moon.

When we think of computers, we sometimes look at them as very complicated devices, when in fact it is not that difficult to understand the basics at least. Computers are composed of hardware, the physical pieces; software, the instructions to the computer, which can be altered; and firmware, which are instructions embedded on a microprocessor. The process includes input, process, output, transmit, and storage. Your cyber security program can be broken down into these elements and each looked at to defend as a separate entity and then in a holistic manner.

> There is a rumor going around that at least one nation-state involved in computer building and sales has embedded into the firmware a code that allows that nation-state to gain access to that sold computer, bypassing security software, when it wants.
>
> It was also rumored that, in the past, there have been covertly installed electrical outlets that allowed the manipulation of the electrical current to turn a desktop computer on, download information, and turn the system back off. Some say that was valid only some years ago; however, today's modern systems have eliminated that risk.

Of course the more a cyber security officer knows about how hardware, firmware, and software work, the better position that person will be in to protect those systems and the information they process, store, display, and/or transmit.

In many of today's information-based nation-states, we have been able to network thousands of systems because of the rapid advances in high technology and cheap hardware. We have built the information systems of the nation-states' businesses and government agencies into major information infrastructures some call national information infrastructures. A stand-alone computer system (one with no external connections between it and other computers) today is relegated to a small minority of businesses and government agencies. We cannot function in today's business world and in our government agencies without being connected to other information systems—both national and international.

The protection of information systems and the information that they process, store, display, and/or transmit is obviously of vital concern in this information world. Many nation-states are already in the Information Age, progressing into what some call the "Knowledge Age," with many other nation-states now entering the Information Age and yet many more close behind. This will obviously complicate the problems of the cyber security officer, as in this case the phrase "the more the merrier" describes something a cyber security officer does not want to deal with, because it means more threats, more vulnerabilities, simply by connecting to their systems.

> The cyber security officer must remember that the cyber security program must be service and support oriented. This is of vital importance.

The cyber security officer must understand that the cyber security program, once it is too costly, is outdated, and does not meet the service and support needs of the business or government agency, will be discarded or ignored. So, one of the cyber security officer's challenges is to facilitate the networking of systems nationally and internationally while protecting company information and systems, but mitigating the risks in a cost-effective manner.

To provide a cost-effective cyber security program, the cyber security officer must continually keep up with high technology. That person must be familiar with technological changes in general and intimately familiar with the technology being planned for installation within his or her business or government agency.

The cyber security officer must understand how to apply information protection (cyber security) and integrate it around, and onto, the new high technology. Failure to do so would leave the information and his or her systems vulnerable to attack. In that case, the cyber security officer would have a serious problem—possibly a job security problem—if a successful attack occurred owing to the new-found vulnerability brought on by the newly implemented technology.

> Management in businesses and government agencies will hold the cyber security officer responsible for any successful attacks, whether or not it was management or the technical staff that was clearly responsible for the vulnerability that allowed the successful attack. Such is the nature of the position.

The cyber security officer could delay installation of the new high technology until a suitable information protection "umbrella" could be installed. However, in most businesses, this would be considered a career-limiting or career-ending move. In today's business world, the phrase "time is money" is truer than ever. In today's and tomorrow's highly technology-based environment, innovation and flexibility are key words for the cyber security officer to understand and apply to the company's or government agencies' information protection program.

Thus, the cyber security officer has very little choice but to support the installation of the new high technology and incorporate information protection as effectively and efficiently as possible. And one of the ways to successfully provide that service and support is to keep up with technological changes.

GLOBAL INFORMATION INFRASTRUCTURE

The importance of information protection continues to grow, as we become more and more dependent on high-technology systems. The networking of systems around the world is continuing to expand the global information infrastructure (GII). Today, because of the microprocessor and its availability, power, and low cost, the world is "building" the GII. The GII is the massive international connections of world computers that are carrying business and personal communications as well as those of the social and government sectors of nation-states. Some say it could connect entire cultures, erase international borders, support "cyber economies," establish new markets, and change our entire concept of international relations.

The GII is based on the Internet and much of the growth of the Internet. The GII is not a formal project; rather, it is the result of the need of thousands of individuals, corporations, and governments to communicate and conduct business by the most efficient and effective means possible.

The importance of information protection takes on added meaning because of the increased threats to the systems and the information they store, process, display, and transmit owing to this expanded connectivity provided by the GII. After all, it will come as no surprise that there are people and nation-states in the world that consider your company and your country an adversary—the enemy. That being the case, they will do whatever they can to meet their own objectives—generally at the expense of your company or nation-state.

NATIONAL INFORMATION INFRASTRUCTURE

The national information infrastructure (NII) is basically the network of computers upon which the nation-state and its people rely in this information–knowledge age. The NII is the high-technology, critical information infrastructure of a nation-state. The critical infrastructures, according to several nation-states, are generally defined as systems whose incapacity or destruction would have a debilitating impact on the defense or economic security of the nation-state. They include:

- Telecommunications,
- Electrical power systems,
- Gas and oil,
- Banking and finance,
- Transportation,
- Water supply systems,
- Government services, and
- Emergency services.

Many have been sounding the alarm for some time now of the vulnerability to and the catastrophic results of some adversary such as terrorists hacking into such systems and setting off a nuclear meltdown, opening the floodgates of dams, and other catastrophes.

HOW DID WE GET FROM ADAM TO THE INTERNET?[3]

The use of the Tofflers' model of technological evolution provides a useful framework for discussing changes arising from the impact of technology, generally, and the Internet specifically. For those of you who have never heard of Alvin and Heidi Toffler, read their books. Yes, they were written maybe before you were born, but the Tofflers are excellent futurists who looked into the future, which is now ours, and their books point to where we have been and what may be coming.

The model begins by describing the Agricultural Age, which lasted from about the time of Adam until about 1745 in the United States. Manual labor and a focus on accumulating a minimum food surplus to allow for governance characterized this long period. During this time, technological progress was very limited, slow, and laborious. The major lack of understanding of even the most basic concepts of science impeded progress.[4]

---

[3] This information was taken from the author's coauthored book, *Internet Robbery: Crime on the Internet*, published by Butterworth–Heinemann.

[4] The time of the agricultural period varies by progress of individual nations.

Warfare, although common, was generally short in duration and was often decided by major battles or campaigns lasting less than a year, with some exceptions, such as the Hundred Years' War and the Crusades. Although large armies were possible (at one point the Roman Empire fielded more than 700,000 soldiers), there were limited and relatively ineffective methods for communicating and controlling more than a small percentage of these forces. Runners and horse-borne message couriers supplemented by flags and other visual media were the major methods of remote communication.

The "Industrial Age," in the United States, lasted a much shorter time, only from approximately 1745 until about 1955. The defining event of the Industrial Age was the introduction of the steam engine, which allowed mechanical equipment to replace muscle-powered efforts of both humans and animals. These devices introduced a new and much accelerated pace of technical innovation. During this 200-year period, there was a dramatic expansion of human knowledge and understanding of the basic principles of physical science. Enhanced agriculture allowed nations to accumulate huge food surpluses. Upon the foundation of the food surplus, the nation-states increased their power, which was driven by mass production. Mass production of weapons and the mass slaughter of both combatants and noncombatants characterized the conflicts of this period.[5]

Communications technology evolved from primitive signaling involving lanterns and reflected lights (heliograph) to supplement the continued use of human couriers, whether riding horses, trains, or waterborne craft. The inventions of the telegraph in the early 1800s, followed in the late 1890s by the telephone and then by wireless radio in the early 1900s, were essential evolutionary steps toward today's telecommunications infrastructure.

The "Information Age" in the United States, according to the Tofflers, began about 1955, which is the first year that the number of white-collar employees exceeded the number in blue-collar production jobs. This has been the era with the most explosive growth in human knowledge. More has been discovered in the past 50 years in both science and engineering than in the thousands of years of recorded human history. In the information age, knowledge is growing exponentially.

The pace of evolution in communications and other technologies accelerated during the early years of the Information Age with the advent of

---

[5] As with the Agricultural Age, dates vary for individual nations.

satellites, fiber-optic connections, and other high-speed and high-band-width telecommunications technologies.

It is in the context of this phenomenal growth of technology and human knowledge that the Internet arises as one of the mechanisms to facilitate sharing of information and as a medium that encourages global communications.

In the past, the U.S. General Accounting Office, in a report to Congress, detailed the rapid development of the telecommunications infrastructure in the United States, resulting in the creation of three separate and frequently incompatible communications networks:[6]

- Wire-based voice and data telephone networks,
- Cable-based video networks, and
- Wireless voice, data, and video networks.

From that past until now, look how far we have come, and imagine, as a cyber security officer, what is yet to come. It behooves all cyber security officers to always project into the future and plan now to address the future environment in which the cyber security officer will work and wage war again all adversaries to their networks (hardware, software, information, data, users, and other entities) for which they are responsible.

Birth of the Internet[7]

It is vital to understand the history and ever-changing environment if the cyber security officer is to succeed in fulfilling all duties and responsibilities through a cyber security program that defends his or her networks against "all enemies, foreign and domestic."

The global collection of networks that evolved in the late twentieth century, and continue to evolve in the twenty-first century, to become the Internet represents what could be described as a "global nervous system," transmitting from anywhere to anywhere facts, opinions, and opportunity. However, when most security and law enforcement professionals think of the Internet, it seems to be something either vaguely sinister or of such complexity that it is difficult to understand. Popular culture, as manifested by Hollywood and network television programs, does little to dispel this impression of danger and out-of-control complexity.

The Internet arose out of projects sponsored by the Advanced Research Project Agency in the United States in the 1960s. It is perhaps one of the

---

[6] "Information Superhighway: An Overview of Technology Challenges." GAO-AIMD 95-23, p. 12.

[7] See the book *I-Way Robbery: Crime on the Internet*, published by Butterworth–Heinemann, 2000, and coauthored by Dr. Gerald L. Kovacich and William C. Boni, for more details about the Internet and criminal activities.

most exciting legacy developments of that era. Originally an effort to facilitate sharing of expensive computer resources and enhance military communications, over the 10 years from about 1988 until 1998 it rapidly evolved from its scientific and military roots into one of the premier commercial communications media. The Internet, which is described as a global metanetwork, or network of networks, provides the foundation upon which the global information superhighway will be built.[8]

It was not until the early 1990s, however, that Internet communication technologies became easily accessible to the average person. Prior to that time, Internet accesses required mastery of many arcane and difficult-to-remember programming language codes. However, the combination of declining microcomputer prices, enhanced microcomputer performance, and the advent of easy-to-use browser software created the foundation for mass Internet activity. When these variables aligned with the developing global telecommunications infrastructure, they allowed a rare convergence of capability.[9]

It has now become a simple matter for average people, even those who had trouble programming their VCRs, to obtain access to the global Internet and with the access search the huge volume of information it contains. The most commonly accessed application on the Internet is the World Wide Web (Web). Originally developed in Switzerland, the Web was envisioned by its inventor as a way to help share information. The ability to find information concerning virtually any topic via search engines from among the rapidly growing array of Web servers is an amazing example of how the Internet increases the information available to nearly everyone. One gains some sense of how fast and pervasive the Internet has become as more TV, radio, and print advertisements direct prospective customers to visit their business or government agency Web sites.

An important fact to understand, and which is of supreme importance for security and law enforcement professionals, is that the Web is truly global in scope. Physical borders as well as geographical distance are almost meaningless in "cyberspace"; the distant target is as easily attacked as a local one. This is an important concept for security and law enforcement professionals to understand because it will affect their ability to successfully do their jobs. The annihilation of time and space makes the Internet an almost perfect environment for Internet robbers. When finding a desired server located on the other side of the planet is as easy and convenient as calling directory

[8] *Ibid.*, p. 11.
[9] Software that simplifies the search and display of information supplied by the World Wide Web.

assistance to find a local telephone number, Internet robbers have the potential to act in ways that we can only begin to imagine. The potential bonanza awaiting the Internet robber, who is undeterred by distance, borders, time, or season, is a chilling prospect for those who are responsible for safeguarding the assets of a business or government agency. As the ISSO, you have responsibility for deterring these miscreants, as well as helping security and law enforcement personnel investigate them.

"Future Shock"

With appreciation for the Tofflers' book *Future Shock*, the reaction of people and organizations to the dizzying pace of Internet progress has been mixed. Although some technologically sophisticated individuals and organizations have been very quick to exploit the potential of this new technology, many have been slower, adopting more of a wait-and-see posture. The rapid pace of evolution of the Internet does raise some questions as to how much a society can absorb and how much can actually be used to benefit organizations in such a compressed time frame. Sometimes lost in the technological hype concerning the physical speed of Internet-enabled communications or the new technologies that are making it easier to display commercial content is the reality of the Internet's greatest impact: It provides unprecedented access to information. The access is unprecedented in terms of the total volume of information that is moving online and may be tapped for decision-making.

It also is unprecedented when we consider the increasing percentage of the world's population that enjoys this access. More and more information moves online and becomes available to more and more people, causing fundamental changes in how we communicate, do business, and think of the world we live in. Consequently, there are also fundamental changes in how criminals and miscreants commit crimes.

Throughout much of human history, the educated elites of every culture have jealously guarded their knowledge. Access to knowledge, whether in written or spoken form, was often the source of the elite's privileged position and often allowed them to dominate or control the great uninformed masses of uneducated humanity—information was and still is a means to power. "Outsiders" were never granted accesses to the store of wisdom unless they were inducted into the privileged elite. Now, however, the average Internet traveler, wherever resident, with little more than a fast modem and a mediocre microcomputer, can access, analyze, and/or distribute information around the world on almost any topic.

Some pundits decades ago had concluded that we now live in an era in which there are "no more secrets." By some estimates, early in this century there will be more information published and available online than has ever been accessible in all the libraries on earth. How this torrent of information will be managed to ensure that Internet robbers do not wreak havoc and dominate the Internet, or have power over others, is now (or should be) the primary objective of every security and law enforcement professional whose business or government agency travels the Internet.

So, what do you think of our current environment? Are we winning or losing the cyber security battles and wars?

Road Map for the Internet

The Internet can be compared in some ways to a road map for a superhighway. Some basic examples will help explain it in common terms.

When multiple computers (whether microcomputers or larger) are linked together by various communications protocols to allow digital information to be transmitted and shared among the connected systems, they become a network. The combination of tens of thousands of organizational networks interconnected with high-capacity "backbone" data communications and the public telephone networks now constitutes the global Internet. However, there is a major difference in this environment that is important to consider for security and law enforcement professionals.

When the isolated byways of individual business or government agency networks become connected to the global Internet, they become an "off-ramp" accessible to other Internet travelers. The number and diversity of locations that provide Internet "on-ramps" are vast and growing. Today, one can access the Internet from public libraries, cybercafés in many cities around the world, even kiosks in some airports. These and other locations provide Internet on-ramps to anyone who has a legitimate account—or an Internet robber can hijack one from an authorized user.

Typically a business or government agency will use centrally controlled computers, called servers, to store the information and the sophisticated software applications used to manage and control its information flow. These systems could be equated to a superhighway interchange.

Commonly business and government agency networks are considered private property and the information they contain as proprietary for the exclusive use of the organization. These business and government agency networks are connected to large networks operated by Internet service providers who provide the equivalent of toll roads and turnpikes—the highways for the flow of information.

The Internet: No Traffic Controls

The Internet challenges the security and law enforcement professional with an array of new and old responsibilities in a new environment. From the perspective of managing risks, this new access to information creates new kinds of dangers to businesses and government agencies. It also allows well-understood security issues to recur in new or unique ways. No longer can organizations assume they will obtain any security through obscurity, no matter where they are physically located. In other words, because there is an Internet off-ramp, they will be visible to Internet robbers. Everything from a nation's most critical defense secrets to business information is vulnerable to easy destruction, modification, and compromise by unauthorized Internet travelers.

Too often careless managers fail to take adequate measures to safeguard sensitive information, which results in premature disclosure with attendant adverse impact. The major part of the controllable risk arises from inadvertent disclosure to the ever-vigilant eyes of Internet robbers and others, such as competitive intelligence analysts with Internet access.

When the Internet was limited to scientists, academic researchers, and government employees, such a collaborative framework was probably a very cost-effective means of controlling the virtual world. However, in the early 1990s, for the first time there were more commercial sites than educational and governmental sites using the Internet. Since that time matters have become increasingly complex. The informal array of social sanctions and technical forums for cooperation is no longer capable of ensuring a modicum of civilized behavior.

What Has Been the Impact of the Internet?

It is apparent that the Internet has rapidly become a significant element in modern society, figuring in advertising, films, and television, even facilitating the rapid dissemination of investigative reports involving a U.S. president. The Internet has provided many additional information services, and they are all becoming easier to access. The two primary new avenues for increased volume of information access are the Web browser and net-enabled e-mail. This increased access to information has been principally an advantage for law-abiding citizens and legitimate businesses, but it also offers both hardened and prospective Internet robbers new, high-speed venues for perpetrating their crimes and schemes.

Almost everyone working in America has been exposed to some form of computer technology. From the front-line retail clerk at the local fast-food franchise, to the Wall Street analyst, to the farmer planning his crop rotations, individual work performance has been substantially enabled by the widespread proliferation of microcomputer technologies. But the macro impacts on organizations are in some ways less remarkable than they have been for individuals. Go to any good computer store, or better yet, if you have Internet access, browse the Web sites of major microcomputer manufacturers. You will discover a wide range of systems with memory, speed, and storage capabilities that would have been descriptive of large, mainframe-type computers in the early 1980s. For example, a large regional bank in southern California in the late 1980s operated its electronic wire/funds transfer machine with only 48 MB of RAM and 120 MB of disk storage, and the system transferred billions of dollars nightly for the bank. Now a much greater performance is available to anyone with a few hundred dollars in a cell phone.

In business, it has become in some ways a David versus Goliath world, in which the advantages do not always accrue to the organization that can field the bigger battalions. Advanced information technology was once the province exclusively of governments, the military, universities, and large corporate entities. This is no longer true. Now anyone with a modest investment in hardware and software can acquire a powerful processor and attach it to the Internet. It should be obvious that criminals and those with criminal intentions also have access to powerful information technology. The question remains: How will they use it?

As we consider the potential for criminal actions directed against organizations, it is critically important to consider these factors. The same information technology we use to manage our organizations can and will be used by savvy Internet robbers to the detriment of governments, businesses, and others.

When powerful microcomputers are networked, the communication capabilities inherent in these arrangements multiply their value. A single microcomputer standing alone is little more than a sophisticated typewriter or calculating machine. The real power comes when individual machines link together to create networks that will allow the flow of information from one person to the entire world. As a case in point, consider the story of Russia's transition from communism. When the military coup against Gorbachev occurred in the early 1990s, the military plotters seized control of all the classic means of communication: newspapers, telephones, and radio and TV stations. However, the anti-coup forces quickly drove their message on the Internet to get word to the outside world of the situation, and timely communications played a significant part in defeating an attempt by the most powerful military and police apparatus on earth to regain power over the Russian people.

The capabilities brought to the individual by the Internet are considerable and growing almost daily. One example is the ability to sign up for investment services from low-cost brokerages and stock market advisors and enjoy the kind of timely advice that for generations has been the perquisite of the rich and powerful classes. Grass-roots political organizing and civic action are also enabled. For example, in California, a concerned parent scanned into a database and posted on a Web page the details of the state's list of sexual predators/pedophiles, thus allowing average people to determine whether there was a registered sex offender residing in their neighborhood.

From shopping for homes and automobiles, where online services promise to eliminate the brokers' monopoly of information, to traffic, weather forecasts, and directions prior to trips, the Internet is providing more information to more people every day, and we are only at the beginning of that process! The major trend here is clear: There will be more information accessible to more people than has ever been possible in the past. How this information power will be used ultimately depends on the ethics and motives of the individual: Internet robbers can use such power negatively.

Organizational Impacts

The major benefits to organizations of the Internet and related technologies are significant and far ranging. In large part, the impacts may be characterized as dramatically lower costs for transmitting and sharing information. To appreciate how far we have come, before electronic mail became ubiquitous, it took as long as a week for first-class postal mail, derisively called "snail mail" by Internet aficionados, to travel from one coast of the United States to the other. Even the fax machine, which itself was a significant improvement over postal and overnight courier services, requires dedicated fax equipment and operates only from point to point. Contrast these with the capabilities of Internet e-mail. E-mail, which may transit the globe in seconds, allows the recipients to obtain the message when it is convenient; they need not be present to receive it. Through the use of digital attachments, e-mail can carry more information in a convenient compression of transmission times.

Whereas the innocent e-mail user sees only increased speed and volume of communication, security and law enforcement professionals must understand how damaging even one message could be to a business or government agency. A single e-mail message could contain the whole strategic business plan of the organization or the source code to a breakthrough product and could be transmitted anywhere on earth in a nanosecond.

To show that this threat is much more than theoretical, consider the allegations involving two leading Silicon Valley software companies, A and B. Company A accused rival Company B of theft of trade secrets and proprietary source code. Company A's management alleged as one element in their complaint that a former Company A employee used his company-provided Internet access to transfer source code of key products to his own, personal account. The employee then tendered his resignation. Upon arrival at his home-based office, the now-former Company A employee allegedly downloaded the stolen source code to his home computer system. Employed as a programmer consultant by rival startup Company B, he reportedly used the purloined source code as the foundation for a remarkably similar product created at Company B.[10]

Another example is a former employee of Company X who was accused of transmitting the source code for a new digital device to rival Company Y. This scheme apparently was discovered only by accident when the highly confidential materials created such a long message that it caused the e-mail system to crash and allowed a system administrator to discover the purported scheme.

These two incidents are drawn from press reports in the media, and it is likely that they are only the very tip of the iceberg. In fact, many organizations do not have the security systems and technologies to detect similar incidents. Because of the adverse publicity and the prospect of a lengthy criminal justice process, even those businesses and government agencies that have been victimized by Internet robbers frequently do not report similar incidents to the proper authorities.

Using the Internet to Share Information

One of the truly remarkable developments in information technology has been the widespread use of the Web browser and related technology to deliver information both to internal employees and to the external

---

[10] Although based on actual cases, the names have not been used because, as of this writing, the cases are still being adjudicated through the criminal justice process.

customers of an organization. If e-mail could be described as a virtual dupli-
cation of the postal services into the global Internet environment, then Web
servers can be thought of as kiosks or bulletin boards. On these "virtual
bulletin boards," an organization can make accessible to target populations
the information they need to make decisions and perform administrative,
operational, or other functions. For example, one very common intranet
(internal company Internet) application is to provide a central "forms page"
on which employees find the most current version of a form to be downloaded and printed for everything from payroll deductions to medical reim-
bursements. Another use is to front-end a database in which is stored
information that must be accessible to a widely dispersed population of
users or broad cross section of Internet travelers.

Currently the most common and growing destination for the Internet
traveler is the business or government agency Web site. For the Internet
traveler, Web sites are a combination of superhighway billboards, banks,
shopping malls, rest stops, and even fast-food delivery services. All of these
services as well as hundreds of others can be found located at the on- and
off-ramps to the Internet.

These Web sites are used by businesses for advertising, public relations,
and marketing, as well as to sell or deliver products or services to Internet
travelers.

Web sites may contain and dispense government information concerning everything from how to prepare and submit forms, to descriptions of
the most wanted criminal fugitives, to recruiting advertisements for future
employees. Even the most secretive U.S. government agencies such as the
Central Intelligence Agency, the National Security Agency, and others have
established Web sites that provide useful information to Internet travelers.

Business and government agency Web sites are often the targets of miscreants, juvenile delinquents, and other Internet robbers. Successful attacks
against these Web sites can be disruptive and destructive of the reputation of
the sponsoring organization. Therefore the protection of the Web site
should be an important part of the business or government agency plan for
using this technology.

CHANGING CRIMINAL JUSTICE SYSTEMS

Thus far, it appears that information protection will increase in importance.
If so, the world's criminal justice systems and processes undoubtedly will
also be affected. The question is, will they change for the better or for the

worse? If the United States is any indication, they will worsen. Why, in such a technologically advanced country? Ironically, technology brings with it rapid social change as well.

One may wonder, what is the impact of the criminal justice system on the cyber security officer and cyber security. The answer is simple: The people who steal business or national secrets; damage, destroy, or modify information and systems; and commit other criminal acts are the main reasons the cyber security officer and information protection program exist. After all, if no one violated laws or company policies, and everyone protected information and systems, why would businesses or government agencies need a cyber security officer or an information protection program?

At some point in your career, you will become involved in a high-technology crime investigation and thus will become actively involved in the criminal justice system. You must understand how that system operates, or you will not only be at a disadvantage, but probably disappointed as well!

In the global marketplace that your company undoubtedly works in and is affected by, you as the cyber security officer must understand the international and foreign nation-state laws that have an impact on your business, especially those related to privacy and security. For example, your company may operate in a foreign country. If so, that country's government may not allow the encryption of transmissions through their country. If this is the case, do you violate that law, understanding its entire ramifications, to protect company secrets, or do you not encrypt and understand the risks of others reading the "company mail"?

As society embraces the Third Wave, as described by the Tofflers, it does not wait for the two prior waves' processes to catch up. Thus, one can see the continuing trend of a disintegrating U.S. criminal justice system in which crime increases faster than the criminal justice system can deal with it. More discretionary arrests, plea-bargaining prosecutions, overburdened court systems, and the release of convicted criminals from jails and prisons are indications of this change to a Third Wave society. We seem to be trying to use Second Wave criminal justice system processes and functions to handle Third Wave problems, and it does not seem to be working.

One of the disadvantages of being a leading technology-based country such as the United States is that one does not have the opportunity to learn from the mistakes of others who are more advanced. This is an extremely important point, especially when discussing the criminal justice system, because the criminal justice system is the primary system responsible for the prevention of crime and the promotion of social stability of a nation.

If a nation is to be strong economically to compete in the world, it must have stability in which businesses can operate and people can have a secure and peaceful life. Lack of security and peace leads to increases in crime. It follows that high-technology crimes would be likely to increase. In addition, without a good criminal justice system, frauds and other crimes not only will be more frequent, but also will sap the economic strength from the people, businesses, and the country.

We know that technology is increasing at a rapid rate. Computer-based technology has become a necessary and integral part of businesses, government agencies, and our personal lives. No longer can we efficiently function without the use of today's modern, computer-based technology.

As with any tool, computers, including telecommunication systems, can be a target or used as a tool by criminals, also known as techno-criminals. The threats to society, businesses, and government agencies by techno-criminals are increasing as our technology and our dependence on technology increase.

The techno-criminals, vis-à-vis the world's criminal justice systems, are also faced with a system that provides them some measure of immunity to techno-crimes. For example, the attacks against U.S. computer systems are becoming more internationally oriented. Today's techno-criminal can attack any place in the world from any place in the world.

What is worse, because of our complicated communication systems, it is difficult to trace the attacks back to the attackers. Also, many countries' laws do not even address the issue of techno-crimes, making it almost impossible to prosecute anyone attacking a U.S. computer from outside the United States. And because of the political ramifications alone, extradition of these attackers to the United States, or any other country, for prosecution is a complicated and generally impossible task! After all, what nation-state wants to give up sovereignty over its citizens?

For the cyber security officer, it is imperative to understand the criminal justice systems of the United States and other countries in which the company or government agency does business. The problems with the criminal justice systems, conflicts, and changes, will continue to be an underlying force whose impact on information protection functions will extend into the twenty-first century.

The fact that white-collar crimes, frauds, are being perpetrated more and more through the use of computers and telecommunications systems seems to be an obvious result of the rapid changes in societies and our reliance on information systems. This is understandable, as alluded to earlier, because what once was done by paper and pencil has now been automated, for example, accounting systems. Therefore, although today's criminals have the same motive as in the past, they must now operate in a new environment, a technological environment. If criminals want to steal money, they must use and attack information systems. To paraphrase an old-time bank robber: "Because that's where the money is!"

Since it appears that more crimes are being committed by using the computer as a tool to attack other computers, and that trend is likely to continue, the cyber security officer's responsibilities include an information protection program, which will assist in minimizing the opportunities for frauds and other crimes through the systems. If such crimes do occur, it is expected that the cyber security officer will play a vital role in the investigation and in any disciplinary action or prosecution of the offenders—thus offering another challenge and opportunity to the cyber security profession.

THE HUMAN FACTOR

With all the talk of high technology, the need for information protection, computer crimes, and the like, there is one important factor to remember. It is the human being who uses the tools for good or bad purposes, and it is the human being whom the cyber security officer often loses sight of when trying to protect information and high technology.

Yes, it is true that for the cyber security officer to be successful, that person must understand not only information systems—computers and their associated networks—but also other forms of high technology, for example, cellular phones, faxes, and pagers. However, one must never lose sight of the human element—usually the most neglected factor in information protection. To be sure, one talks about information protection awareness programs, but the human factor must be addressed in more detail and given more emphasis if the cyber security officer is to protect information.

Laws, Regulations, Standards, and Legal Issues

There are many laws and government regulations such as those related to protecting the stockholders' interests in publicly traded corporations in which you may work. There are too many of them to discuss here, except to say that just because a law or regulation exists, it does not mean that the entity where you work is complying with them. Therefore, it is important to determine what the laws are, and to do so, one should develop a working relationship with the corporation's legal staff.

After all, you must be in compliance with the laws, so obviously, you first must know what they are. In addition, knowing them and working with the legal staff will help support your case to executive management when you show the connection of why you are running a cyber security program or particular parts of it. You should be able to get the legal staff to support your case by having them explain what happens when you do not safeguard the corporate owners' assets. Yes, assets protection insurance is one way to handle risks; however, the corporation must still be in compliance. An insurance corporation should obviously demand it, as security would still be required.

As the cyber security officer, you should search the Internet and identify such laws and regulations. There are also international standards to consider. Know them and implement them in a cost-effective manner using risk management/risk analyses methodologies.

ISO/IEC 27001[11] is the international standard for information security management. By implementing the standard, organizations can identify security risks and put controls in place to manage or eliminate them, gain stakeholder and customer trust that their confidential data are protected, and help achieve preferred supplier status, helping to win new business.

[11] bsigroup.com.

Another example is from the National Institute of Standards & Technology (The Framework Core):

The Framework Core is a set of cyber security activities and references that are common across critical infrastructure sectors organized around particular outcomes. The Core presents standards and best practices in a manner that allows for communication of cyber security risk across the organization from the senior executive level to the implementation/operations level. The Framework Core consists of five functions— Identify, Protect, Detect, Respond, Recover—which can provide a high-level, strategic view of an organization's management of cyber security risk. The Framework Core then identifies underlying key categories and subcategories for each of these functions and matches them with example informative references such as existing standards, guidelines, and practices for each subcategory. This structure ties the high-level strategic view, outcomes, and standards-based actions together for a cross-organization view of cyber security activities. For instance, for the Protect function, categories include Data Security, Access Control, Awareness and Training, and Protective Technology. ISO/ IEC 27001 Control A.10.8.3 is an informative reference that supports the subcategory "Data during transportation/transmission is protected to achieve confidentiality, integrity, and availability goals" of the Data Security category in the Protect function.

SUMMARY

To be a successful cyber security officer, you must:

Understand today's world of business, politics, various cultures, people, threat agents, technology—in other words the world of external forces that have an impact on your working world.

Understand your corporation or government agency and its culture, people, policies, laws, regulations, international and nation standards, procedures, attitudes relative to cyber security, systems, processes, political dynamics—everything there is to know about your government agency or corporation.

CHAPTER 2

Understanding the Past and Present Global Business and Management Environment

Contents

Chapter Objective

The objective of this chapter is to provide the reader with a basic understanding and philosophy of cyber security within the business environment, including how to communicate with management in "their language."

> As we transition from the Information Age to the Knowledge Age, successful organizations are the ones that actively manage their information environment.[1]
>
> [1] Quote from my coauthored book with Dr. Andy Jones, Global Information Warfare, second edition, published by CRC Press.

This combines old and new aspects of this environment, as it is important to know the past as well as the present, as that combination of knowledge of today's environment is where the cyber security officer works, lives, and plays. The past provides a look down the road traveled and helps explain the logic used to get to the present. Furthermore, it provides the foundation on which the cyber security officer can project and plan a cyber security program that will meet the current and future needs of the business and the expectations of management.

THE CHANGING BUSINESS AND GOVERNMENT ENVIRONMENTS

Businesses and the societies in which they operate need stability to prosper. Prosperity brings jobs, reduces crimes, and leads to more security for all. Security brings more stability. You can't have one without the other.

Many of the changes in the world environment are the basis for the rapid shifts in the way we do business, both nationally and internationally. Businesses can, and do, adapt to these changes quite rapidly. However, in government agencies, these changes come more slowly and sometimes threaten the agencies' very existence. For example, a day may come in the not too distant future when the post offices of the world will be unnecessary. E-mails may take the place of letters even for the poorest people of the world, as they will have access to Internet networks. As for packages, commercial firms such as DHL, FedEx, and UPS have already been providing that service for some time. Even contracts these days are electronically signed and there is no need to mail hard copies. However, to be legal, they must be secured to stand up in court.

Clear examples of these changes are the "global marketplace," business-to-business networks, electronic commerce, electronic business, and the like.

Massive, growing networks such as the Internet, national information infrastructures (NIIs), and global information infrastructures (GIIs) are adopted, and must continually be adapted, by businesses if they are to maintain a competitive advantage—or at least compete—in today's marketplace. As a cyber security officer, you must find ways to facilitate such growth in a secure and yet invisible manner. That is a challenge for all of us in the profession.

As a cyber security officer, if you try to slow down business and global communications, you will be run over by "progress" and will soon be updating your resume. Business comes first, and if you do not provide a professional cyber security service that supports and enhances the business, what good are you? After all, business is about profits—and remember, you are a "parasite" on the profits of most companies, since your function is identified as an overhead cost.

There is some business, for example, with government agencies, for which the cyber security function is a direct charge to the contract. The problem is that one must meticulously keep track of time spent on the contract work, as charging to a contract when not working on that specific contract results in a fraud against the government, which in turn could lead to being investigated, never to work in the profession again. Why? Because you may be in jail.

As an overhead cost, you do not have direct, hands-on experience in building your company's widgets, for example. Yeah, yeah, yeah, we all have tried to explain that without cyber security and us, as professional cyber security officers, companies can lose their business and their competitive edge through loss of trade secret information, etc. However, the bottom line is that it appears that most of today's business executives are in it for the short term, not the long term. Their concern is the "bottom line" for the next quarter to one year. They can easily terminate a cyber security program and take their chances by having auditors audit for compliance with laws and policies and recommend cyber security policies that information technology people can write. Then they can just buy insurance to cover any potential losses and, by the way, the business of buying such insurance is supposedly booming.

So, as today's cyber security officer, you must do a better job of making yourself part of the "company team" and finding ways to provide value-added and integral services to the company.

In the private sector, telecommunications businesses have become Internet providers as well as leading the drive into mobile communications from laptops, to cell phones, to tablets—and soon wearable devices from watches to other wrist-band gadgets to clothing. As we look into the future, we see more and more people making use of the long-distance voice telephone capabilities of the Internet, at very little additional cost. Then there are the enhanced versions using Skype and FaceTime, for example. The day has arrived when we no longer need a separate telephone in the home or office, except maybe in rural areas. It is becoming a thing of the past.

Speaking of Internet service providers (ISPs), let us take a moment to look at this new business born out of the Internet and see how well it is supporting cyber security and cyber security standards.[2]

---

[2] Previously written by the author under the name ShockwaveWriter and published by Reed Elsevier in their magazine *Computer Fraud & Security* (2002), as the article "Internet Service Providers and InfoSec Standards."

First a little history of how we got to where we are: The Internet was born in the 1960s and arose out of projects sponsored by the Advanced Research Project Agency in the United States. It was originally a project to facilitate the sharing of computer resources and enhance military communications. As the Internet was maturing, there were conflicts between the "haves," who had the use of the Internet, and the "have-nots," who did not. The haves were computer scientists, engineers, and some others. They argued that the Internet should not be made available to the public. Well, they lost that battle, especially after the business sector found out what a lucrative marketing and public relations tool the Internet could be for reaching potential customers, suppliers, etc. Thus, the ISPs were born.

From that time until now, the Internet has rapidly grown from an experimental research project and tool of the U.S. government and universities to the tool of everyone in the world with a computer. It is the premier global communications medium. With the subsequent development of search engines and, of course, the World Wide Web (Web), the sharing of information has never been easier.

There are many, many ISPs operating and connected all around the globe. We all should know by now that our e-mails don't go point to point, but hop around the Internet, where they can be gleaned by all those with the resources to read other people's mail and steal information to commit crimes such as identity theft or collect competitive intelligence information, etc.

So, what's the point? The point is that there still are ISPs all over the world with few regulations and few, if any, global cyber security standards. Happily, this is gradually changing. So, some ISPs may do an admirable job of protecting our information passing through their systems while others may do little or nothing. Furthermore, as we learn more and more about Netspionage (computer-enabled business and government spying), we learn more and more about how our privacy and our information are open to others to read, capture, change, and otherwise misuse.

In addition, with such "oldies but goodies" programs as SORM in Russia, Internet monitoring in China and elsewhere, global Echelon, and the U.S. FBI's Carnivore (still Carnivore no matter how often they change the name to make it more "politically correct" or to try to "hide" it from the public), we might as well take our most personal information, tattoo it on our bodies, and run naked in the streets for all to see. Although that may be a slight exaggeration, the point is we have no concept of how well ISPs, or any network connected to your corporation's networks, are protecting our information.

Now, we are quickly expanding into the world of instant communications through such things as Skype, Twitter, Facebook, and the like. After all, the more rapidly our world changes, the more rapidly we want to react and we want everything—now! Of course there are perhaps hundreds, if not thousands, of examples of ISPs being penetrated or misused, as well as corporate Web sites and their networks. They are in the news on a regular basis and also our networks are constantly under attack from multiple sources—from teenagers to terrorists to competitors to organized criminals.

UNDERSTANDING THE BUSINESS ENVIRONMENT

A cyber security program and its supporting organization are not the reason that a business or government agency exists. In the case of a business, the company usually provides a service or a product. The business has certain information or systems networks that are vital to performing its service and producing its product. The purpose of a cyber security program, therefore, is to provide service and support to the business.

To meet the needs of its customers, both internal and external to the company, it is imperative for the cyber security officer to understand the company and the company's business. This includes the following:

- History
- Products
- Business environment
- Competition
- Long-range plans
- Short-range plans
- Cost of business
- Product value

These are some of the most important parts of a business. Remember, in general, the cyber security program is not a product to be sold in the global marketplace unless that is the business of the corporation; it does not bring in revenue. In fact, cyber security is a cost to the business—unless you can prove that the cyber security program is a value-added service that financially supports the business, assisting in bringing in revenue.

> Your cyber security program should, as much as possible, be seamlessly integrated into the systems and processes of at least the core business and all systems connected to that core business.

In this globally competitive economy, there is increasing competition for market shares in the worldwide marketplace. It is important for the cyber security officer to understand this competition and what can be done by the cyber security officer through the cyber security program to enhance business, increasing such things as profits, market shares, and income.

Kenichi Ohmae, in his book, *The Mind of the Strategist*,[3] discusses product/service differentiation in the form of "the strategic three C's": the corporation, the customers, and the competition. Corporations and competitors are differentiated by costs. Customers differentiate between the corporation and the competitors by value.

Customers will buy a product that they want (consider of value), if it is a quality product at the right price. Therefore, it is important that the cyber security program add value to the product, and do so at the lowest cost, in order for the business to remain competitive in the marketplace. So, treat the cyber security program as a product that adds value and minimizes costs. Since it is your product, market it and sell it!

Fast, accurate, and complete information provides the opportunity to gain a competitive advantage—assuming of course that the information is correctly acted upon in time to provide that advantage. The responsibility of the cyber security officer is to support this process by assisting in storing, processing, transmitting, and displaying that fast, accurate, and complete information in a secure manner. This support is necessary to assist in providing the company competitive advantage opportunities.

These opportunities to take advantage of information were summarized by Colonel John R. Boyd, U.S. Air Force, as a strategy based on the "OODA loop" (observe–orient–decide–act). Although put forth some time ago, the points made are still valid. The idea is to look at it from the viewpoint that whoever can be the quickest to move through this loop can gain a competitive advantage. Information has always been time dependent and probably is more so today than ever before. That is why it is crucial to be able to have a tighter (using less time) OODA loop than one's adversaries, whether they be a nation-state, a business, or an individual.

In addition, this advantage is created because the competitor becomes more confused and uncertain over events, and that may influence the competitor's judgment and decisions. In *Patterns of Conflict*,[4] Boyd concluded that operating inside an opponent's OODA loop generates uncertainty, doubt, mistrust, confusion, disorder, fear, panic, and chaos.

---

[3] Ohmae, Kenichi, *The Mind of the Strategist*. Penguin Books, Ltd., Middlesex, UK, 1982.
[4] John Boyd, http://www.ausairpower.net/JRB/poc.pdf. Patterns of Conflict, December 1986.

Case Study

In his book *Following the Equator*,[5] Mark Twain wrote about how one can take advantage if one has information before the competitor and knows how to act on that information. At the time of Twain's world travels, sharks populated the harbor of Sydney, Australia. The government paid a bounty on sharks. A young man was down on his luck and walking around the harbor when he met an old man who was a shark fisher, who had not caught a shark all night. The old man asked the young man to try his luck. The young man caught a very large shark. As was the custom, the shark was disemboweled, as sometimes one found something of value. As it happened this young man did.

The young man went to the house of the richest wool broker in Sydney and told him to buy the entire wool crop deliverable in 60 days. They formed a partnership based on what the young man found in the shark. It seems that the shark had eaten a German sailor in the Thames River. In the belly of the shark were found not only his remains, some buttons, and a memorandum book discussing the German's returning home to fight in the war, but also a copy of the *London Times* that had been printed only 10 days before. At that time, news from London came by ship that took about 50 days. However, sharks traveled faster than the ships of that time. The *Times* stated that France had declared war on Germany, and wool prices had gone up 14% and were still rising. No other Australian wool brokers or wool producers would know that wool prices were skyrocketing for at least 50 days. By then the young man and his partner the wool broker would own all the wool, purchased at the "normal lower price," and could ship it to Europe for a very handsome profit.

[5] A Tramp Abroad, Following the Equator, Other Travels (Library of America No. 200) March 4, 2010 by Mark Twain (Author), Roy Blount Jr. (Editor), 1050 pages, Publisher: Library of America; First Printing edition (March 4, 2010), Language: English, ISBN-10:1598530666, ISBN-13:978-1598530667.

This case study is an example of how accurate information received and acted upon within the competitor's OODA loop can give one a tremendous advantage in business. So, the old saying "information is power" is probably more true today than ever before, again provided that:

- The information is accurate,
- It is acted upon correctly, and
- It is acted upon before it is acted upon by your competitor.

MANAGEMENT RESPONSIBILITIES AND COMMUNICATING WITH MANAGEMENT

One of the biggest mistakes made by cyber security officers is to assume that they "own" the systems and information. The cyber security officer must remember that the owners of the business, whether it be private ownership or public ownership through the stockholders, make the decisions as to how the business is run. The stockholders do it through the elected members of the company's board of directors, who are the risk takers. Their responsibilities include making decisions relative to company risks.

As a cyber security officer, you are there because the management believes you have the expertise they need to protect the business's information systems and the company's information.

All too often, the cyber security officer gets into the "tail wagging the dog" situation in which the cyber security officer can't understand why management does not provide the cyber security officer with the support that is needed or wanted. The cyber security officer must keep in mind that if management did not provide at least some support, the company would not employ the cyber security officer!

When decisions are made to process, store, display, or transmit information that goes against the desires of the cyber security officer, many cyber security officers take that personally. Remember, it is not your information! It belongs to the business owners.

Of course, depending on your responsibilities and the authority delegated to you by management, you will probably be responsible for making the majority of decisions that involve cyber security. However, even with that responsibility and authority, the cyber security officer must gain the support and concurrence of others within the company. You were hired to safeguard these valuable systems, networks, information, etc., with the goal of doing so at the lowest cost based on the threats, vulnerabilities, and risks to these systems. You determine that by doing formal risk analyses.

When a cyber security decision must be made and that decision is outside the purview of the cyber security officer, the cyber security officer must elevate the final decision to a higher level of management. Although each company's culture and policies will dictate when and how that process will be implemented, the cyber security officer should be sure to provide complete staff work on which the management can base the required decision. In other words, the person making the decision must be provided with all the necessary information on which to base the decision. If that information is not provided to upper management, the wrong decision could be made, which may jeopardize the protection of the company's information and/or systems or may cause the company to incur unnecessary costs.

If you have done your homework—if you have assessed the risks to the information and systems, the protection alternatives, the costs involved, and the benefits involved, and you are in a position to make your recommendations accordingly—then you have done your job.

Before you bring a problem and decision to management, you, the cyber security officer, should be sure that you have addressed the problem by providing management with clear, concise information, using nontechnical language, on which they can base their decision. The following, as a minimum, should be included in that process:

- Identification of the problem
- Possible problem solutions, including cost and benefits
- Recommended solution to the problem, and why
- Identification of who should fix the problem (it may not be a cyber security issue, or it may be one outside your authority)
- Consequences of no decision (no action/no decision is always an option, and sometimes the right one)

Whether it is the responsibility of the cyber security officer to fix the problem or not, the cyber security officer should follow up. Once the problem is fixed, it is always good to contact the other personnel who were at the meeting at which the problem was discussed and the decision made, and advise them either verbally or in writing when the corrective action is completed or the project is closed out.

An excellent gesture would be to send a letter of appreciation to those involved in fixing the problem, with appropriate copies to management. This is especially important if others fixed the problem outside your organization, or if staff outside your organization assisted you in fixing the problem.

It is the responsibility of the business management to make the final decision, unless of course they abdicate that responsibility to you. They, in turn, are held accountable to the owners of the business.

Remember that managers are usually authorized to make decisions related to accepting cyber security-associated risks for only the organizations under their authority. They should not be allowed by the business to make decisions that affect the entire company. If that appears to be occurring, you are obligated to ensure that the manager as well as upper management knows that information. This is of course a sensitive matter and must be handled that way.

A word of caution: Some managers will abdicate their management responsibility to the cyber security officer. As the cyber security officer, you may be flattered by such a gesture, but beware! You may also be getting set up to take the blame for the consequences. These consequences may be due to a decision that you may not have recommended—in fact, it may be a case in which you were in total disagreement with management as to the correct course of action to be taken.

The responsibility of business management is a serious one. Under current laws in many nation-states, managers can be held personally responsible, and possibly liable, for any poor decisions that affect the value of the business. So, your responsibility as a service and support information security (InfoSec) professional is to give management the best advice you can. When their decision is made, do your job by supporting that decision and by ensuring that the information and systems are protected based on that decision.

> "JPMorgan spending $250 million on cyber security and going to double it to $500 million in the coming years."[6]
>
> [6] Fox News interview of Jamie Dimon, January 13, 2015.

There may be times when, in the opinion of the cyber security officer, management makes the wrong decision relative to protection of information. The cyber security officer then has several additional choices:

- Meet with the decision-maker in private to try to convince that person of the consequences of the decision and why it may not be right,
- Appeal the decision to the next level of management,
- Quit the job, or
- Quit the company.

Another word of caution is needed here. Whether the decision is right or wrong, the cyber security officer should document that decision process. The documentation should answer the typical security/investigative questions of who, how, where, when, why, and what.

This is important, not from the standpoint of just another bureaucratic process, but to have a history of all actions taken that are related to cyber security. Thus, when similar instances occur a year or more after the last decision, it can be used as a precedent. This not only helps in making subsequent decisions based on similar instances, but also helps ensure consistency in the application of InfoSec. Inconsistent InfoSec decisions lead to confusion, which leads to not following sound InfoSec policy and causes increased costs to the business. This process follows the process used by the legal community, in which case law is used to argue a current illegal issue. Precedence is a logical process to follow—assuming that the decisions previously made were the correct ones, of course.

If it is subsequently shown that the last decision had unexpected, adverse consequences, then it will help the decision-maker not to make the same mistake again—one would hope. People come and go, but a good historical file will ensure consistency and keep you from having to rely on the memories of people involved—assuming they are even still employed by the company.

For example, assume that a major decision had to be made concerning cyber security, and the decision was determined to be that of management. You, as the cyber security officer, should do the following:

- Lead the effort to resolve the issue,
- Request a meeting,
- Ensure all the applicable personnel are invited, and
- Brief those at the meeting on the situation as stated above.

If you as the cyber security officer are to keep minutes of the meeting, the minutes should include:

- Why the meeting was held,
- When the meeting was held,
- Where the meeting was held,
- Who was at the meeting,
- What information was presented and discussed,
- What the decision was,
- How management made their decision, and
- Who made the decision.

Someone in management should sign the minutes of the meeting showing the results of the meeting—preferably the person who made the final decision. You will find that such decisions are usually verbal, and most managers do not want to sign any document that will place them at risk. So, how do you deal with such issues? There are several methods that can be used, all of which may cause your position as the cyber security officer to be questioned: "not a team player," "you don't understand the big picture," or "you are not a business person, so you don't understand the situation." By the way, having an MBA may help in winning this argument.

Even though you have the best interest of the company at heart and it is the basis for your recommendation, and even though you consider yourself a dedicated and loyal employee, in the eyes of some in management you're not a team player. In other words, you are not on their team.

You will soon find that the position of the cyber security officer is sometimes a risky one. Even if you do the best professional job that can be done or has been done in the history of the cyber security officer profession, office politics must be considered. Such non-cyber security situations will often cause many more problems than the cyber security officer will face in dealing with InfoSec issues, hackers, and the like.

If the you do not know about such things as "turf battles" and "protecting rice bowls," the local bookstore is the place to go. There, you will find numerous books that will explain how to work and survive in the "jungle" of office politics. You may know cyber security, but if you do not know office politics, you may not survive—even with the best cyber security program ever developed. Always remember: "It's a jungle out there!"

Why is it that way? There are many reasons, but for cyber security officers the primary reason is that you make people do things that they do not consider part of their job. And if they do not follow the cyber security policies and procedures, they could face disciplinary action. So, you, like corporate security personnel and auditors, are not always popular.

Obviously, as the cyber security officer, you want to eliminate or at least minimize that type of image—the "cop" image. It is hard work, but you must constantly try to overcome the negativism that people tack onto the cyber security officer and cyber security. Some ways of countering that negative image can be found throughout this book.

Many business meetings require that minutes be taken. If so, and if you are not responsible for taking the minutes, obtain a copy and ensure that your recommendations are noted in them, as well as who made what decisions. This is the best method of documenting what went on in the meeting.

If the minutes do not adequately describe what has taken place—if, for example, they lack details of what was presented, the potential risks, or who made the final decision (all crucial pieces of information)—then annotate the minutes. Attach any of your briefing charts, sign and date the minutes, then place them in a file in case you want to use them as a reference at a later date.

Another method that can be used, but is more confrontational, is to send a memo to the manager who made the decision in which you document the cyber security options, costs, benefits, and associated risks. You then conclude with a sentence that states, for example, "After assessing the risks I have concluded that the best course of action is option 2." Leave room for a date and the signature block of the manager you want to sign the document.

The document should be worded professionally and should be as non-intimidating to the manager as possible. Even so, in most cases, you may find that you won't get a signed copy returned to you if you send it in the company mail.

You should hand carry this document to the manager and discuss it with that person. Imagine yourself in the manager's position. When you put your signature on such a document, there can be no mistake. You made the decision. If something goes wrong, that letter may document the fact that in retrospect it was a poor decision. No manager—no one—ever wants to be put in that position. Remember that the manager does not have to sign the cyber security document. In fact, no matter how it is presented, you will find most managers will find some way not to sign the document if there is the slightest chance of being second-guessed later. In today's environment of "touchy-feely don't-hold-me-responsible" management, today's cyber security officers are more challenged than ever before to get management to own up to their decisions.

Asking a manager to sign such a document, especially if you have voiced disagreement about the decision, should be a last resort. It should be done only if you feel so strongly about the decision that you are willing to put any possible raise or promotion, or even your employment, on the line. So, you'd better be right, and you'd better strongly believe that it is worth it. Also, as the cyber security officer, you must do this as a cyber security officer professional, a person of integrity and principles.

Even so, you may end up being right, but also right out of a job. Well, no one said that being a cyber security officer professional is easy.

CREATING A COMPETITIVE ADVANTAGE THROUGH A CYBER SECURITY PROGRAM

To ensure that the cyber security program supports the company's business services and products, the cyber security officer must think of methods, philosophies, and processes that will help the company in gaining a competitive advantage. Such methods and philosophies should include a team approach. That is, have the company employees and especially management support your cyber security program.

To help in that endeavor, you should strive to insert, in appropriate company policy documents, policies that can help support your efforts. The following are some examples that may be useful in incorporating into company policy documents support for your cyber security program and your quest to assist the company in gaining a competitive advantage through cyber security:

- Managers will ensure a compliant cyber security program within their organization.
- Managers will develop our customers' trust that their sensitive information will be effectively protected while under our control.

- Managers will employ cost-effective cyber security systems and strive to help keep the price of our company's services and products as low as possible relative to our competitors.
- Managers will help keep the company's overhead down through effective loss prevention and assets protection processes.
- Managers will minimize the adverse impact of our cyber security controls on the efficiency of the company's operational functions by working with the cyber security staff to find the most cost-effective ways of protecting our information assets.
- Managers will proactively find ways to securely and efficiently provide the company's services and products.

The Cyber Security Officer as a Business Manager

The role of the cyber security officer in managing a cyber security program is somewhat different from the role of the cyber security officer as a manager of the company.

All company managers have some role to play that applies regardless of the manager's area of responsibility. This also applies to the cyber security officers in management positions. The following items should be considered for implementation by the cyber security officer as a manager within the company:

- Comply with all company policies and procedures, including the intent of those policies and procedures.
- Take no action that will give the appearance of violating applicable company policies, procedures, or ethical standards.
- Implement applicable management control systems within the cyber security organization to ensure the efficient use of resources and effective operations.
- Identify business practices, ethics, and security violations/infractions; conduct inquiries; assess potential damage; direct and take corrective action.
- Communicate with other departments to provide and receive information and guidance for mutual benefit.
- Plan, organize, direct, coordinate, control, report, assess, and refine business activities to achieve quality, cost, schedule, and performance objectives, while retaining responsibility for the results.
- Exercise due diligence to prevent fraud, waste, or abuse.
- Establish and maintain a self-audit process to identify problem areas and take corrective action to eliminate deficiencies.

These items, if made part of the cyber security officer's philosophy and goals, will not only benefit the company, but also assist the cyber security officer in professionally meeting the cyber security duties and responsibilities as a valued member of the company's management team. Remember that the cyber security program is a company program. That means you need help from everyone in the company to ensure its success.

SERVICE, SUPPORT, AND A BUSINESS ORIENTATION

In any business, the cyber security officer must strive to balance the required "user friendly" systems demands of management and users with those of cyber security. After all, cyber security, unless it can be proven to be "value added," thus at least paying for itself, is a parasite on profits or, at the least, has an adverse impact on budgets. This will be a factor to consider as you, the cyber security officer, establish the company's cyber security processes, programs, plans, projects, budgets, etc.

Remember that the cyber security program must be service and support oriented. This is of vital importance. The cyber security officer must understand that the cyber security program, if it becomes too costly or outdated or does not meet the service and support needs of the business or government agency, will be discarded or ignored. Each of these possibilities will eventually lead to the dismissal of the cyber security officer.

The dismissal of any cyber security officer affects all cyber security officers. The cyber security officer profession is thus damaged, as is our professional credibility and our opportunities to protect vital information for our internal and external customers. It is difficult enough, even in today's environment, to "sell" a cyber security program. It makes our jobs as cyber security officers harder when one of us fails. The failure of a cyber security officer could be a lesson learned for all cyber security officers. Learn not only from your own failures, but also from those of others.

The word of a cyber security officer's dismissal and failures does get around within the industry and government agencies, making it much more difficult for the cyber security officer's replacement to develop a professional InfoSec program. You may be that replacement.

As the cyber security officer, you must constantly update your cyber security program and its processes. You must continuously look at changes in society and technology, plan for those changes, and be prepared to address cyber security ramifications of the installation of new technology into the business before it is installed. You must implement cyber security measures before someone can take advantage of a system vulnerability.

So far, cyber security officers for the most part have been in a reactive mode, with little time to be proactive and put cyber security defenses in place before they are needed! How to do that will be discussed in the following chapters.

BUSINESS MANAGERS AND CYBER SECURITY

Some cyber security officers may want to talk "techie" to keep business managers in the dark about the "mysteries" of cyber security. They think that it will make the cyber security officer invaluable to the corporation and, therefore, always needed. That is illogical and also works against the cyber security officer. The more the managers and all employees understand about the concepts and philosophies of cyber security, the more they will understand cyber security officer decisions—and also the more supportive they will be.

Corporate management's knowledge may also challenge a cyber security officer, causing him or her to rethink some decisions and the logic that led to them. That's good, except for those cyber security officers who do not want to excel and accept such a challenge—in other words, the lazy and unprofessional people in cyber security officer positions. However, in the long run, such criticisms and recommendations are good for the corporation. Why? Because it means that management is actually looking at cyber security and becoming, as they should, a part of the cyber security team.

As a cyber security officer, you should know that the more input you get and the more interested corporate management and employees are in cyber security, the better your cyber security program will become, and the better it will meet the needs of the corporation. It is true that you will probably spend more time in discussions with corporate management, but that is really a good thing. In the long run, your job, if you do it right, will actually be easier.

It should come as no surprise to company managers that they are responsible for the protection of company assets. In today's information-dependent and information-based companies, it should also come as no surprise that these assets include information. These are facts of business life today and are probably concurred with by 99.9% of the company managers that one could survey. I would say 100%, except that there are always some managers (many of us have met them in our careers) who just don't seem to get it. So, let's allot the 0.1% to those managers that just don't get it.

So, if most company managers agree with that premise, why do so many either battle to negate information and information systems protection (cyber security) instead of supporting cyber security? Maybe they don't care for anything beyond their paychecks and bonuses. It seems today that there are many of those. It is ironic, but it seems in many companies around the world today that the truly company-loyal people are mostly the "regular employees" and not the managers. Employees are out there working hard and doing their best to help the company succeed. They have a loyalty—though somewhat less than in earlier years—to the company that it seems most of today's managers do not.

Today's managers either are so self-centered that they care only about their careers—you see, managers have "careers," while employees have "jobs"—or are ignorant as to their responsibilities. Let us assume ignorance is their problem. Perhaps they have been promoted into management but no one has ever explained their assets protection responsibilities. That may be because their boss did not know—it was not explained to him or her. Maybe it is because the managers try to avoid that responsibility by hiring someone to provide cyber security. Thus the problem is delegated to someone else. Therefore, when things go wrong, it is not the company manager's fault; it is the fault of those hired to protect the assets.

Then what can be done about it? Whatever the reason, it is up to the company managers to know their responsibilities and the cyber security professionals to politely remind them of those responsibilities. As the saying goes, "You can delegate authority but not abdicate your responsibilities."

If you are a company manager reading this, other than a security professional of some kind, congratulations! You are one of the few who are interested in cyber security. May your career rise above the stars. For you others out there, it is assumed you have some responsibility for cyber security or cyber security-related tasks such as fraud prevention or other asset protection. If so, you should provide your company managers information that politely and professionally explains to them that they have some very basic and direct cyber security responsibilities. Lay out those responsibilities to them as part of some awareness e-mail, on an internal company Web page or newsletter—whatever communication form works best in your environment.

The first things that company managers should be made aware (or reminded) of is that they do have a responsibility for protecting company assets—and some of the most important of those assets are sensitive information and information systems within their organization.

Company managers should understand the basics of cyber security. It is not rocket science. It is common sense. They should know that the purpose of cyber security is to do the following:
- Minimize the probability of a successful attack on the company's information,
- Minimize the damage if an attack occurs, and
- Provide a method to quickly recover in the event of a successful attack.

The three basic principles that are the foundation of cyber security are:
- Access control,
- Individual accountability, and
- Audit trails.

These are rather basic and should be easy enough for company managers not versed in cyber security to understand. Once managers understand the cyber security purpose and the three basic principles, the cyber security professional must be able to explain the concepts in detail and how they apply to the individual company managers. Obviously, there is not sufficient space in this entire book to adequately cover that topic. Furthermore, I hope that, as a cyber security officer responsible for protecting these valuable assets within your company, you do understand these concepts and can easily explain them to company managers. If not, failure to clearly communicate and gain support for your program may be your downfall.

WHAT COMPANY MANAGERS SHOULD ASK OF THEIR CYBER SECURITY PROFESSIONALS

Company managers should also be sufficiently knowledgeable to ask intelligent questions about cyber security-related matters, and ideally the company cyber security officer can answer them. Some questions company managers should ask, and some possible answers that the InfoSec can give and then explain in more detail, include the following:
- Question: How do you know you are actually under attack and not the victim of misconfigured systems? Answer: You may not know until it is too late; you may never know; you may know, but can't stop it.
- Question: What are the warning signs of potential or actual attacks? Answer: There may not be any.
- Question: Is it possible to know of pending attacks? Answer: Yes. No. Maybe—depending on conditions.

- Question: What can you do to set up an "imminent" attack warning system? Answer: Base it on history, on the latest techniques identified in CERTs, on target visibility, on your defenses, on your countermeasures, on your use of technology, and on vendor products.
- Question: What is the basis of deploying intrusion detection to assist in countering the attacks? Answer: What is normal activity? What is abnormal? One can compare activity against known attack methods and establish countermeasures, and one must have, as a minimum, a cyber security policy, procedures, and awareness program.
- Question: What must be considered when deploying the intrusion detection system and processes? Answer: Any available tools should be adapted to your unique environment. The intrusion detection process must be always secure, operating, and "foolproof." It must detect all anomalies and misuse, must have audit-based systems for history, must have real-time monitoring and warnings, and must take immediate action based on each unique attack. Also, one must know what to do if attacked.
- Question: Any other things to consider? Answer: Audit entry ports, especially to critical areas; prioritize processes, shut down others; isolate the problem; and establish alternate routing paths.

WHAT CYBER SECURITY PROFESSIONALS SHOULD DO

If the company managers are able to ask such questions and understand the answers and the details provided, the cyber security officer professional has gone a long way to help protect their information and systems from attacks and external fraud. The cyber security officer has also gone a long way in gaining some basic, active support from company managers.

As part of the above, to be successful, the cyber security officer professional should do at least the following:

- Collect information on attacks from all available sources;
- Develop and maintain a threat tool kit containing strategies, tactics, tools, and methodologies used to attack systems;
- Continuously maintain a current tool kit and methodologies that can threaten systems through attack methods;
- Model the capabilities of the potential intruders against real-time attacks;
- Collect information related to the corporation's information systems' vulnerabilities;
- Establish systems simulating intruder attacks using threat tools in a simulations and testing environment; and
- Establish defenses accordingly.

QUESTIONS TO CONSIDER

Based on what you have read, consider the following questions and how you would reply to them[7]:

- Do you understand the company for which you have cyber security responsibility—its history; what products and services it produces; its environment, culture, competition, and business plans; the impact of the cyber security program on profits; and the like?
- Are you absolutely clear as to what management expects of you?
- Are you absolutely clear that management understands your cyber security program?
- Is management clear as to what you expect from them, such as support?
- Do you have good communication channels with management?
- Are there managers who are against your cyber security program, and if so, do you avoid them or try to understand their position and work with them?
- If you do not work with them, why not?
- Do you understand your business management responsibilities?
- Are you trying to make the cyber security program a value-added function?
- If so, are you succeeding, and how do you know?
- Does management also think the cyber security program is a value-added program, and if so, how do you know?

SUMMARY

As we are now well on our way into the twenty-first century, a cyber security officer faces many more challenges than existed only a decade ago. The environment is faster, more technical, and much more challenging. The twenty-first-century cyber security officer must understand the global marketplace and the company's business environment much more than was necessary only a decade or so ago:

- Cyber security officers must understand their company's business, including its history, products, competition, plans, costs, and product value.
- Cyber security officers must understand business, management, and how to communicate with management in management's language—not in "computerese"!

---

[7] Obviously, if you answer No to any of these questions, you have some additional work to do.

- Cyber security officers must document major cyber security decisions to provide a historical file that can be used in the future when considering similar situations.
- Cyber security officers must also think and act as business managers of the company.
- Cyber security officers must be service and support oriented.
  - Cyber security officers must understand today's NII and GII and where the corporation's networks are connected to that system—weakest point and all that.
  - Cyber security officers must understand the threats, vulnerabilities, and risks associated with the corporation's systems
  - Cyber security officers must know where the systems are and where they are connected inside and outside the corporation.

Company managers must understand their assets protection responsibilities. That is especially important today, when information protection and crime prevention should be a major responsibility of every company manager. For it is only with that understanding, support, and action that companies can respond to attacks against them from competitors, nation-states, and techno-spies.

CHAPTER 3

An Overview of Related World Views of Cyber Security

The world is a dangerous place to live; not because of the people who are evil, but because of the people who don't do anything about it[1]

Albert Einstein

Contents

Chapter Objective

This chapter will provide a short overview of world views of cyber security broken down by regions of the world. We live in an interconnected world of computer networks, all having the ability to positively and negatively affect those attached to them.

Therefore, the purpose of providing these global views is so the cyber security officer has an overview of what others are thinking and doing to protect parts of the global information infrastructure (GII) and how that may affect the cyber security officer's responsibilities as they relate to his or her part of the GII, national information infrastructure (NII), and related networks.

As with any subject matter these days, a search of the Internet will find more information than you ever wanted to know on a topic. This topic is no different. Therefore, it is not the intent to provide everything you always wanted to know on what

---

[1] http://www.brainyquote.com/quotes/keywords/world_2.html.

the United Nations (UN) and other entities are doing but, as the chapter title says, provide an "overview" of what others are thinking and doing vis-à-vis cyber security.

Remember that in today's world of global corporations, the cyber security officer may have to follow the cyber security policies and procedures in the various nations where his or her corporation does business. So, as a cyber security officer, it is crucial that you understand such laws, rules, regulations, etc., and work with your corporation's legal staff to be sure that any issues identified relative to these matters are addressed.

EVOLUTION OF LAWS, STANDARDS, POLICIES, AND PROCEDURES

In general, the evolution of laws followed the evolution of "civilization" (some argue that we have yet to be truly "civilized") from primitive to feudal to agricultural to industrial to today's information age, and some say that a few nations are beginning to enter the knowledge age.

Cyber security-related laws, standards, policies, and procedures have, as can be expected, evolved as the threats, vulnerabilities, and risks to computers, systems, networks, the NII, the GII, and their related information have evolved. However, they seem to have always been updated as a reaction to attacks and not using a proactive approach. In addition, even when a nation-state, for example, the United States, passes cyber security-related laws and policies, they do not seem to be followed.

> The January 1, 2015, report revealed and concluded that the Department of Homeland Security's (DHS's) cyber security practices and programs are so bad, the DHS fails at even the basics of computer security and is "unlikely" to be able to protect both citizens and government from attacks.[2]
>
> [2] www.zdnet.com/.../new-report-the-dhs-is-a-mess-of-cybersecurity.

Of course such things as the Cold War, political revolutions, economic revolutions, revolutions in military affairs, human evolution and revolution, and revolutions in technology all continue to have major impacts on the need and demand for new laws, standards, policies, and procedures. This will obviously continue as various evolutions and revolutions continue.

In this overview, this topic will be broken down as follows:

* Global via the UN,
* European Union (EU),
* Asia,
* South America,
* Africa,
* Canada,
* United States.

GLOBAL VIA THE UN

The UN appears to be heavily involved in cyber security-related matters regarding associations, committees, treaties, and the like. This is of course logical since cyber security is a global problem and needs global solutions. After all, if some cyber criminal in a foreign nation commits a cyber crime in another nation, the victim nation must have a way to bring the criminal to justice. If the criminal resides in a nation without an extradition treaty with the victim nation, and especially one that does not have any cyber laws, the chance of that criminal being brought to justice runs from slim to none, as they say.

> The UN system's collective engagement in addressing cyber threats is critical. The International Telecommunications Union (ITU) is leading the call for stakeholders to work together to set international policies and standards and to build an international framework for cyber security.[3]
>
> [3] http://www.un.org/en/ecosoc/cybersecurity/summary.pdf.

What view you may have of the UN in general will of course taint your view of their efforts relating to cyber security. For example, are they trying to set the "laws" for the world? Do they want to control the Internet, maybe in a manner used by the UN Security Council, with permanent members such as Russia and China, as well as rotating members, for example, Saudi Arabia, Libya?

How will such a structure affect the freedom of the world's users? Some may rejoice in such a move but others may cringe at the idea, fearing the loss of freedom that in general the Internet now provides. Even the United States has designs on more control. In fact, all government agencies around the world for the most part cannot stand to have their citizens be free to live, speak their minds, and write whatever they want without some government controls, and certainly that applies to the citizens of the world's use of the Internet.

We all must be on guard when our Internet—yes it is *ours*, the users'—and other networks are to be controlled by laws, standards, rules, regulations, policies, and procedures in the name of protecting us through cyber security-related controls. Yes, some controls are needed to avoid chaos and rampant carnage of information stolen, destroyed, and such. However, we must all be vigilant when presented with controls for "our own good." Unfortunately most people would probably prefer a little more security, sacrificing some freedoms, but when is enough enough? Will we realize it only when it is too late?

So, what has the UN been up to as relates to cyber security matters? A search of the UN's website disclosed the following result of a Special Event on Cyber Security and Development, December 9, 2011, 10:00 a.m. to 1.00 p.m., ECOSOC Chamber, UN, New York, which provides an overview.

As a cyber security officer, you should search online for the most current UN, nation-state, and regional associations dealing with cyber security and, as used here, get an understanding of what is happening on a global basis when it comes to cyber security matters. After all, as a cyber security officer, you probably work in a global environment and, like it or not, your networks are connected to the world and, as we all know, the world is not a safe place, and that goes for our global, information- and networked-based environment.

Even as far back as 2011, which is a lifetime in cyber security, the UN stated that:

> Cyber security is one of the greatest issues of our times, and it will continue to grow in importance. It is our collective duty to ensure that ICTs are safe and secure so that the 7 billion people of this planet can reap the benefits of ICTs. Today, everything is dependent on ICTs and we are all vulnerable—cyber security is a global issue that can be solved only with global solutions. Cyber security is an area that affects each and every agency and program of the UN. As we push forward the UN agenda for peace and security, we must remember that cyber security is part of this. The UN system's collective engagement in addressing cyber threats is critical. The ITU is leading the call for stakeholders to work together to set international policies and standards and to build an international framework for cyber security.

As with the suggestion of online research on cyber security matters related to the UN, the same applies for all other areas of the world as shown below. This is important as probably at one time or another, whether you are a cyber security officer for a government agency or a corporation or association, or just an Internet user, you are likely to be connected in one form or another outside your own country. In fact, these days that is pretty much a certainty.

So, what happens in another part of the world may have an adverse impact on you personally, your association, your business, or your government agency.

THE EU

The following provides some insight into the direction that the EU and United States are going. Note that this was the first meeting and was just held in December of 2014. The question is, "What's taken them so long to meet?"

On December 5, 2014, an EU and U.S. cyber security-related meeting was held in Brussels. The purpose of the meeting was to discuss foreign policy related to the cyber environment and of course cyber security, as quoted below:[4]

International Security in Cyberspace

The participants welcomed the landmark consensus of the 2012–2013 Group of Governmental Experts on Developments in the Field of Information and Telecommunications in the Context of International Security, including its affirmation of the applicability of existing international law to cyberspace.

Internet Governance Developments in 2015

The two sides reiterated that no single entity, company, organisation or government should seek to control the Internet, and expressed their full support for multi-stakeholder governance structures of the Internet that are inclusive, transparent, accountable and technically sound....

U.S.–EU Cyber Security-Related Cooperation

They would work through their EU–U.S. working group on cyber security and cyber crime. Their cooperation would encompass issues related to raising awareness, "cyber incident management," cyber issues related to sex offenders, cooperation to fight cyber crime, and working with other Internet organizations that share mutual interests.

ASIA

The following provides an Asian overview of cyber security as it relates to the Association of Southeast Asian Nations[5]

---

[4] http://eeas.europa.eu/statements-eeas/2014/141205_05_en.htm.
[5] http://www.nbr.org/publications/asia_policy/Free/AP18/AsiaPolicy18_Heinl_July2014.pdf.

The Octopus Conference: Cooperation against Cybercrime was held on December 4, 2013, in Strasbourg, France,[6] and included a statement entitled "Statement on Cooperation in Fighting Cyber Attack and Terrorist Misuse of Cyber Space, Kuala Lumpur, July 28, 2006." The statement included:

> ... endeavor to enact and implement cyber crime and cyber security laws in accordance with their national conditions and by referring to relevant international instruments and recommendations/guidelines for the prevention, detection, reduction, and mitigation of attacks to which they are a party.

They also agreed to address criminal, terrorist, and other issues associated with cyber security and use of the Internet.

That included the following.

1. *Acknowledge the importance of a national framework for cooperation and collaboration in addressing criminal, including terrorist, misuse of cyber space and encourage the formulation of such a framework.*
2. *Agree to work together to improve their capabilities to adequately address cyber crime, including the terrorist misuse of cyber space.*
3. *Commit to continue working together in the fight against cyber crime, including terrorist misuse of cyber space, through activities aimed at enhancing confidence among the various national Computer Security Incident Response Teams (SIRIs), as well as formulating advocacy and public awareness programs.*

SOUTH AMERICA

Symantec and the Organization of American States (OAS) Secretariat of Multidimensional Security (SMS) and the Inter-American Committee against Terrorism (CICTE) released a report analyzing cybersecurity trends and government responses in Latin America and the Caribbean.[7]

The co-sponsored report explores various cybersecurity trends including the overall increase in data breaches:

- Rise of Ransomware and Cryptolocker
- ATM fraud
- Social media and mobile computing vulnerabilities
- Malware
- Spam
- Spear phishing

[6] http://www.coe.int/t/DGHL/cooperation/economiccrime/cybercrime/cy_octopus2013/Octopus2013_en.asp.

[7] http://www.symantec.com/page.jsp?id = cybersecurity-trends; http://www.symantec.com/content/en/us/enterprise/other_resources/b-cyber-security-trends-report-lamc-annex.pdf.

AFRICA

African Union adopts framework on cyber security and data protection[8]
8:30am | 22 August 2014 | by Access Policy Team,

> Without much media attention, the heads of state of the African Union (AU) agreed to a landmark convention this summer affecting many aspects of digital life.
>
> In June, leaders in the AU, a group of 54 African governments launched in 2002, met at the 23rd African Union Summit and approved the African Union Convention on Cyber Security and Personal Data Protection.
>
> The Convention covers a very wide range of online activities, including electronic commerce, data protection, and cybercrime, with a special focus on racism, xenophobia, child pornography, and national cybersecurity ...

CANADA[9]

In Canada, they developed a three-pillar strategy as follows:

- *Securing government systems*
- *Partnering to secure vital cyber systems outside the federal Government*
- *Helping Canadians to be secure online*

UNITED STATES

The United States has developed the "Comprehensive National Cybersecurity Initiative,"[10] which is described below.

> President Obama has identified cyber security as one of the most serious economic and national security challenges we face as a nation, but one that we as a government or as a country are not adequately prepared to counter. Shortly after taking office, the President therefore ordered a thorough review of federal efforts to defend the U.S. information and communications infrastructure and the development of a comprehensive approach to securing America's digital infrastructure.
>
> In May 2009, the President accepted the recommendations of the resulting Cyberspace Policy Review, including the selection of an Executive Branch Cybersecurity Coordinator, who will have regular access to the President. The Executive Branch was also directed to work closely with all key players in U.S. cyber security, including state and local governments and the private sector, to ensure an organized and unified response to future cyber incidents, strengthen public/private partnerships to

---

[8] https://www.accessnow.org/blog/2014/08/22/african-union-adopts-framework-on-cyber-security-and-data-protection.
[9] http://www.publicsafety.gc.ca.
[10] https://www.whitehouse.gov/issues/foreign-policy/cybersecurity/national-initiative.

find technology solutions that ensure U.S. security and prosperity, invest in the cutting-edge research and development necessary for the innovation and discovery to meet the digital challenges of our time, and begin a campaign to promote cyber security awareness and digital literacy from our boardrooms to our classrooms and begin to build the digital workforce of the twenty-first century. Finally, the President directed that these activities be conducted in a way that is consistent with ensuring the privacy rights and civil liberties guaranteed in the Constitution and cherished by all Americans.

The activities under way to implement the recommendations of the Cyberspace Policy Review build on the Comprehensive National Cybersecurity Initiative (CNCI) launched by President George W. Bush in National Security Presidential Directive 54/Homeland Security Presidential Directive 23 (NSPD-54/HSPD-23) in January 2008. President Obama determined that the CNCI and its associated activities should evolve to become key elements of a broader, updated national U.S. cyber security strategy. These CNCI initiatives will play a key role in supporting the achievement of many of the key recommendations of President Obama's Cyberspace Policy Review.

The CNCI consists of a number of mutually reinforcing initiatives with the following major goals designed to help secure the United States in cyberspace:

- **To establish a front line of defense against today's immediate threats** by creating or enhancing shared situational awareness of network vulnerabilities, threats, and events within the federal government—and ultimately with state, local, and tribal governments and private sector partners—and the ability to act quickly to reduce our current vulnerabilities and prevent intrusions.
- **To defend against the full spectrum of threats** by enhancing U.S. counterintelligence capabilities and increasing the security of the supply chain for key information technologies.
- **To strengthen the future cyber security environment** by expanding cyber education, coordinating and redirecting research and development efforts across the federal government, and working to define and develop strategies to deter hostile or malicious activity in cyberspace.

In building the plans for the CNCI, it was quickly realized that these goals could not be achieved without also strengthening certain key strategic foundational capabilities within the government. Therefore, the CNCI includes funding within the federal law enforcement, intelligence, and defense communities to enhance such key functions as criminal investigation; intelligence collection, processing, and analysis; and information assurance critical to enabling national cyber security efforts.

The CNCI was developed with great care and attention to privacy and civil liberties concerns in close consultation with privacy experts across the government. Protecting civil liberties and privacy rights remains a fundamental objective in the implementation of the CNCI.

In accord with President Obama's declared intent to make transparency a touch-stone of his presidency, the Cyberspace Policy Review identified enhanced informa-tion sharing as a key component of effective cyber security. To improve public understanding of federal efforts, the Cybersecurity Coordinator has directed the release of the following summary description of the CNCI.

CNCI Initiative Details

Initiative 1. *Manage the Federal Enterprise Network as a single network enterprise with Trusted Internet Connections (TIC). The TIC initiative, headed by the Office of Man-agement and Budget and the DHS, covers the consolidation of the federal govern-ment's external access points (including those to the Internet). This consolidation will result in a common security solution, which includes facilitating the reduction of exter-nal access points, establishing baseline security capabilities, and validating agency adherence to those security capabilities. Agencies participate in the TIC initiative either as TIC access providers (a limited number of agencies that operate their own capabili-ties) or by contracting with commercial Managed Trusted IP Service providers through the GSA-managed Networx contract vehicle.*

Initiative 2. *Deploy an intrusion detection system of sensors across the federal enterprise. Intrusion detection systems using passive sensors form a vital part of U.S. government network defenses by identifying when unauthorized users attempt to gain access to those networks. The DHS is deploying, as part of its EINSTEIN 2 activities, signature-based sensors capable of inspecting Internet traf-fic entering federal systems for unauthorized accesses and malicious content. The EINSTEIN 2 capability enables analysis of network flow of information to identify potential malicious activity while conducting automatic full packet inspection of traffic entering or exiting U.S. government networks for malicious activity using signature-based intrusion detection technology. Associated with this investment in technology is a parallel investment in manpower with the expertise required to accomplish the DHS's expanded network security mission. EINSTEIN 2 is capable of alerting US-CERT in real time to the presence of malicious or potentially harm-ful activity in federal network traffic and provides correlation and visualization of the derived data. Owing to the capabilities within EINSTEIN 2, US-CERT analysts have a greatly improved understanding of the network environment and an increased ability to address the weaknesses and vulnerabilities in federal network security. As a result, US-CERT has greater situational awareness and can more effectively develop and more readily share security-relevant information with network defenders across the U.S. government, as well as with security profes-sionals in the private sector and the American public. The DHS's Privacy Office has conducted and published a Privacy Impact Assessment for the EINSTEIN 2 program.*

Initiative 3. *Pursue deployment of intrusion prevention systems across the federal enterprise. This initiative represents the next evolution of protection for civilian departments and agencies of the federal Executive Branch. This approach, called*

EINSTEIN 3, will draw on commercial technology and specialized government technology to conduct real-time full packet inspection and threat-based decision-making on network traffic entering or leaving these Executive Branch networks. The goal of EINSTEIN 3 is to identify and characterize malicious network traffic to enhance cyber security analysis, situational awareness, and security response. It will have the ability to automatically detect and respond appropriately to cyber threats before harm is done, providing an intrusion prevention system supporting dynamic defense. EINSTEIN 3 will assist the DHS US-CERT in defending, protecting, and reducing vulnerabilities of federal Executive Branch networks and systems. The EINSTEIN 3 system will also support enhanced information sharing by US-CERT with federal departments and agencies by giving the DHS the ability to automate alerting of detected network intrusion attempts and, when deemed necessary by the DHS, to send alerts that do not contain the content of communications to the National Security Agency (NSA) so that DHS efforts may be supported by NSA exercising its lawfully authorized missions. This initiative makes substantial and long-term investments to increase national intelligence capabilities to discover critical information about foreign cyber threats and use this insight to inform EINSTEIN 3 systems in real time. The DHS will be able to adapt threat signatures determined by the NSA in the course of its foreign intelligence and Department of Defense information assurance missions for use in the EINSTEIN 3 system in support of the DHS's federal system security mission. Information sharing on cyber intrusions will be conducted in accordance with the laws and oversight for activities related to homeland security, intelligence, and defense to protect the privacy and rights of U.S. citizens.

As of this writing, the DHS is conducting a exercise to pilot the EINSTEIN 3 capabilities described in this initiative based on technology developed by the NSA and to solidify processes for managing and protecting information gleaned from observed cyber intrusions against civilian Executive Branch systems. Government civil liberties and privacy officials are working closely with the DHS and US-CERT to build appropriate and necessary privacy protections into the design and operational deployment of EINSTEIN 3.

Initiative 4. Coordinate and redirect research and development (R&D) efforts. No single individual or organization is aware of all of the cyber-related R&D activities being funded by the government. This initiative is aimed at developing strategies and structures for coordinating all cyber R&D sponsored or conducted by the U.S. government, both classified and unclassified, and redirecting that R&D where needed. This initiative is critical to eliminate redundancies in federally funded cyber security research and to identify research gaps, prioritize R&D efforts, and ensure the taxpayers are getting full value for their money as we shape our strategic investments.

Initiative 5. Connect current cyber operations centers to enhance situational awareness. There is a pressing need to ensure that government information security offices and strategic operations centers share data regarding malicious activities *against federal systems, consistent with privacy protections for personally identifiable and other protected information and as legally appropriate, to have a better understanding of the entire threat to government systems and to take maximum advantage of each organization's unique capabilities to produce the best overall national cyber defense possible. This initiative provides the key means necessary to enable and support shared situational awareness and collaboration across six centers that are responsible for carrying out U.S. cyber activities. This effort focuses on key aspects necessary to enable practical mission bridging across the elements of U.S. cyber activities: foundational capabilities and investments, such as upgraded infrastructure, increased bandwidth, and integrated operational capabilities; enhanced collaboration, including common technology, tools, and procedures; and enhanced shared situational awareness through shared analytic and collaborative technologies.*

The National Cybersecurity Center within the DHS will play a key role in securing U.S. government networks and systems under this initiative by coordinating and integrating information from the six centers to provide cross-domain situational awareness, analyzing and reporting on the state of U.S. networks and systems, and fostering interagency collaboration and coordination.

Initiative 6. *Develop and implement a government-wide cyber counterintelligence (CI) plan. A government-wide cyber CI plan is necessary to coordinate activities across all federal agencies to detect, deter, and mitigate the foreign-sponsored cyber intelligence threat to U.S. and private sector information systems. To accomplish these goals, the plan establishes and expands cyber CI education and awareness programs and workforce development to integrate CI into all cyber operations and analysis, increase employee awareness of the cyber CI threat, and increase CI collaboration across the government. The Cyber CI Plan is aligned with the National Counterintelligence Strategy of the United States of America (2007) and supports the other programmatic elements of the CNCI.*

Initiative 7. *Increase the security of our classified networks. Classified networks house the federal government's most sensitive information and enable crucial warfighting, diplomatic, counterterrorism, law enforcement, intelligence, and homeland security operations. Successful penetration or disruption of these networks could cause exceptionally grave damage to our national security. We need to exercise due diligence in ensuring the integrity of these networks and the data they contain.*

Initiative 8. *Expand cyber education. While billions of dollars are being spent on new technologies to secure the U.S. government in cyberspace, it is the people with the right knowledge, skills, and abilities to implement those technologies who will determine success. However, there are not enough cyber security experts within the federal government or private sector to implement the CNCI, nor is there an adequately established federal cyber security career field. Existing cyber security* *training and personnel development programs, while good, are limited in focus and lack unity of effort. To effectively ensure our continued technical advantage and future cyber security, we must develop a technologically skilled and cyber-savvy workforce and an effective pipeline of future employees. It will take a national strategy, similar to the effort to upgrade science and mathematics education in the 1950s, to meet this challenge.*

Initiative 9. *Define and develop enduring "leap-ahead" technology, strategies, and programs. One goal of the CNCI is to develop technologies that provide increases in cyber security by orders of magnitude above current systems and that can be deployed within 5–10 years. This initiative seeks to develop strategies and programs to enhance the component of the government R&D portfolio that pursues high-risk/high-payoff solutions to critical cyber security problems. The federal government has begun to outline Grand Challenges for the research community to help solve these difficult problems that require "out-of-the-box" thinking. In dealing with the private sector, the government is identifying and communicating common needs that should drive mutual investment in key research areas.*

Initiative 10. *Define and develop enduring deterrence strategies and programs. Our nation's senior policy makers must think through the long-range strategic options available to the United States in a world that depends on ensuring the use of cyberspace. As of this writing, the U.S. government has been implementing traditional approaches to the cyber security problem—and these measures have not achieved the level of security needed. This initiative is aimed at building an approach to cyber defense strategy that deters interference and attack in cyberspace by improving warning capabilities, articulating roles for the private sector and international partners, and developing appropriate responses for both state and non-state actors.*

Initiative 11. *Develop a multipronged approach for global supply chain risk management. Globalization of the commercial information and communications technology marketplace provides increased opportunities for those intent on harming the United States by penetrating the supply chain to gain unauthorized access to data, alter data, or interrupt communications. Risks stemming from both the domestic and the globalized supply chain must be managed in a strategic and comprehensive way over the entire life cycle of products, systems, and services. Managing this risk will require a greater awareness of the threats, vulnerabilities, and consequences associated with acquisition decisions; the development and employment of tools and resources to technically and operationally mitigate risk across the life cycle of products (from design through retirement); the development of new acquisition policies and practices that reflect the complex global marketplace; and partnership with industry to develop and adopt supply chain and risk management standards and best practices. This initiative will enhance federal government skills, policies, and processes to provide departments and agencies with a robust tool set to better manage and mitigate supply chain risk at levels commensurate with the criticality of, and risks to, their systems and networks.*

Initiative 12. *Define the federal role in extending cyber security into critical infrastructure domains. The U.S. government depends on a variety of privately owned and operated critical infrastructures to carry out the public's business. In turn, these critical infrastructures rely on the efficient operation of information systems and networks that are vulnerable to malicious cyber threats. This initiative builds on the existing and ongoing partnership between the federal government and the public and private sector owners and operators of critical infrastructure and key resources (CIKR). The DHS and its private sector partners have developed a plan of shared action with an aggressive series of milestones and activities. It includes both short-term and long-term recommendations, specifically incorporating and leveraging previous accomplishments and activities that are already under way. It addresses security and information assurance efforts across the cyber infrastructure to increase resiliency and operational capabilities throughout the CIKR sectors. It includes a focus on public–private sharing of information regarding cyber threats and incidents in both government and CIKR.*

SUMMARY

The above provides a short overview of what is being considered and implemented throughout the world. The important point is this: all the nation-states of the world that are depending on technology, to whatever degree, are at least talking about cyber security-related matters and many are at least trying to start to address the issues of cyber security, cyber terrorism, and cyber crime. They also seem willing to cooperate to address the issues, as the issues are as global as are the networks.

It is recommended that the cyber security officer identify all the businesses that the corporation is connected to and the nation-states that they are in and conduct research and analyses to see what they are doing as it relates to cyber security and how it affects his or her corporation.

This is just the start, but at least it gives the cyber security officer a basic understanding of the state of cyber security throughout the world. Also, the nation-states that are censoring users should also be evaluated. Furthermore, take it for granted that nation-states are monitoring your transmissions into their country and may be censoring them.

Working with corporate management, the legal staff, and the audit staff, the cyber security officer should identify key issues related to the protection of the corporation's information in foreign countries. A project plan should then be developed and implemented to conduct risk analyses related to that connectivity. Furthermore, the cyber security officer should meet with his or her counterparts in those nation-states and establish a line of communication to address issues of mutual concern.

CHAPTER 4

A Glimpse at the History of Technology

What hath God wrought?
Samuel F.B. Morse (When the first telegraph message ever was sent, 1844)

Contents

Chapter Objective

In this chapter, technology will be discussed, as obviously the cyber security officer must understand technology, which includes hardware, software, firmware, and all related aspects.

The revolution in technology has obviously caused nation-states, corporations, and individuals to become more technology-driven, technology-supported, and technology-dependent.

63

It is not the intent here to provide a detailed history of technology. The intent is to provide a brief overview. This overview is provided because it is obviously important for those involved in cyber security to understand their working environment as much as possible. It may seem obvious, but it is amazing how many cyber security officers have little knowledge of technology and how we got to where we are.

WHAT IS TECHNOLOGY?

According to one dictionary,[1] technology is defined as follows:

tech·nol·o·gy [tek   näl'   ə   jē] (plural tech·nol·o·gies) noun

1. Application of tools and methods: the study, development, and application of devices, machines, and techniques for manufacturing and productive processes • recent developments in seismographic technology

2. Method of applying technical knowledge: a method or methodology that applies technical knowledge or tools • a new technology for accelerating incubation "…Maryland-based firm uses database and Internet technology to track a company's consumption of printed goods…." *Forbes Global Business and Finance*, November 1998.

(Early seventeenth century. From Greek tekhnologia, literally "systematic treatment," literally "science of craft," from tekhne "art, craft.")

FROM CAVE MAN TO CYBER SECURITY PROFESSIONAL AND INFORMATION WARRIOR

The world is rapidly changing. We humans are in the midst of, or have gone through, a hunter–gatherer period, an agricultural period, an industrial period, and now the modern nation-state, and our society is in an information-based and information-dependent period. Some are saying that we are approaching the Knowledge Age—not to be confused with a "smarter age"!

Our global society can no longer function without the aid of automated information and high technology—computers and networks. With computers and global networks such as the Internet come opportunities to make life better for all of us. However, it also makes each of us more vulnerable and increases the risk to the high technology we depend on, as well as increasing risks to cyber security, our personal freedoms, and our privacy.

---

[1] *Encarta World English Dictionary*, 1999, Microsoft Corporation. All rights reserved. Developed for Microsoft by Bloomsbury Publishing Plc.

Throughout human history, technology has played a role in the development of our species, and it has played a major role in our lives. Even the making of fire was probably seen as a technological wonder in the early history of the human race—and also used as a weapon of war such as by setting fire to the enemy's fortifications, houses, and crops. It was also used to help forge tools as weapons of war.

A short look back at that history is appropriate, for as someone once said: "If you don't know where you've been, you don't know where you are going"—and one might add, "you don't even know where you are." And if you do not know where you are, your survivability in a cyber security environment is not good.

> *Technology drives change.*
>
> **Andrew Grove, CEO, Intel Corporation**

REVOLUTIONS AND EVOLUTIONS IN HIGH TECHNOLOGY

As was previously mentioned, one cannot address the issue of cyber security without first addressing the changes brought on by technology and its impact on businesses, government agencies, societies, global and economic competition, and the world in general. Technology obviously has a major impact on cyber security and the cyber security officer's ability to successfully protect information and networks.

Technology has many uses, and over the centuries it has driven how we humans work, live, and interact. In a speech televised on the program *BookTV*, as far back as April 4, 2002, Michael Eisner, Chairman and CEO, The Walt Disney Company, discussed the impact of technology on the world and used the following timeline of the beginnings of communication-related "devices"—which is as relevant today as it was then:

- 1455: Gutenberg Bible
- 1689: Newspapers
- 1741: Magazines
- 1892: Movies
- 1907: Radio broadcasts
- 1927: TV
- 1975: Microsoft

Look how far we've come in the last 40-plus years. All these forms of technology and communication systems have had a major impact on our lives throughout history. They not only entertain us, but also provide us with information. Some of the information processed, stored, and transmitted will be sensitive information that a company or government agency may want to keep private and not release to the general public. Consider this as a cyber security officer: If that private, sensitive information communicated to the public is about your company, how that information is obtained may indicate a vulnerability in an information protection process. If so, you have a serious problem. The freer a society is, the freer the news media will be, and consequently, the more challenging your job to protect sensitive business information. However, with that said, remember that as a cyber security professional, your job is also to protect the privacy of individuals in your company.

> *Some day, on the corporate balance sheet, there will be an entry which reads "Information"; for in most cases the information is more valuable than the hardware which processes it.*
>
> **RADM Grace Murray Hopper, U.S. Navy**

FROM THE TWENTIETH CENTURY TO TODAY: TECHNOLOGY AND THE ADVENT OF HIGH TECHNOLOGY

The use of technology during the agricultural and industrial periods saw great numbers of new inventions and improvements in old technologies. This was also the time of the building of the great cities of the world, as well as their total destruction in global wars. Thus, technology for warfare had truly come of age. With the advent of the atomic and subsequent bombs, the entire world could now literally be destroyed. The period also saw great improvements in technology inventions and new inventions such as the telegraph, telephone, air transportation, and computers. This period saw increases in education, mass transportation, and exponential growth in communications—the sharing of information.

During this period, the sharing of information became easier owing to the improvement of communications systems, new communications systems, and increased consolidation of people into large cities. This also made it easier to educate the people in the needed skills for working in the more modern factories and offices of the period and for developing, improving, and implementing technologies.

The transition period from the Industrial Age to the Information Age in world history varies with each nation-state. In the United States, the well-known authors the Tofflers estimated the transition to take place about 1955, when the number of white-collar workers began to outnumber the blue-collar workers. Some nation-states are still in various phases of transition from the agricultural period to the industrial period to the information period.

No matter when a nation experiences this technology-driven transition, however, it will see, as the United States and other modern nation-states have seen, the most rapid changes in all aspects of human existence since humans first walked on this Earth—including how wars are prosecuted.

The twentieth century saw the rapid expansion and use of technology more so than all past centuries combined. It was also the beginning of the concentrated development of technology specifically to develop new and improved networks on a massive scale. This ushered in the era of modern warfare, an era that was sponsored primarily by governments and globally committed businesses that had the will and the means for such development, and these entities were able to use these new technologies to their agendas on a global scale.

Thus, the twentieth century was the true beginning of technology-based warfare. Owing to the technological improvement of older inventions (e.g., submarine, machine gun) and new inventions such as nuclear weapons, never before could so many be killed by so few. There were also the tanks, hand grenades, poison gases, and land mines that gave way to the chemical/biological/nuclear weapons, carpet bombings, smart bombs, and the beginning of true cyber security.

In 1962 … the CIA quietly contracted the Xerox Company to design a miniature camera, to be planted inside the photocopier at the Soviet Union's embassy in Washington. A team of four Xerox engineers … modified a home movie camera equipped with a special photocell that triggered the device whenever a copy was made. In 1963, the tiny Cold War weapon was installed by a Xerox technician during a regular maintenance visit to the Soviet embassy.[2]

[2] From an article by Dawn Stover in the January 1996 issue of Popular Science, entitled "The CIA's Xerox Spy-cam." Although dated, this indicates how far back government agencies have been involved in covert cyber operations. Imagine the progress they have made since then.

This period included many significant technology-driven inventions too numerous to mention here in their entirety. In the medical field alone, we have seen the rapid invention of literally thousands of new drugs, procedures, and devices, many of which saved possibly millions of lives over the years. Some other significant technologically driven inventions during this century include:

- Zeppelin
- Radio receiver
- Polygraph machine
- Airplane
- Gyrocompass
- Jet engine
- Synthetic rubber
- Solar cell
- Short-wave radio
- Wirephoto

The twentieth century saw the development and improvement of our modern era's amazing electronic inventions leading to the computer and its peripherals:

Electronic amplifying tube (triode)	Photocopier
Radio tuner	Computer
Robot	Integrated circuit
Digital computer	BASIC language
UNIVAC I	FORTRAN
Sputnik	Compact disk
Explorer I satellite	Computer mouse
Laser	Computer with integrated circuits
OS/360 IBM operating system	RAM, ROM, EEPROM
Minicomputer	ARPANET
Optical fiber	Daisy wheel printer
Cray supercomputer	Floppy disk
Space shuttle	Dot-matrix printer
IBM personal computer	Liquid-crystal display
Videotape recorder	Computer hard disk
Graphic user interface	Modem
Cathode ray tube	Mobile phone
Television	Transistor
FM radio	World Wide Web
Voice recognition machine	Browsers

Other Significant Twentieth-Century Technological Developments and Events

Some of the other significant technological events and inventions that took place in the twentieth century and have led to our rapidly changing information-based societies and information dependency, and assisted in the development of new methods of prosecuting warfare, include the following:[3]

1930: Shannon's doctorate thesis explains the use of electrical switching circuits in modern Boolean logic.

1934: Computing–Tabulating–Recording becomes IBM.

1936: Burack builds the first electric logic machine.

1940: Atanasoff and Berry design a computer with vacuum tubes as switching units.

1943–1946: Mauchley, Eckert, and Von Neumann build the ENIAC, the first all-electronic digital computer.

1947: The transistor is perfected.

1955: Shockley Semi-Conductor founded in Palo Alto, California; Bardeen, Shockley, and Brattain share the Nobel Prize for the transistor.

1957: Fairchild Semi-Conductor is founded.

1962: Tandy Corporation buys chain of RadioShack electronic stores.

1964: Kemeny and Kurtz, Dartmouth College, develop the BASIC computer language.

1968: Intel is founded.

1969: Intel produces integrated circuits for Japanese calculators; Data General releases Nova.

High-Tech: A Product, a Process, or Both?

There is no universally accepted definition of "high-tech," nor is there a standard list of industries considered to be high-tech. Today nearly every industry contains some element of technology, and even the most technologically intensive industry will include low-tech elements.

Nevertheless, several groups have developed lists of industries they consider high-tech using U.S. Standard Industrial Classifications (SIC).

The breadth of these lists depends on two factors: (1) the goals of the organization and its customers and (2) whether the organization ascribes to the argument that only industries that produce technology can be considered high-tech or to the argument that industries that use advanced technology processes can also be categorized as high-tech.

Any industry-based definitions of high-tech will be imperfect, but none of the definitions discussed here should be considered incorrect. The important factor to consider is the perspective from which any list is derived.

---

[3] See P. Freiberger and M. Swaine's book, *Fire in the Valley: The Making of the Personal Computer*, Osborne/McGraw, Berkeley, CA, 1984.

Most high-tech industry classifications have common elements, yet may vary significantly in scope. Let's consider four classifications of high-tech industries developed by the following respected and often quoted organizations: the American Electronics Association (AEA), RFA (formerly Regional Financial Associates), One Source Information Services, Inc. (formerly Corp Tech), and the U.S. Bureau of Labor Statistics (BLS).

The different missions of these four organizations influence how they define high-tech. The AEA is a trade association made up of mostly electronics and information technology companies. Its members generally produce technology and ascribe to the limited definition of high-tech based only on the nature of an industry's product rather than its process. RFA is a national consulting firm. Its clients include builders and contractors, banks, insurance companies, financial services firms, and government. The industries with the greatest growth potential and those reflective of their clients' interests are included in RFA's list of high-tech industries. While both the AEA and RFA have narrowly defined high-tech, One Source and the BLS use broader definitions that include industries with both high-tech products and processes.

One Source gathers and sells corporate information on technology firms for use in sales and marketing. As it has built its database of firms, One Source has expanded its list of what should be considered a high-tech industry. The BLS is a federal agency responsible for collecting and analyzing data on the national labor force. It has defined those industries with the highest concentration of technology-based occupations, such as scientists and engineers, as high-tech industries.

The Trade Association: AEA

The AEA released Cyberstates 4.0, its annual report on technology employment, based on the AEA's limited definition of high-tech industries, which fall into three categories: (1) computers, communications, and electrical equipment; (2) communication services; and (3) computer-related services. The AEA's list is the most restrictive of the four classifications. Absent from the list are areas such as drug manufacturing, robotics, and research and testing operations.

The Consulting Group: RFA

RFA's high-tech sectors are similar to those selected by the AEA. However, RFA does not include household audio and video equipment or telephone communications, but adds drugs and research and testing services.

Information Provider: One Source

Unlike the short lists compiled by the AEA and RFA, the One Source list classifies 48 sectors as high-tech. Major additions include a number of manufacturing industries, such as metal products and transportation equipment, and several service industries.

The Research Group: BLS

BLS has further refined its high-tech industry definition by separating sectors into two groups. Those industries with a high concentration of research-oriented occupations are labeled intensive, while those with a lower concentration are considered nonintensive. The differences shown here illustrate why knowing how data are defined is essential to understanding what the data mean. Once again, those wishing for a simple answer will be frustrated. It is not the data that have failed them, but the reality of a complex system (the economy) and the human factor that must determine how to best reflect that system using data.

As we have found, trying to get a handle on this thing called technology, any kind of technology, is like grabbing air. Even low technology was once considered high technology in its day. For example, when the first plow was invented, it was probably considered a technological wonder. Then, after being hooked up to a horse or water buffalo, it increased the productivity of the farmers and it certainly drastically changed farming methods. When the wooden plow was integrated with a steel blade, certainly that was considered high technology in its day. One must remember that high technology today will undoubtedly be considered low technology 25–50 years from now. So, high technology is also based on a reference point and that reference point is time—perception and time are also key factors in cyber security.

As we see, it is not easy to come to grips with this phenomenon called high technology. For our purposes, a narrowly focused definition is better. In today's world, the microprocessor drives the technological products that drive the Information Age and cyber security. So, we will define high technology based on the microprocessor. High technology is defined as technology that includes a microprocessor.

The Microprocessor

In 1971, Intel introduced the Intel 4004 microprocessor. This was the first microprocessor on a single chip and included a central processing unit, input and output controls, and memory. This made it possible to program "intelligence" into inanimate objects and was the true beginning of the technology revolution that has caused so many changes in the world and ushered in the beginnings of the age of cyber security.

The microprocessor was developed through a long line of amazing inventions and improvements on inventions. Without these dramatic and often what appear to be new, miraculous breakthroughs in microprocessor technology, today's cyber security phenomenon would still be only in the dreams of science fiction writers, the likes of Jules Verne and George Orwell. However, because of the amazing developments in the microprocessor, cyber security is beginning to come to the forefront in modern-day governments and businesses.

Today, because of the microprocessor and its availability, miniaturization, power, and low cost, the world is rapidly developing new high-technology devices, procedures, processes, networks, and, of course, cyber security and conventional warfare weapons. The global information infrastructure (GII) is just one example of what microprocessors are making possible. The GII is the massive international connections of world computers that carry business and personal communication as well as that of the social and government sectors of nations. Some say that GII will connect entire cultures, erase international borders, support "cyber economies," establish new markets, and change our entire concept of international relations.

The GII is based on the Internet and much of the growth of the Internet is in developing nations. The GII is not a formal project but it is the result of thousands of individuals', corporations', and governments' need to communicate and conduct business by the most efficient and effective means possible. The GII is also a battlefield in the cyber security arena.

Moore's Law

No discussion of high technology and cyber security weapons would ever be complete without a short discussion of Moore's Law. In 1965, Gordon E. Moore, Director of Research and Development Laboratories, Fairchild Semiconductor, was asked by *Electronics* magazine to predict the future of semiconductors and its industry during the next 10 years. In what became known as Moore's Law, he stated that the capacity or circuit density of semiconductors doubles every 18 months or quadruples every 3 years.[4]

---

[4] Schaller, Bob, "The Origin, Nature, and Implications of 'MOORE'S LAW': The Benchmark of Progress in Semiconductor Electronics," September 26, 1996, http://research.microsoft.com/en-us/um/people/gray/moore_law.html.

The interesting thing about Moore's comments is that they became sort of a high-technology driver for the semiconductor industry and, even after all these years, it has been pretty much on track as to how semiconductors have improved over the years. Its power, of course, depends on how many transistors can be placed in how small a space. The mathematical version of Moore's Law is:

Bits per square inch $= 2(\text{time} - 1962)$[5]

Some of the-high technology "inventions" of the twentieth century that depended on the microprocessor include the following:

Ethernet (1973)
Laser printer (1975)
Ink-jet printer (1976)
Magnetic resonance imager (1977)
VisiCalc (1978)
Cellular phones (1979)
Cray supercomputer (1979)
MS-DOS (1981)
IBM personal computer (PC) (1981)
Scanning tunneling microscope (1981)
Apple Lisa (1983)
CD-ROM (1984)
Apple Macintosh (1984)
Windows operating systems (1985)
High-temperature superconductor (1986)
Digital cellular phones (1988)
Doppler radar (1988)
World Wide Web/Internet protocol (HTTP); HTML (1990)
Pentium processor (1993)
Java computer language (1995)
Digital versatile disk or digital video disk (1995)
Web TV (1996)

The Pioneer 10 spacecraft used the 4004 microprocessor. It was launched on March 2, 1972, and was the first space flight and microprocessor to enter the Asteroid Belt.

---

[5] Winfred Phillips, "Chapter 2 - Computers and Intelligence," The Mind Project, http://www.mind. ilstu.edu/curriculum/extraordinary_future/PhillipsCh2.php?modGUI=247&compGUI=1944&ite mGUI=3397.

Other Significant Twentieth Century High-Technology Developments and Events

Some of the significant high-technology computer events and inventions that took place in the twentieth century and led to our rapidly changing methods of prosecuting a war include:[6]

1971: Intel develops the 8008; Wozniak and Fernandez build the "Cream Soda Computer."

1972: Kildall writes PL/1, the first programming language for the Intel 4004 microprocessor; Gates and Allen form "Traf-O-Data"; Wozniak and Jobs begin selling Blue Boxes.

1973: Wozniak joins HP; Kildall and Cooper build "astrology forecasting machine."

1974: Intel invents the 8080; Xerox releases the Alto; Torode and Kildall begin selling microcomputers and disk operating systems.

1975: Microsoft (previously known as "Traf-O-Data") writes BASIC for the Altair; Heiser opens the first computer store in Los Angeles.

1976: Kildall funds Digital Research; work on the first RadioShack microcomputer started by Leininger and French; first sale of the CPM operating system takes place.

1977: Apple introduces the Apple II; TRS-80 developed.

1978: Apple ships disk drives for the Apple II and begins development of the Lisa computer.

1980: HP releases the HP-85; Apple III is announced; Microsoft and IBM sign an agreement for IBM's PC operating system.

1981: Osborne I developed; Xerox comes out with the 8010 Star and the 820 computers; IBM presents the PC.

1982: Apple Lisa is introduced; DEC develops a lines of personal computers (e.g., DEC Rainbow 100).

1983: IBM develops the IBM PC Jr.; Osborne files for Chapter 11 as the microcomputer market heats up.

1984: Apple announces the Macintosh microcomputer.

1986: Intel develops the 8086 chip.

1987: Intel develops the 8088 chip.

1990s: Intel, already the leader in microprocessors, announces the 286, 386, and 486 chips, followed rapidly by the Pentium chips now reaching speeds of 1.7 GHz as we enter the twenty-first century.

---

[6] See P. Freiberger and M. Swaine's book, *Fire in the Valley: The Making of the Personal Computer*, Osborne/McGraw, Berkeley, CA, 1984, and http://www.swaine.com/wordpress/tag/mike-swaine/ for additional details of computer history.

Moore's Law is still holding true although some believe we will soon hit the silicon wall, based on the laws of physics. Some of these doomsayers have been saying such things for years. Others are more optimistic and believe that other materials will be found to replace silicon or that silicon will be somehow enhanced to "defy" the laws of physics. If the past is any clue to the future, the future of high technology will not be impaired by such minor impediments as the laws of physics.

THE INTERNET

The real issue is control. The Internet is too widespread to be easily dominated by any single government. By creating a seamless global-economic zone, anti-sovereign and unregulatable, the Internet calls into question the very idea of the nation-state.[7]

John Perry Barlow

[7] John Perry Barlow, "Thinking Locally, Acting Globally," *Time*, January, 1996, p.57; as quoted on p. 197, *The Sovereign Individual*, by James Dale Davidson and Lord William Rees-Mogg, published by Touchstone, New York, 1999.

It is in the context of this phenomenal growth of high technology and human knowledge that the Internet arises as one of the mechanisms to facilitate sharing of information and as a medium that encourages global communications. The Internet has already become one of the twenty-first century's cyber security battlefields.

The global collection of networks that evolved in the late twentieth century to become the Internet represents what could be described as a "global nervous system," transmitting from anywhere to anywhere facts, opinions, and opportunity. However, when most people think of the Internet, it seems to be something either vaguely sinister or of such complexity that it is difficult to understand. Popular culture, as manifested by Hollywood and network television programs, does little to dispel this impression of danger and out-of-control complexity.

The Internet arose out of projects sponsored by the Advanced Research Project Agency (ARPA) in the United States in the 1960s. It is perhaps one of the most exciting legacy developments of that era. Originally an effort to facilitate sharing of expensive computer resources and to enhance military communications, it has, since about 1988, rapidly evolved from its scientific and military roots into one of the premier commercial communications media. The Internet, which is described as a global meta-network, or network of networks,[8] provides the foundation on which the global information superhighway has been built.

However, it was not until the early 1990s that Internet communication technologies became easily accessible to the average person. Prior to that time, Internet access required mastery of many arcane and difficult-to-remember programming language codes. However, declining microcomputer prices combined with enhanced microcomputer performance and the advent of easy-to-use browser[9] software as key enabling technologies created the foundation for mass Internet activity. When these variables aligned with the developing global telecommunications infrastructure, they allowed a rare convergence of capability.

E-mail. Although e-mail was invented in 1972, it was not until the advent of the "modern Internet system" that it really began to be used on a global scale. In 1987, there were approximately 10,000 Internet computer hosts and 1000 news messages a day in 300 newsgroups. In 1992, there were more than 1,000,000 hosts and 10,000 news messages a day in 1000 newsgroups. By 1995, the number of Internet hosts had risen to more than 10 million, with 250,000 news messages a day in over 10,000 newsgroups.[10] By 2014, the majority of e-mail traffic originated from the business world, which accounted for more than 108.7 billion e-mails that were sent and received every day.[11]

Internet protocols. In the 1970s, the Internet protocols were developed to be used to transfer information.

Usenet newsgroup and electronic mail. Newsgroups and electronic mail were developed in the 1980s.

Gopher. In 1991, personnel at the University of Minnesota created the Gopher as a user-friendly interface that was a menu system for accessing files.

World Wide Web. In 1991, Tim Berners-Lee and others at the Conseil Européene pour la Recherche Nucleaire developed the Web. In 1993, the Web had approximately 130 sites; in 1994, about 3000 sites; in April 1998, this had grown to more than 2.2 million and in January 2015 it had reached 1,169,228,000.[12]

---

[8] Ibid., p. 11.

[9] Software that simplifies the search and display of World Wide Web-supplied information.

[10] *Internet Guide* by Microsoft Personal Computing, http://www.microsoft.com/magazine/guides/internet/history.htm.

[11] "Email Statistics Report, 2014–2018," The Radicati Group, http://www.radicati.com/wp/wp-content/uploads/2014/01/Email-Statistics-Report-2014-2018-Executive-Summary.pdf.

[12] Internet live stats, http://www.internetlivestats.com/total-number-of-websites/.

The most commonly accessed application on the Internet is the World Wide Web (WWW). Originally developed in Switzerland, the Web was envisioned by its inventor as a way to help share information. The ability to find information concerning virtually any topic via search engines, such as Google, Bing, Alta Vista, HotBot, Lycos, InfoSeek, and others, from among the rapidly growing array of Web servers is an amazing example of how the Internet increases the information available to nearly everyone. One gains some sense of how fast and pervasive the Internet has become as more TV, radio, and print advertisements direct prospective customers to visit their business or government agency Web site. Such sites are typically named www.companyname.com, where the business is named "companyname," or www.governmentagency.gov for government agencies.

From the past century until now, the Internet has rapidly grown from an experimental research project and tool of the U.S. government and universities to the tool of everyone in the world with a computer. It is the premier global communications medium. With the subsequent development of search engines and, of course, the Web, the sharing of information has never been easier. Sites such as Google.com state that, in 2013 they searched through 30 trillion Web pages!

It has now become a simple matter for average people—even those who had trouble programming their VCRs—to obtain access to the global Internet and with the access search the huge volume of information it contains. Millions of people around the world are logging in, creating a vast environment often referred to as cyberspace and the GII, which has been described as the virtual, online, computer-enabled environment, as distinct from the physical reality of "real life."

By the end of the twentieth century, worldwide revenues via Internet commerce had reached perhaps hundreds of billions of dollars, an unparalleled growth rate for a technology that has been really effective only since the early 1990s! The "electronic commerce" of the early twenty-first century already includes everything from online information concerning products, purchases, and services to the development of entirely new business activities (e.g., Internet-enabled banking and gambling).

An important fact for everyone to understand, and which is of supreme importance to those interested in cyber security, is that the Web is truly global in scope. Physical borders as well as geographical distance are almost meaningless in cyberspace; the distant target is as easily attacked as the local one.

The annihilation of time and space makes the Internet an almost perfect environment for cyber crime and warfare. When finding a desired adversary's[13] server located on the other side of the planet is as easy and convenient as calling directory assistance to find a local telephone number, information warriors have the potential to act in ways that one can only begin to imagine. Undeterred by distance, borders, time, or season, the potential bonanza awaiting the information warrior is a chilling prospect for those who are responsible for safeguarding and defending the assets of a business or government agency.

Because of religious beliefs in many faiths, Internet access to material considered pornographic is generally not acceptable. One of society's struggles will be how to provide access to the world's information without causing some moral decay of society. This will be a struggle for many countries and it is believed that the information warriors will have a major impact on the society of such developing countries.

The Internet is the latest in a series of technological advances that are being used not only by honest people to further their communication, but also by miscreants, juvenile delinquents, and others for illegal purposes. As with any technological invention, it can be used for good or for illegal purposes. It is really no different from other inventions such as the handgun. The handgun can be used to defend and protect lives or to destroy them. It all depends on the human being who is using the technology.

THE HIGH-TECHNOLOGY-DRIVEN PHENOMENON

There are thousands of Internet service providers (ISPs) operating and connected all across the globe. It is hoped that we all know by now that our e-mails do not go point to point, but hop around the Internet. They are susceptible to being gleaned by all those with the resources to read other people's mail or steal information to commit crimes (e.g., identity theft, competitive intelligence information collections, and, of course, useful information for information warriors).

So, what is the point? The point is that there are ISPs all over the world with few regulations and absolutely no protection and defensive standards. Some ISPs may do an admirable job of protecting our information passing through their systems, while others may do nothing. Furthermore, as we learn more and more about "Netspionage" (computer-enabled business and government spying), we learn more and more about how our privacy and our information are open to others to read, capture, change, and otherwise misuse.

---

[13] The term "adversary" is used more often these days to describe an enemy than the word "enemy" because it seems it is not as harsh a term, although the intent is still to disable or kill them.

In addition, with such programs as SORM in Russia, Internet monitoring in China and elsewhere, global Echelon, and the U.S. FBI's Carnivore (still Carnivore no matter how often they change the name to make it more politically correct), we might as well take our most personal information, tattoo it on our bodies, and run naked in the streets for all to see. Well, that may be a slight exaggeration; the point is that we have no concept of how well ISPs are protecting information belonging to governments, businesses, individuals, or associations. Through your ISP, how susceptible are you to the threats of cyber security? Do you know if your ISP is protecting or monitoring you? If it is monitoring you, for whom?

FASTER AND MORE MASSIVE HIGH-TECHNOLOGY-DRIVEN COMMUNICATIONS

We are quickly expanding into a world of instant messages (IMs) through ISPs. After all, the more rapidly our world changes, the more rapidly we want to react and we want everything—now! A 2014 report by Juniper networks stated that instant messaging apps will account for 75% of mobile messaging traffic, or 63 trillion messages, by 2018. Furthermore, they can be used to transfer files, send graphics, and, unlike the telephone and normal e-mails, with IM one knows whether the person being contacted is there. Interesting ramifications—check to see if a person is online; if not (after already setting up a masquerade or spoof), take over that person's identity and contact someone posing as the other—instantly. Of course, there are perhaps hundreds, if not thousands, of examples of ISPs being penetrated or misused. As far back as approximately November 1995, for example, the *Wall Street Journal* ran a story entitled "America Online to Warn Users about Bad E-mail." We all know about the basic issues of viruses and other malicious codes being sent via ISPs. So, the problem has existed for quite some time.

Solar Storms Could Affect Telecommunications. Intense storms raging on the sun … could briefly disrupt telecommunications …. The eruptions triggered a powerful, but brief, blackout Friday on some high-frequency radio channels and low-frequency navigational signals … forecast at least a 30 percent chance of continuing disruptions …. In addition to radio disruptions, the charged particles can bombard satellites and orbiting spacecraft and, in rare cases, damage industrial equipment on the ground, including power generators and pipelines.[14]

[14] "Solar Flare Goes Off the Charts," http://www.tldm.org/News3/Solar_flare.htm.

High technology is vulnerable to nature and the universe in general. What a great time to launch a cyber security attack on an adversary, including maybe competitors. Is it sunspots or an adversary causing these outages? By the time the adversary finds out it is you and not three days of sunspots, the war could be over.

THE BENEFICIAL EFFECT OF HACKER TOOLS AND OTHER MALICIOUS SOFTWARE ON NETWORK SECURITY WITH DUAL ROLES AS CYBER SECURITY TOOLS

The following examples of malicious software were selected as a representative sample of those that are available and for their range of functionality and, additionally, for their range through time from 1991 to present. These tools can be and are being adapted and adopted for use in cyber security.[15]

Hacker tools. Of the hacker tools that were reviewed, while the intentions of the originators of the tools were mixed, with some being malicious and some well intentioned, they can all be used to strengthen the security of a network or to monitor the system for illicit activity. This can be achieved if the system owner uses hacker tools to identify the weaknesses that exist in the security of the system, to identify appropriate remedial action, before a person with malicious intent attempts to exploit the weaknesses. A number of the tools can also be used to monitor the system for illicit activity, even before software patches are available, so that the system owner can make informed decisions on appropriate action to prevent or minimize damage to his or her system. As a cyber security officer, how will you defend against such attacks?

Viruses. Viruses have no direct beneficial effect on the security of a system except to provide a visible indication that there has been a breakdown in procedures for the transfer of software or data between systems. The negative effect of viruses is the cost in terms of time and the antivirus software to check data and software being imported or exported to and from the system, as well as the cost of rectifying a problem when an infection has occurred, which can be considerable.

In an abstract way, the advent of the virus has actually been beneficial to the cyber security officer because the impact of a virus on the user is a visible and constant reminder of the need to observe good cyber security practices.

---

[15] A number of other tools were reviewed but contained no obvious property or functionality that was considered to be both beneficial and a potential cyber security weapon; that is, they modified the system to exploit vulnerabilities or they were purely malicious and caused a denial of service. These are tools that are "pure" cyber security tools.

In the majority of cases, the virus is detected before it can activate its payload, so the damage is normally limited to the inconvenience and cost of the cleaning up the system to remove the virus. As a cyber security weapon, it is a valuable and cheap weapon that can cause devastating results against your unprepared information systems.

Worms. The release onto the Internet on November 2, 1988, of the Internet worm written by Robert T. Morris, Jr., quickly caused widespread disruption and the failure of a large proportion of the network that existed at that time. The problem was compounded by the fact that some of the servers that had not been affected were taken offline to prevent them from becoming infected, thus placing a higher load on already-affected sections of the system and denying those elements of the network that had gone offline access to the patches that would protect them, as the normal distribution method for patches was over the Internet itself. To date, there have been no security benefits derived from worms, other than, in the case of the Robert T. Morris worm, to highlight the urgent need for effective and early communication of information on incidents.

The potential for the use of this type of program in a way that would aid the security of systems has been postulated, in the form of autonomous intelligent agents that would travel through the system and report back predefined information, such as the system assets, the condition and identity of system elements, and the presence or absence of specific types of activity. As a weapon for prosecuting cyber security, worms have excellent potential and may even be considered a "weapon of mass destruction" because of the damage they can cause a high-technology, information systems-dependent adversary. Of course, we now have many "colored" worms being written and traveling around the GII, NIIs, and other networks.

Easter eggs. Easter eggs have no beneficial effect other than to highlight that even proprietary software can have large sections of code included in them that are redundant to the functionality for which they were intended and also that the quality control procedures for the production of software by well-known organizations is poor if the Easter eggs were not detected during production. Can you think of any way to use these "eggs" in a cyber security battle?

Trojan horses. The Trojan horse, by definition, carries out actions that are normally hidden from the user while disguising its presence as a benign item of software. They are difficult to detect because they appear to be a legitimate element of the operating system or application that would normally be found on the system. Given that the purpose of a Trojan horse is to hide itself and its functionality from legitimate users, there have been no beneficial effects derived from them—unless you are an information warrior. As a cyber security officer, you must defend against them.

Logic bombs. Logic bombs, as with Trojan horses, carry out actions that are unexpected and undesirable. Some may cause relatively minor damage, such as writing a message to a screen, while others are considerably more destructive. They are normally inserted by disaffected staff or by people with a grudge against the organization. Again, they are difficult to detect before they have been activated and, as a result, can be expensive to rectify. Logic bombs are correctly named as they can have the same effect against the system of an adversary as a physical bomb might have against a building—Boom! It is gone!

The clear implication from the issues discussed above is that some hacker tools can have a beneficial effect on the security of computer systems if they are used by the system staff before they are used by personnel either within the organization or outside it to identify shortcomings or flaws in the operating system or applications software, the configuration of the system, or the procedures used to secure it. Viruses, while providing no direct benefit, do provide a detectable indication that there has been a breach in the security of the system, either by an exploitation of a flaw in the security procedures or by a shortcoming in the system software (it allowed a virus through any barriers that had been created to prevent access to the system).

Worms currently have no beneficial effect on system security management. However, the concept that was used to disseminate the Robert T. Morris worm may have an application in the mapping of large networks if applied to autonomous agents. The Trojan horse and the logic bomb, which, by their very nature, are covertly inserted into the system without the owner's knowledge, have no beneficial effect and have only malicious applications.

OTHER HIGH-TECHNOLOGY TOOLS IN CYBER SECURITY

Cyber wars (information warfare) through technology are being fought on many fronts—on the personal privacy, corporate Netspionage,[16] and nation-state battlefields of the world. Even such innocent-sounding words as "cookies" take on new meaning in the cyber security arena.

These cookies—the computer kind, not the ones you eat—are beneficial, except when they are used to profile customer habits and gather an individual's

---

[16] See the book, *Netspionage: The Global Threat to Information*, published by Butterworth–Heinemann in September 2000.

private information, which is then sold. High-technology cookies are files that a Web site can load onto a user's system. They are used to send back to the Web site a user's activity on that Web site, as well as what Web sites the user has previously visited. They are also a potential tool of the information warrior.

Intel's Pentium III included a unique processor serial number (PSN) in every one of its new Pentium III chips. Intel claimed that the PSN could identify an individual's surfing through electronic commerce and other Internet-based applications. It was noted that by providing a unique PSN that can be read by Web sites and other application programs, it could make an excellent cyber security tool. Although this number is designed to be used to link user activities on the Internet for marketing and other purposes, one can easily imagine other uses, from a cyber security perspective, that can be made of this high-technology application. And as for Microsoft's new operating system, XP, imagine the IW possibilities.

Steganography is another use of high technology that can be used in cyber security:[17]

Hiding information by embedding a file inside another, seemingly innocent file is a technique known as "steganography." It is most often used with graphics, sound, text, HTML, and PDF files. Steganography with digital files works by replacing the unused bytes of data in a computer file with bytes that contain concealed information.

Steganography (which translated from Greek means covered writing) has been in use since about 580 B.C. One technique was to carve secret messages into wooden objects and then cover the etched words with colored wax to make them undetectable to an uninitiated observer. Another method was to tattoo a message onto the shaved messenger's head. Once the hair grew back, the messenger was sent on his mission. Upon arrival, the head was shaved, thus revealing the message—obviously not time-dependent. The microdot, which reduced a page of text to the size of a typewriter's period so that it could be glued onto a postcard or letter and sent through the mail, is another example.[18]

Two types of files are typically used when embedding data into an image. The innocent image that holds the hidden information is a "container." A "message" is the information to be hidden. A message may be plaintext, ciphertext, other images, or anything that can be embedded in the least significant bits of an image.[19]

---

[17] Excerpt taken from the book, *Netspionage: The Global Threat to Information*, published by Butterworth–Heinemann in September 2000, and reprinted with permission.

[18] Steganography, http://www.webopedia.com/TERM/S/steganography.html.

[19] Steganography, http://www.jjtc.com/Steganography/.

Steganographic software has some unique advantages as a tool for Netspionage agents. First, if the agents use regular cryptographic software on their computer systems, the files may not be accessible to investigators but will be visible, and it will be obvious that the agents are hiding something. Steganographic software allows agents to "hide in plain sight" any valuable digital assets they may have obtained until they can transmit or transfer the files to a safe location or to their customer. As a second advantage, steganography can be used to conceal and transfer an encrypted document containing the acquired information to a digital dead drop. The agents could then provide the handler or customer with the password to unload the dead drop but not divulge the steganographic extraction phrase until payment is received or the agents are safely outside the target corporation. As a final note, even when a file is known or suspected to contain information protected with steganographic software, it has been almost impossible to extract the information unless the passphrase has been obtained.

WELCOME TO THE TWENTY-FIRST-CENTURY TECHNOLOGY

As we left the twentieth century and began the twenty-first century, our dependence on technology continued to increase as well as our interconnectivity on a global basis, our integration of devices–or platforms–and use of wireless, mobile technology. This has increased our vulnerability to successful attacks on a global scale. It has also made protection of our systems, information, etc., much more difficult—maybe even impossible.

As we progress into the twenty-first century, we continue to fall behind in our defenses and ability to react quickly and successfully to attacks from around the world. As the sophistication of attacks continues to increase so do the vulnerabilities of our vital information infrastructures.

Top cyber security experts echoed a dire warning from a top intelligence chief on the vulnerability of the U.S. power grid, with one telling FoxNews.com that state-sponsored hackers could send America's nerve centers on an "uncontrollable, downward spiral."[20]

[20] "Intel boss' warning on cyber attacks no joke, say experts," http://www.foxnews.com/world/2014/11/23/intel-boss-warning-on-cyber-attacks-no-joke-say-experts/.

Defending our information has been made more difficult by advances in technology and also in social networks of all kinds, through which users continue to innocently provide information that is very useful to competitors and other adversaries and that leaves individuals, groups, corporations, and governments more open to attacks.

Let's Look at Some of the Major Technology Advances Thus Far in the Twenty-first Century:

The power of cell and Wi-Fi phones as they have become not only telephones, but more all-in-one communication devices, for example, voice, text, e-mail, storage devices, and video and digital cameras. Not far behind are the tablets, which offer the same mobility as cell phones but bigger screens and often more power, storage, memory capacity, and speed.

Twitter, Facebook, You Tube, blogs, and others offer social connectivity as never before by which individuals, businesses, and governments on a global, mobile scale share information that includes accidentally or purposefully posting sensitive or maybe even classified information as users go unchecked. It is also a great platform for blackmail, marketing, and spreading false information or propaganda and of course for collecting information useful in GIW and conventional wars and battles.

More sophisticated game machines and games that can be used to help train info-warriors and in fact are being used to do so.

Driverless vehicles, including trams, trains, and cars, that are turning into computers on wheels. They are loaded with technology. Imagine once they are taken over, controlled by a terrorist, they can easily be turned into weapons, giving new weapons status as car bombs with which the drivers do not have to sacrifice their lives.

Electric vehicles over time will become more prevalent. Since we are unable to store electricity as well as we can gas, what would happen to our ability to use electric vehicles, especially for emergencies, once our power grids go down and they cannot be recharged. As we race to be "eco-friendly," are we considering what to do to mitigate this up-and-coming vulnerability? No, of course not.

We are also approaching the time when we will truly be able to use artificial intelligence and possibly become dependent on it. What happens when that happens and it is taken over and changed by info-warriors and made into weapons support?

The use of nano-technology will continue to be enhanced and as it is, it can be embedded in our infrastructures to destroy them or injected into our bodies. Also, as we depend more on robotics from manufacturing to medical devices, even for surgeries, what happens when they are taken over by info-warriors?

Looking back at what has been accomplished just in our short lifetimes, imagine the twenty-first-century technology and the cyber security-related implications coming in the future.

SUMMARY

If you are involved in any activity in which technology is used as a tool to help you accomplish your work, you are aware of the tremendous and very rapid advances that are being made in that arena. It is something to behold. We are in the middle of the most rapid technological advances in human history, but this is just the beginning. We are not even close to reaching the potential that technology has to offer, nor its impact on all of us—both good and bad.

It is said that there have been more discoveries in the past 50 years than in the entire history of mankind before that time. We have just to read the newspapers and the trade journals to look at every profession and see what technology is bringing to our world. There are new discoveries in medicine, online and worldwide information systems, the ability to hold teleconferences across the country and around the globe, and hundreds of other examples that we can all think of.

High technology is the mainstay of both our businesses and our government agencies. We can no longer function in business or government without them. Pagers, cellular phones, e-mail, credit cards, teleconferences, smart cards, tablets and notebook computers, networks, and private branch exchanges (PBXs) are all computer based and all are now common tools for individuals, businesses, and public and government agencies. Information warriors are also relying more and more on computers. As computers become more sophisticated, so do the information warriors. As international networks increase, so does the number of international information warriors.

Networking and embedded systems, those integrated into other devices (e.g., automobiles, microwave ovens, medical equipment), are increasing and drastically changing how we live, work, and play. According to a study financed by the U.S. ARPA and published in the book *Computers at Risk:*

> Computers have become so integrated into the business environment that computer-related risks cannot be separated from normal business risks or those of government and other public agencies.
>
> Increased trust in computers for safety-critical applications (e.g., medical) leads to the increased likelihood that attacks or accidents can cause deaths. (Note: It has already happened.)
>
> Use and abuse of computers are widespread with increased threats of viruses and credit card, PBX, cellular phones, and other frauds.
>
> An unstable international political environment raises concerns about government or terrorist attacks on information and high-technology-dependent nations' computer and telecommunications systems.
>
> Individual privacy is at risk owing to large, vulnerable databases containing personal information, thus facilitating increases in identity theft and other frauds.

If I want to wreak havoc on a society that, in some cases, has become complacent, I am going to attack your quality of life.
Curt Weldon, R-PA. U.S. House, Armed Services Committee[21]

[21] Speaking at an InfoWar Conference in Washington, D.C., in September 1999.

Personal computers have changed our lives dramatically and there is no end in sight. High technology in general has improved the quality of life for societies and made life a little easier, and yet it makes an information-dependent way of life more at risk than ever before. The use of modems has become commonplace, with all newly purchased microcomputer systems[22] coming with an internal modem already installed and ready for global access through the Internet or other networks. Wireless networks are being increasingly used and there are now millions of Wi-Fi "hot spots" to which people can connect their phone,

[22] Microcomputers had been a term used to differentiate them from minicomputers and mainframe computers. The computers' power and what the manufacturers decided to call them differentiated these systems. However, with the power of today's microcomputer equaling that of larger systems, the issue is unclear and basically no longer very relevant. What these systems are called, coupled with notebooks, PDAs, workstations, desktops, etc., is not that important because they all basically operate the same way.

laptop, or tablet wherever they are. Therefore, these devices and the networks that they are using potentially represent some of the most serious and complex crime scenes of the Information Age. This will surely increase as we begin the twenty-first century.

> ... it is computerized information, not manpower or mass production that ... will win wars in a world wired for 500 TV channels. The computerized information exists in cyberspace—the new dimension created by endless reproduction of computer networks, satellites, modems, databases, and the public Internet.[23]
>
> **Neil Munro**

[23] Neil Munro, "The Pentagon's New Nightmare: An Electronic Pearl Harbor," *Washington Post*, July 16, 1995, p. C3.

High-technology development continues to play a dual role in information-based nation-states. The high-technology devices have been turned into tools that have been used to determine the adequacy of cyber defenses and have been adopted and adapted by global hackers, terrorists, and other miscreants. They now have been using those tools for probing and attacking systems, especially through the Internet interfaces of corporations and nation-states, as well as the GII and NIIs of nation-states. These same hacker techniques have been readily adopted and enhanced by the information warriors of nation-states and others.

CHAPTER 5

Understanding Today's Threats in the Cyber Vapor—"War Stories" from the Front Lines[1]

[2]*Existing and potential threats in the sphere of information security are among the most serious challenges of the twenty-first century. Threats emanate from a wide variety of sources and manifest themselves in disruptive activities that target individuals, businesses, national infrastructure, and governments alike. Their effects carry significant risk for public safety, the security of nations, and the stability of the globally linked international community as a whole*

Contents

When discussing the various aspects of cyber security, the cyber security officer must understand that he or she is also an information warrior and is working in the midst of global information warfare (GIW). It is important to also be aware of the actual, various types of information warfare attacks that are currently being conducted 24/7 around the world against individuals, groups, businesses, and governments.

Being aware of such attacks, one can get a better appreciation of the massive challenges ahead for those cyber security professionals, sometimes also called info-warriors throughout this chapter, trying, often in vain, to protect the information and information systems being used today.

It is also important to know of the latest technologies being developed and by whom, as well as understanding the politics of the time, because as

---

[1] Much of this chapter is quoted with permission from the author and his coauthor's book, *Global Information Warfare*, second edition, published by CRC Press.
[2] Report (A/65/201) of the Group of Governmental Experts on Developments in the Field of Information and Telecommunications in the Context of International Security.

tensions rise among people, businesses, groups, and nations, they are more apt to become aggressively involved in GIW.

As you read through these actual attacks and their related commentaries[3], think of how to defend against them and also how to use them, piggyback off of them, when conducting maybe "aggressive defensive" operations against adversaries. Knowing the who, how, where, when, why, and what will help defend against GIW attacks as well as providing a basis that can be used for enhancing your corporation's or government agency's defenses.

As you read through them, consider that one or more of these attacks are happening 24/7 and your corporation or government agency is now under attack, has been, or will be. Details are not provided, as the point is to get an understanding of these attacks, similar to old warfare bombardment of our defenses, if you were in a physical war zone. Details of each of these attacks or other information provided can be found at referenced Web sites. As you know, all information online is subject to being perishable. Even so, you can search the topic and find information you need on each threat to help you build your defenses.

REPORTED DIGITAL BATTLEFIELD ATTACKS AND RELATED STORIES

Let us start off with one of the most sophisticated attacks, allegedly made in July 2010 against Iran's nuclear program using a program called "Stuxnet."

Stuxnet is a computer worm that was discovered in June 2010. It was designed to attack industrial programmable logic controllers (PLCs). PLCs allow the automation of electromechanical processes such as those used to control machinery on factory assembly lines, amusement rides, or centrifuges for separating nuclear material.[4]

Allegedly, this program was the work of the United States and Israel, although this is just speculation. The worm entered the Iranian network and destabilized over 1000 of their centrifuges.

Now, one can only speculate how it entered a "closed" network. Some allege it was inserted via a CD/DVD or a flash drive by an insider. Others speculate a disk or flash drive was left in a place where someone working in the Iranian facility found it and entered it into the closed Iranian nuclear network just to see what was on the medium and thus unleashed the worm.

[3] All stories are edited, generally direct quotes from the cited Web sites, except where otherwise noted.
[4] http://en.wikipedia.org/wiki/Stuxnet; Razvan, Bogdan. "Win32.Worm.Stuxnet.A". Retrieved March 28, 2014.

The "Regin" malware—allegedly the most powerful to date, even more powerful than Stuxnet, targets mostly Russian and Saudi telecommunication companies. It has been out there since 2008 and even when detected, you cannot tell what it is doing. It is supposedly in 10 countries, including India and Iran, with half of its attacks in Russia. Some say it is so good it is believed it could be developed only by a nation-state—a Western nation-state. Interestingly, attacks are now being reported in the United States.

- Varney & Company, business news program, Fox Business TV Channel, November 24, 2014

Now, let us talk about a simple attack:

A journalist tells the story[5] of his devices allegedly being hacked and his photos, e-mails—basically his entire cyber life—were deleted. He was able to contact the hackers, who were teenagers, and they said they just did it for "fun." He agreed not to press charges, not to identify them, but wanted to know how they did it.

They allegedly told him that they did not hack his passwords, but basically did the following: They began by "social engineering" their way into his accounts taking advantage of loopholes in the system.

- They first called amazon.com as him and gave them a false credit card number.
- They received a temporary password from Amazon.
- Now they owned his Amazon account.
- They got the last four numbers of his actual credit card.
- Apple was using it also as an identity verification method.
- Apple gave "him" (the hackers) a password reset.
- Now they owned his Apple account.
- They then went to Google and then to Twitter.

Note: As you can see, today's GIW attacks can range from the nontechnical, using social engineering techniques, to the more sophisticated covert malware types of attacks, to a combination of both, and everything in-between.

U.S. military academies' information warfare (IW) games: Every year the U.S. military academies of the Army, Navy, Coast Guard, and Air Force put together a group of cadet info-warriors to compete in an IW game using a points system to determine the winner. It begins with each academy selecting a team and building a "secure" network and all are then attacked over a three-day period by a "Red Team." This sophisticated IW game is used to help train the U.S. military info-warriors of the future.[6]

[5] TV Program called "NOVA," October 8, 2014.
[6] Cyber Wargame," August 25, 2014, Fox Business Channel TV.

Do you ever get the feeling you are being watched? If you've got a webcam, you might be right ... It's stunningly easy since most companies, in an effort to be helpful, put installation manuals online, manuals that make public the default passwords for their products.

- http://www.foxnews.com/tech/2014/11/21/hacked-webcams-is-your-home-next/?intcmp=ob_homepage_tech&intcmp=obnetwork

The Taiwanese government is investigating whether Xiaomi, Inc., China's leading smartphone company ... is a cyber security threat ... as governments become increasingly wary of potential cyber security threats from the world's second-biggest economy. ... The smartphone maker recently came under fire for unauthorized data access.

- https://ca.news.yahoo.com/taiwan-government-investigates-xiaomi-potential-cyber-security-concerns-044430946--finance.html

A Syrian Twitter user appeared to break the news of U.S.-led air strikes in Syria overnight before the Pentagon announced it had launched them.

- http://news.yahoo.com/us-syria-air-strikes-live tweets-130215331.html

Home Depot said Thursday a recent cyber attack on its computer network affected a colossal 56 million customer payment cards ... is believed to be the biggest ever hack of a retail firm's computer systems ... used malware to collect customer information.

- http://www.foxnews.com/tech/2014/09/19/home-depot-malware-attack-even-bigger-than-targets-56m-payment-cards-affected/?intcmp=obnetwork

Hackers would love to weasel their way onto your smartphone or tablet ... mobile gadgets are a bit harder to crack ... hackers have to be even sneakier and use malicious apps or hidden Wi-Fi attacks or simply walk off with your gadget.

- http://www.foxnews.com/tech/2014/10/19/essential-security-apps-for-your-smartphone-and-tablet/?intcmp=obnetwork

Governments all around the world use malware and spyware to keep tabs on people, from visitors to residents.

The Detekt tool was developed and supported by several human rights groups. Detekt checks for malware that is often used against journalists, activists, and others.

- http://www.foxnews.com/tech/2014/11/21/free-tool-detects-government-spyware/?intcmp=ob_homepage_tech&intcmp=obnetwork

A company Web site, along with 1.2 billion other Web sites, was targeted by Russian hackers utilizing a massive "bot" attack. These bots aggressively attempted access to Web sites with user name and password options.

- http://www.foxbusiness.com/personal-finance/2014/08/29/why-your-passwords-should-be-at-least-24-charcters-long/?intcmp=obnetwork

Voting machines that switch Republican votes to Democrats are being reported in Maryland.

- http://www.foxnews.com/politics/2014/10/27/calibration-issue-pops-up-on-maryland-voting-machines/

Australian defense officials are preparing for what could be a barrage of possible cyber attacks during the G20 leaders' summit this Saturday and Sunday in Brisbane. "Targeting of high profile events such as the G20 by state-sponsored or other foreign adversaries, cyber criminals and issue-motivated groups is a real and persistent threat ..."

- http://www.foxnews.com/tech/2014/11/13/australia-braces-for-g20-cyber-attacks/?intcmp=features

Some of the "FBI's Cyber's Most Wanted" show that this problem is global in nature as those wanted come from all parts of the world. (See their photos and descriptions on their Web site—also note that they are from all over the world—http://www.fbi.gov/wanted/cyber.)

Their offenses include such things[7] as conspiracy to commit wire fraud, money laundering, passport fraud, and trafficking in counterfeit service marks; wire fraud; money laundering; passport fraud; and trafficking in counterfeit service marks. Reward: The U.S. Department of State's Transnational Organized Crime Rewards Program is offering a reward of up to $1 million for information leading to the arrest and/or conviction ... conspiring to commit computer fraud; accessing a computer without authorization for the purpose of commercial advantage and private financial gain; damaging computers through the transmission of code and commands; aggravated identity theft; economic espionage; and theft of trade secrets.

On May 1, 2014, a grand jury in the Western District of Pennsylvania indicted five members of the People's Liberation Army (PLA) of the People's Republic of China (PRC) on 31 criminal counts, including conspiring to commit computer fraud, accessing a computer without authorization for the purpose of commercial advantage and private financial gain, damaging computers through the transmission of code and commands, aggravated identity theft, economic espionage, and theft of trade secrets.

The subjects were allegedly officers of the PRC's Third Department of the General Staff Department of the PLA, Second Bureau, Third Office, Military Unit Cover Designator 61398, at some point during the investigation. The activities executed by each of the individuals allegedly involved in the conspiracy varied according to his specialties. Each provided his individual expertise to an alleged conspiracy to penetrate the computer networks of six American companies while those companies were engaged

[7] Taken from the FBI's Web site.

in negotiations or joint ventures or were pursuing legal action with, or against, state-owned enterprises in China. They then used their illegal access to allegedly steal proprietary information including, for instance, e-mail exchanges among company employees and trade secrets related to technical specifications for nuclear plant designs. One subject, Sun, who held the rank of captain during the early stages of the investigation, was observed both sending malicious e-mails and controlling victim computers.

One individual is wanted for his alleged involvement in manufacturing spyware, which was used to intercept the private communications of hundreds, if not thousands, of victims. As part of the scheme, the suspect ran a Web site offering customers a way to "catch a cheating lover" by sending spyware masquerading as an electronic greeting card. Victims who opened the greeting card would unwittingly install a program onto their computers. The program collected keystrokes and other incoming and outgoing electronic communications on the victims' computers. The program would periodically send e-mail messages back to the purchaser of the service containing the acquired communications, including the victims' passwords, lists of visited Web sites, intercepted e-mail messages, and keystroke logs. The program in question was initially called "e-mail PI" and renamed "Lover Spy" in July/August 2003. The suspect allegedly hosted the Web site, as well as creating the computer program. He ran the operation from his San Diego residence in 2003.

He was charged with the following crimes: manufacturing a surreptitious interception device, sending a surreptitious interception device, advertising a surreptitious interception device, unlawfully intercepting electronic communications, disclosing unlawfully intercepted electronic communications, unauthorized access to protected computer for financial gain, and aiding and abetting.

This suspect was in the United States on a travel visa and then obtained a student visa while he was taking college courses. He has ties to San Diego, California, and his last known location is San Salvador, El Salvador.

One security expert noted that healthcare.gov is a still a huge ripe target … and that unlike the private sector, no law requires the federal government to even inform you if your information has been hacked.
• http://www.foxnews.com/politics/2014/10/27/is-your-obamacare-information-safe/

Throughout the flood of hacks and data breaches at retailers, restaurants, health care providers, and online companies this year—Home Depot, Target, Subway, Adobe, and eBay were just a handful …
• http://www.foxnews.com/tech/2014/11/01/5-steps-to-keep-your-accounts-safe-from-hackers-and-scammers/?intcmp=ob_homepage_tech&intcmp=obnetwork

Defense Advanced Research Project Agency leaders told lawmakers the agency is making progress with an ongoing cyber security project known as Plan X to increase cyber visibility and provide a new foundation for the fast-developing world of cyber warfare moving into the future.

- http://defensetech.org/2014/05/14/darpa-sets-cyber-foundations-with-plan-x/#ixzz32V4YPy00

Information warfare is one of the hottest topics in current discussions of battlefield and geopolitical conflict. It has been addressed in writings, conferences, doctrines and plans, and military reorganizations, and it has been proposed as a fundamental element of twenty-first-century conflict. In a way, the IW situation is reminiscent of the concept of logistics as a military discipline, c.1940:

- Elements of the concept had been known and used for millennia.
- The value of integrating those elements into a coherent discipline was just beginning to be recognized.
- The discipline was to become a central element of modern warfare—it is now said that "amateur generals [that is, Saddam Hussein] talk strategy, professional generals talk logistics."
- From L. Scott Johnson, who works for Tera Research, Inc., a contractor performing analysis on behalf of the Directorate of Intelligence.

General Zhu's comments were echoed during a spirited question-and-answer session following Hagel's speech. In the session, PLA Major General Yao Yunzhu questioned America's repeated claim that it doesn't take sides in territorial disputes, asking how that can be true when the United States also claims the disputed islands in the East China Sea are covered by a U.S. treaty with Japan.

- http://www.foxnews.com/world/2014/05/31/chinese-general-warns-that-us-is-making-imporant-mistakes-in-region/?intcmp=HPBucket

Virtual Battlespace 3 ... Using the system, the Army can build battlefield scenarios and tailor the game to reflect specific requirements. Soldiers, for example, can simulate driving a Stryker, conduct patrols, engage in close combat, and drive down to the firing position to practice gunnery in realistic terrain.

- http://www.foxnews.com/tech/2014/05/22/army-battles-with-brawn-and-beer-bellies/?intcmp=features

The U.S. Department of Homeland Security is investigating about two dozen cases of suspected cyber security flaws in medical devices and hospital equipment that officials fear could be exploited by hackers ...

- http://www.foxnews.com/tech/2014/10/22/us-government-probes-medical-devices-for-possible-cyber-flaws/?intcmp=features

BlackBerry has announced a deal to acquire German anti-eavesdropping specialist SecuSmart ... provides its technology to German Chancellor Angela Merkel, who is at the center of a controversy over an alleged National Security Agency phone tap.

- http://www.foxnews.com/tech/2014/07/29/blackberry-launches-cyber-snooping-counter-attack/?intcmp=obnetwork

Between traffic-light cameras, blue-light cameras that scan neighborhoods for violent crime, cameras on board city trains and buses—not to mention private security cameras—there are few places you can go in Chicago without being monitored.

- http://www.foxnews.com/politics/2014/05/12/security-camera-surge-in-chicago-sparks-concerns-massive-surveillance-system/

The United States plans to "keep up the pressure" on China as it gauges that nation's response to this week's indictment of five Chinese military officials for allegedly hacking into American corporate computers ... If China doesn't begin to acknowledge and curb its corporate cyber espionage, the United States plans to start selecting from a range of retaliatory options.

- http://www.foxnews.com/politics/2014/05/24/us-to-rev-up-hacking-fight-against-china/

There are at least 19 bogus cell phone towers operating across the United States that could be used to spy upon, and even hijack, passing mobile phones.

- https://us-mg6.mail.yahoo.com/neo/launch?.partner=ftr&.rand=701bmckq23kk8#mail

More than 1000 U.S. retailers could be infected with malicious software lurking in their cash register computers, allowing hackers to steal customer financial data, the Homeland Security Department ...

- http://www.foxnews.com/tech/2014/08/22/malicious-software-in-cash-registers-could-affect-more-than-1000-us-retailers/?intcmp=obnetwork

The director of the CIA, in a rare apology, has acknowledged an internal probe's findings that CIA employees in the Executive Branch improperly spied on the Legislative Branch by searching Senate computers earlier this year.

- http://www.foxnews.com/politics/2014/07/31/cia-director-apologizes-to-senate-leaders/?intcmp=latestnews

In the field of artificial intelligence, there is no more iconic and controversial milestone than the Turing Test, when a computer convinces a sufficient number of interrogators into believing that it is not a machine but rather is a human. Having a computer that can trick a human into thinking that someone, or even something, is a person we trust is a wake-up call to cyber crime.

- https://www.yahoo.com/tech/a-computer-passed-the-famous-turing-test-for-the-first-88270310244.html

The mission data packages now being developed by the Air Force's 53rd Wing are designed to accommodate new information as new threat data become available. The database is loaded with a wide range of information to include commercial airliner information and specifics on Russian and Chinese fighter jets.

- http://www.foxnews.com/tech/2014/06/19/air-force-develops-threat-data-base-for-f-35/?intcmp=obnetwork

The National Security Agency's (NSA) surveillance machinery is again in the spotlight after a media report claimed that it is secretly providing data to almost two dozen U.S. government agencies via a powerful "Google-like" search engine.

- http://www.foxnews.com/tech/2014/08/26/google-like-search-engine-puts-nsa-snooping-back-in-spotlight/

The federal government is spending nearly $1 million to create an online database that will track "misinformation" and hate speech on Twitter … monitor "suspicious memes" and what it considers "false and misleading ideas," with a major focus on political activity online.

- http://www.foxnews.com/politics/2014/08/26/feds-creating-database-to-track-hate-speech-on-twitter/

The Secret Service has confirmed what you've probably suspected for a long time: Public computers at hotels are ridiculously insecure, and you're taking a gamble with your personal data each time you use one.

- http://www.foxnews.com/tech/2014/07/14/secret-service-warns-hotels-data-theft/?intcmp=obnetwork

Israeli's secret service intercepted Secretary of State John Kerry's phone calls during 2013 Middle East peace negotiations, according to the German publication *Spiegel*.

- http://www.foxnews.com/politics/2014/08/03/israel-spied-on-kerrys-calls-during-2013-peace-talks-magazine-reports/

China took its investigation of "alleged monopoly actions" by Microsoft to a new level this week, raiding four of the company's offices and carrying away internal documents and computers.

- http://www.foxnews.com/tech/2014/07/30/microsofts-china-woes-increase/?intcmp=obnetwork

Samsung Electronics said five of its Galaxy-branded smartphones and tablets that come with its enterprise security software recently received approval from the U.S. Defense Information Systems Agency, allowing them to be listed as an option for officials.

- http://www.foxnews.com/tech/2014/06/09/samsung-devices-get-nod-from-us-defense-agency/?intcmp=obnetwork

As more devices and appliances with Internet capabilities enter the market, protecting those devices from hackers becomes critical. Unfortunately, many of these noncomputer, nonsmartphone devices—from toilets to refrigerators to alarm systems—were not built with security in mind.

- http://www.foxnews.com/tech/2014/08/26/how-to-secure-your-easily-hackable-smart-home/?intcmp=obnetwork

Hot on the heels of the NSA snooping firestorm, a leaked document appears to detail the cyber espionage tricks employed by its U.K. counterpart, GCHQ.

- http://www.foxnews.com/tech/2014/07/15/uk-intelligence-agency-in-cyber-spying-controversy/

The spy agency has relied more on facial-recognition technology in the past 4 years as a result of new software that can process the flood of digital communications such as e-mails, text messages, and even video conferences ...

- http://www.foxnews.com/politics/2014/06/01/nsa-steps-up-digital-image-harvesting-to-feed-its-advancing-facial-recognition/

Concerned over network security following news last year suggesting German leader Angela Merkel had her phone tapped by the NSA, the government said it will transfer all its telecom and Internet-related services to the German firm Deutsche Telekom...

- http://www.foxnews.com/tech/2014/06/27/german-government-ends-contract-with-verizon-following-nsa-revelations/?intcmp=obnetwork

The U.K. Cyber Security Strategy: Protecting and promoting the United Kingdom in a digital world. Our vision is for the United Kingdom in 2015 to derive huge economic and social value from a vibrant, resilient, and secure cyberspace, where our actions, guided by our core values of liberty, fairness, transparency, and the rule of law, enhance prosperity, national security, and a strong society.

- https://www.gov.uk/government/uploads/system/uploads/attachment_data/file/60961/uk-cyber-security-strategy-final.pdf

Many of America's military secrets can be stolen by exploiting the networks over which unclassified information is shared by military contractors and subcontractors ... Chinese hackers are believed to have stolen the designs for "more than two dozen major weapons systems ..."

- http://www.cbsnews.com/news/how-chinese-hackers-steal-us-secrets/2/

... The Pentagon was pushing to expand its cyber security forces. The U.S. military's so-called Cyber Command will grow fivefold over the next few years, from 900 employees at present to about 5000 civilian and military personnel, Orr reported.

- http://www.cbsnews.com/news/china-military-unit-behind-many-hacking-attacks-on-us-cybersecurity-firm-says/

U.S. officials are blaming Chinese hackers for another serious data breach. Someone broke into secure government networks that hold personal information for all federal employees. The target appears to be workers applying for high-level security clearances.

- http://www.cbsnews.com/news/report-chinese-hackers-got-to-federal-workers-records/

On average, the hackers would spend nearly a year perusing a targeted company's systems looking for sensitive information to steal: product development plans, manufacturing techniques, business plans, and the e-mail messages of senior executives. The point is to help Chinese companies be more competitive.

- http://gizmodo.com/why-chinese-hackers-stole-4-5-million-us-hospital-recor-1623284602

Hackers may have breached the Office of Personnel Management's network ... intrusion has been traced to China, although it is not clear that the Chinese government is involved.

- http://www.washingtonpost.com/news/morning-mix/wp/2014/07/09/report-chinese-hacked-into-the-federal-governments-personnel-office/

A Chinese hacking group has been accused of stealing data from Israel's billion-dollar Iron Dome missile system.

The state-sponsored Comment Crew hacking group, thought to operate out of China, was responsible for attacks from 2011 onward on three Israeli defense technology companies, Elisra Group, Israel Aerospace Industries, and Rafael Advanced Defense Systems, all involved with the Iron Dome project.

- http://www.theguardian.com/technology/2014/jul/29/chinese-hackers-steal-israel-iron-dome-missile-data

Ballistic-missile defenses, joint-strike fighters, Black Hawks, and more—Chinese hackers have their hands on plans for these and more of the Pentagon's most sophisticated weapons systems, just the latest sign that the culture of hacking in China continues to put America on the defensive ...

- http://www.thewire.com/global/2013/05/china-hackers-pentagon/65628/

Security attacks/breaches in the U.S. government from July 2014 to November 2014, include Health and Human Services, Energy Department, Postal Service, White House, State Department—those are just the reported ones; there maybe more that are not reported or, worse yet, do not even know they were attacked.[8]

SUMMARY

As you can see, attacks and those issues associated with attacks and defense are numerous and vary in their approach. Learn from these attacks, so your government agency or corporation does not become a casualty of this global information warfare.

---

[8] Cavuto, Fox New TV Program, November 21, 2014.

SECTION II

The Duties and Responsibilities of a Cyber Security Officer

Section I provided a basic understanding of the external world, with all its many threats to information and information systems—all of which have a direct bearing on the cyber security officer and his or her job. Section II provides a more internal, business focus on the world of the cyber security officer.

Section II begins with the identification of the position, duties, and responsibilities of the corporation cyber security officer. It progresses through a discussion of:

- establishing and managing a cyber security program;
- strategic, tactical, and annual plans;
- developing and managing a cyber security organization and its functions;
- measuring cyber security costs, failures, and successes through metrics management;
- supporting the investigative staff; and
- an overview of the cyber security program in a nation-state's national security environment.

CHAPTER 6

The Cyber Security Officer's Position, Duties, and Responsibilities

Responsible, who wants to be responsible? Whenever something bad happens, it's always, who's responsible for this?

Jerry Seinfeld[1]

Contents

Chapter Objective

The objective of this chapter is to define the role that the cyber security officer will play in a corporation or government agency. In this case, it is the role of the cyber security officer in an international corporation. The duties and responsibilities of a cyber

---

[1] *Reader's Digest,* October 2002, p. 73.

security officer vary depending on the place of employment. However, in this case, we are assuming the cyber security officer has the *perfect* position because it is one all cyber security officers should strive to attain in order to "do it right the first time."

INTRODUCTION

The role of the cyber security officer is more demanding now than ever before, owing to advances in technology, especially in miniaturization and mobility; more national and global network interfaces to his or her corporation; and more sophisticated attacks. The challenges have never been greater but they will be over time.

Where It Began and Its Evolution and Revolution

We began with only physical security, as after all, the ENIAC and other computers did not connect to the world. A guard, a paper-authorized personnel access list, an alarm, and such were all that were needed in those early days. But as the computer evolved over time, so did the profession of the cyber security officer.

The security profession at that time was primarily made up of retired or former law enforcement or military personnel, who had no interest in computer security. They knew physical security, investigations, and personnel security. This new thing called a computer was best left to the computer scientists and engineers.

As systems evolved, so did the departments responsible for their support. Departments that were once engineering departments perhaps became information resource management departments and later became known as information technology (IT) departments. The protection of this new technology stayed with the IT people. However, the computer security positions within the IT departments also evolved.

As the microprocessor and its related technology developed, the once-separated telecommunications and computer staffs began their integration. Consequently, the "computer security" profession began to also consider the protection of information as it flowed through telecommunications links. As the Internet evolved, the need for protecting information as it was displayed, such as on Web sites, also became an important task for those responsible for protecting the hardware, software, and firmware.

Information and related systems are some of a business's most valuable assets, one can argue, second only to the employees. In fact, although no one in management within a business would ever prioritize assets to place information and systems above the employees—at least not publicly—people can always be replaced, and replaced at less cost and adverse impact to the business, than trade secrets and information networks. However, that will probably remain an unspoken issue because of the sensitive nature of valuing machines over humans.

When we think about it, though, information really is business's No. 1 asset. After all, employees can be terminated, even replaced by computers, and the business survives. In fact, profits may even increase because of lower labor costs. However, eliminate an intranet or national or global information infrastructure connection and the business could be lost.

Today, the cyber security officer position is generally still part of the IT department's function. Now, the cyber security officer is responsible for the protection of information and the systems that store, process, transmit, and display that information. The cyber security officer profession has matured into a separate profession, and in most large-to-medium companies, it is more than a part-time job or additional responsibility these days. In smaller businesses it remains mostly a part-time job or is outsourced with other security-related functions.

Information systems of various types, such as cellular phones, notebook computers, personal digital assistants, and fax machines, are all used to process, store, transmit, and display information. These devices are becoming more and more integrated into one device. Couple this phenomenon with the hard copies being produced, and one finds that information may be protected on an intranet but leaked through a cellular phone or printed on paper and then taken out of the business's facilities.

Case Study

Cellular phones are becoming smaller and smaller. Digital cameras are also being installed into these cellular phones. Since management wants their employees to have the latest high-technology devices that help support the business in the most efficient and effective way possible, employees are issued cellular phones. The cellular phones with digital cameras integrated into them allow employees to digitally send photographs as part of their business communications processes. It also provides the opportunity for the employee to photograph sensitive documents, facilities, and such and send the photos directly to unauthorized sources. Thus, there is now another method of performing "Netspionage" (network-enabled espionage). As a cyber security officer, do you have policies, etc., in place to mitigate this new threat?

The cyber security officer position must evolve to be responsible not only for protecting information and systems related to, or the responsibility of, the IT department, but also for protecting all of the business's information assets. It is ridiculous to have the business security professional responsible for the security of company assets, including hard-copy documents, people, and facilities, and leave the protection of automated information and systems essentially to IT people. These positions must be integrated to provide a holistic asset protection approach. This may be accomplished through the evolution of the cyber security officer professional into more than a "computer protector" and the security manager into more than a physical security manager. Here in 2016, we are slowly, grudgingly getting there, but ever so slowly, except when it comes to management fixing blame, of course.

The cyber security officer position is evolving, but no real, permanent, standardized "home" has been identified for the cyber security officer position. It depends on the structure and culture of the corporation in which he or she is employed. We do see signs of this changing as this evolution continues, from guard, computer scientist, engineer, IT specialist, computer security specialist, to information security (InfoSec) to cyber security officer, with some indications of change to corporate information assurance officer or corporate information security officer or cyber security officer. In some cases, the evolution of the profession has already led to making the cyber security officer a part of executive management in the position of a vice president. Of course this varies, as can be expected, by the culture of the corporation.

Still, the evolution must continue until all information and systems are integrated into a total business cyber security profession. This requires the combining of business (corporate) security, for example, physical security and personnel security, and the cyber security officer responsibilities. It is the best way to safeguard all business assets in a holistic and cost-effective manner, but again, based on the corporate culture.

THE CYBER SECURITY OFFICER IN A GLOBAL CORPORATION

If you are chosen as the new cyber security officer for a global corporation, you should have determined the history of that position:
- When was it established?
- Why?
- What is expected of you as the cyber security officer?
- What are your responsibilities and duties?
- What are you accountable for?
- What happened to the last one? (You want to know so you can understand the political environment in which you will be working.)

As you begin your new job as the corporate cyber security officer, you must clearly determine what is expected of you. Again, this information should have been asked during your interview process for two reasons:

- So you know what you were getting into by accepting the cyber security officer position and
- So you can better prepare for the position with a more detailed cyber security program prior to beginning your first day at work.

You need a detailed plan prior to beginning your employment because you will be behind schedule from the moment you walk in the corporate door. That is because putting together a cyber security program from the start is a tremendous project. More likely than not, in today's world, you will probably be inheriting someone else cyber security program.

As the new cyber security officer, it is important to review the program you are inheriting, its philosophy, and the logic behind its policies and procedures. Never change anything unless you can make it better based on risk analysis methodology, not just different, as that costs money. Furthermore, there may be very good reasons it is what it is, or the chief executive officer or corporate information officer (CIO) would not have approved it the way you inherited it.

You must also determine the answers to the following:

- What is important and requires protection?
- What is being protected?
- In what manner?
- Is a staff needed?
- If so, how many?
- With what qualifications, for what positions?
- What are the tasks to be performed?
- What are the mandatory, best practices, and optional requirements to be met?
- What processes and functions are necessary to meet those requirements?
- What are the necessary budget allocations?
- What metrics management techniques are required?
  and the list goes on.

On top of all this is the need to learn about the corporate culture, normal corporate policies and procedures, and all that comes with just joining a company. As the new cyber security officer, you cannot afford to waste any time in your 24/7 duties. You must understand and learn your new environment, the key players, and the issues that must be addressed first. Often, cyber security officers tend to isolate themselves from the rest of the corporation and consider it almost a "me against them" situation. In today's corporations this will get you nowhere but possibly out the corporate door. As a cyber security officer, you and your staff must integrate your functions into the corporate mainstream and integrate yourselves into the processes of the business. "Teaming" with others in the corporation is the only way to succeed in today's information-based, information-supported, and information-dependent modern corporations.

The cyber security officer must eventually get into a proactive mode to be successful, that is, identifying problems and solutions *before* they come to the attention of management. Cyber security-related problems will undoubtedly get management's attention when they adversely affect costs and/or schedules. Adverse impacts on costs and schedules run contrary to the cyber security program goal, objectives, etc.

When a cyber security officer is in the position of constantly *putting out fires*, the proactive cyber security program battle is lost. If that battle is lost, the results are adverse impacts on costs and schedules. The goal of a cost-effective cyber security program cannot be attained.

As the cyber security officer, you have been told that you are expected to establish and manage a cyber security program that works and is not a burden on the corporation. You are told to establish a program that you believe is necessary to get the job done. You have the full support of management because they have come to realize how important their information and systems are to the corporation maintaining its competitive advantage in the global marketplace. This honeymoon will last maybe about six months—if you are lucky. So, you must take advantage of it. To do so, you must have a fast start and then pick up speed.

Based ideally on a "management blank check" and your prior experience (or for the inexperienced cyber security officer, the information gained from reading this book), you have evaluated the corporate environment and have decided that the overall goal of the cyber security program is to:

Administer an innovative cyber security program that minimizes risks to these valuable assets at least impact to costs and schedules, while meeting all of the corporation's and customers' reasonable expectations.

If that is what is expected of you, then that is your primary goal. Everything you do as the cyber security officer should be focused and directed toward meeting that goal. That includes incorporating that philosophy into your:
- Cyber security strategic plan,
- Tactical plan, and
- Annual plan.

CYBER SECURITY OFFICER DUTIES AND RESPONSIBILITIES

As a global corporation's cyber security officer, you have certain duties and responsibilities. These include the following:

- *Managing people*, which includes:
  Building a reputation of professional integrity;
  Maintaining excellent business relationships;
  Dealing with changes;
  Communicating;
  Influencing people in a positive way;
  Building a teamwork environment; and
  Developing people through performance management, such as directing and helping the cyber security staff to be result-oriented.
- *Managing the business of the cyber security program*, which consists of:
  A commitment to results;
  Being customer/supplier focused;
  Taking responsibility for making decisions;
  Developing and managing resource allocations, such as budgets;
  Planning and organizing;
  Being a problem-solver;
  Thinking strategically;
  Using sound business judgment; and
  Accepting personal accountability and ownership.
- *Managing cyber security processes*, which includes:
  Project planning and implementation;
  Persistence of quality in everything;
  Maintaining a systems perspective; and
  Maintaining current job knowledge.

GOALS AND OBJECTIVES

Remember that your primary goal is to administer an innovative cyber security *that minimizes information protection risks at the least impact to costs and schedules, while meeting all of the corporation's and customers' reasonable expectations.*

You must have as your objectives at least the following:

- Enhance the quality, efficiency, and effectiveness of the cyber security program.
- Identify potential problem areas and strive to mitigate them before they adversely affect processes, and especially before management and/or customers identify them.

- Enhance the company's ability to attract customers because of the ability to efficiently and effectively protect their information.
- Establish and manage the InfoSec organization as the leader in the widget industry.

LEADERSHIP POSITION

As a cyber security officer, you will be in a leadership position. In that position, it is extremely important that you understand what a leader is and how a leader is to act.

According to the definition of *leadership* found in numerous dictionaries and management books, it basically means the position or guidance of a leader, the ability to lead, the leader of a group; a person that leads; or the directing, commanding, or guiding head, as of a group or activity.

As a cyber security professional and *leader*, you must set the example: create and foster an "information protection consciousness" within the company.

As a *corporate leader*, you must communicate the company's community involvement, eliminate unnecessary expenses, inspire corporate pride, and find ways to increase profitability.

As a *team leader*, you must encourage teamwork, communicate clear direction, create a cyber security environment conducive to teaming, and treat others as peers and team members, not as competitors.

As a *personal leader*, you must improve your leadership skills, accept and learn from constructive criticism, take ownership and responsibility for decisions, make decisions in a timely manner, and demonstrate self-confidence.

Providing Cyber Security Service and Support

As the cyber security officer and leader of a cyber security service and support organization, you must be especially tuned to the needs, wants, and desires of your customers, both internal (those within the company) and external (those who are outside the company and are usually the company's customers).

To provide service and support to your external customers, you must:
- Identify their information protection needs;
- Meet their reasonable expectations;
- Show by example that you can meet their expectations;
- Treat customer satisfaction as Priority 1;
- Encourage feedback and listen;

- Understand their needs and expectations;
- Treat customer requirements as an important part of the job;
- Establish measures to ensure customer satisfaction; and
- Provide honest feedback to customers.
  To provide service and support to your internal customers; you must:
- Support their business needs;
- Add value to their services;
- Minimize security impact to current processes; and
- Follow the same guidelines as for external customers.

As the corporate cyber security officer, you will also be dealing with suppliers of cyber security products. These suppliers or vendors are valuable allies because they can explain to you the many new cyber security-related problems being discovered, and how their products mitigate those problems. In addition, they can keep you up-to-date on the latest news within the cyber security officer profession and about the latest InfoSec tools available. Furthermore, you can make yourself available to beta test new cyber security products and provide feedback so the final products will meet your needs.

In dealing with suppliers of cyber security-related products, you should do the following:

- Advise them of your needs and what types of products can help you;
- Assist them in understanding your requirements and the products that you want from them, including what modifications they must make to their products before you are willing to purchase them;
- Direct them in the support and assistance they are to provide you;
- Respect them as team members;
- Value their contributions;
- Require quality products and high standards of performance from them;
- Recognize their needs also.

Use Team Concepts

It is important that as the cyber security officer, you understand that the cyber security program is a company program. To be successful, the cyber security officer cannot operate independently, but as a team leader, with a team of others who also have a vested interest in the protection of the company's information and information systems.

It is important to remember that if the cyber security program and its related functions are divided among two or more organizations (e.g., other asset protection such as physical security of hardware under the security department), there will naturally be a tendency for less communication and coordination—and of course political turf battles. The cyber security officer must be sensitive to this division of functions and must ensure that even more communication and coordination occur between all the departments concerned.

The cyber security procedures must be sold to the management and staff of the corporation. If they are presented as a law that must be followed or else, then they will be doomed to failure. The cyber security officer will never have enough staff to monitor everyone all the time, and that is what will be needed. For as soon as the cyber security officer's back is turned, the employees will go back to doing it the way they want to do it. Everyone must do it the "right security way" because they know it is the best way and in their own interests, as well as in the interest of the corporation.

In many global corporations today, success can be achieved only through continuous interdepartmental communication and cooperation and by forming specialists from various organizations into integrated project teams to solve company problems. The cyber security officer should keep that in mind. Teaming and success go together in today's modern corporation.

VISION, MISSION, AND QUALITY STATEMENTS

Many of today's modern corporations have developed vision, mission, and quality statements using a hierarchical process. The statements, if used, should link all levels in the management and organizational chain. The statements of the lower levels should be written and used to support the upper levels and vice versa.

The following examples can be used by the cyber security officer to develop such statements, if they are necessary. It all depends on the culture of the corporation and the processes in place. It seems that these types of statements are "politically required" but given lip service as they are thrust on the employees by some outsourced marketing firm or internal marketing group.

Vision Statements

In many of today's businesses, management develops a vision statement. As stated earlier in this book, the vision statement is usually a short paragraph that attempts to set the strategic goal, objective, or direction of the company.

The corporation may have a vision statement and require all organizations to have statements based on the corporate statement. Remember that a vision statement is a short statement that:

- Is clear, concise, and understandable by the employees;
- Is connected to ethics, values, and behaviors;
- States where the corporation wants to be (long term);
- Sets the tone; and
- Sets the direction.

The following is an example of a vision statement: *The corporate vision is to maintain its competitive advantage in the global marketplace by providing widgets to our customers when they want them, where they want them, and at a fair price.*

The cyber security officer may report to the CIO, and the CIO's vision statement: *In partnership with our customers, we provide a competitive advantage for the IWC widget by continuous maximization of available technology and innovative information management concepts to enhance productivity and cost-effectively support increased production of corporate products.*

The cyber security vision statement may be: *We provide the most efficient and effective cyber security program for the corporation, which adds value to our products and services, as a recognized leader in the widget industry.*

Mission Statements

Remember that mission statements are declarations of the purpose of a business or government agency. Below are samples:

Mission statement: *The corporate mission is to design, manufacture, and sell high-quality products, thereby expanding our global market share while continuing to improve processes to meet customers' expectations.*

CIO mission statement: *The mission of the corporate information office is to efficiently and effectively manage information and provide low-cost, productivity-enhanced, technology-based services that will assist IWC in maintaining its competitive advantage in the marketplace.*

Cyber security program mission statement: *Administer an innovative program that minimizes information protection risks at the least impact to cost and schedule, while meeting all of IWC's and customers' information and information systems assets requirements.*

Quality Statement

Remember that quality is what adds value to your company's products and services. It is what your internal and external customers expect from you.

Quality statement: *To provide quality widgets to our customers with zero defects by building it right the first time.*

CIO quality statement: *To provide quality information management services and systems support while enhancing the productivity opportunities of the IWC workforce.*

Cyber security program quality statement: *Consistently provide quality cyber security professional services and support that meet the customers' requirements and reasonable expectations, in concert with good business practices and company guidelines.*[2]

CYBER SECURITY PRINCIPLES

The cyber security officer's duties and responsibilities are many and sometimes quite complex and conflicting. However, as the corporate cyber security officer, you must never lose sight of the three basic principles:

- Access control;
- Individual accountability; and
- Audit trails.

This triad of principles must be incorporated into the cyber security program. For just as a three-legged stool requires three strong and level legs to be useful, the cyber security program requires these three strong principles. Without all three, the cyber security program will topple, just as a two-legged stool will topple.

PROJECT AND RISK MANAGEMENT PROCESSES

Two basic processes that are an integral part of a cyber security program are project management and risk management concepts.

Project Management

As the cyber security office and organizational manager and leader for the corporation, you will also provide oversight on cyber security-related projects that are being worked by members of your staff.

The criteria for a project are as follows: Formal projects, along with project management charts, will be initiated where improvements or other changes

---

[2] You will find that the same themes of service, support, cost-effectiveness, customer expectations, etc., continuously run through this book. It is hoped that the constant reinforcement will cause the reader to continuously think of these themes when establishing and managing a cyber security program.

will be accomplished and where that effort has an objective, has beginning and ending dates, and will take longer than 30 days to complete.

If the project will be accomplished in less than 30 days, a formal project management process is not needed. The rationale for this is that projects of short duration are not worth the cost (in terms of time needed to complete the project plan, charts, etc.) of such a formal process.

Risk Management

To be cost-effective, the cyber security officer must apply risk-management concepts and identify:

- Threats to the information and information systems of the corporation;
- Vulnerabilities (information systems' weaknesses);
- Risks; and
- Countermeasures to mitigate those risks in a cost-effective way.

CYBER SECURITY OFFICER AND ORGANIZATIONAL RESPONSIBILITIES

As the cyber security officer, you will be managing and leading a cyber security organization. You will be responsible for developing, implementing, maintaining, and administering a company-wide program. The following is an example scenario for the development of your organizational responsibilities.

You have evaluated the corporate environment and found that a centralized cyber security program is required to cost-effectively *jump-start* the program and its associated processes. Your evaluation of what is needed led you to consider the following program-related functions for development:

- Management of all functions and work that are routinely accomplished during the course of conducting the organization's business in accordance with corporate policies and procedures;
- System access administration and controls, including the direct use and control of system access software, monitoring its use, and identifying access violations;
- Access violation analyses to identify patterns and trends that may indicate an increased risk to systems or information;
- Computer crime and abuse inquiries where there are indications of intent to damage, destroy, modify, or release to unauthorized people information of value to the company (*Note*: this function was coordinated and agreed to by the Director of Security as long as his investigative

organization manager was kept apprised of the inquiries and copies of all reports sent to that manager);

- Disaster recovery/contingency planning, which includes directing the development and coordination of a company-wide program to mitigate the possibility of loss of systems and information and ensure their rapid recovery in the event of an emergency or disaster;
- An awareness program established and administered to all system users to make them aware of the information systems protection policies and procedures that must be followed to adequately protect systems and information;
- Evaluation of the systems' hardware, firmware, and software for impact on the security systems and information;
- Where applicable, conduction of risk assessments, with the results reported to management for risk decisions;
- Conduction of systems' compliance inspections, tests, and evaluations to ensure that all users and systems are in compliance with IWC's CIAPP policies and procedures.

Cyber Security Officer's Formal Duties and Responsibilities

Based on the above and in concert with the executive management of the corporation, the cyber security officer has developed and received approval for formally establishing the following charter of the cyber security officer responsibilities:

Summary of the Purpose of the Cyber Security Officer Position

Develop, implement, maintain, and administer an overall, corporate-wide cyber security program to include all plans, policies, procedures, assessments, and authorizations necessary to ensure the protection of customer, subcontractor, and corporate information from compromise, destruction, and/or unauthorized manipulation while being processed, stored, and/or transmitted by corporate's information systems.

Accountabilities

- Identify all government, customer, and corporate cyber security requirements necessary for the protection of all information processed, stored, and/or transmitted by corporate's information systems; interpret those requirements; and develop, implement, and administer corporate plans, policies, and procedures necessary to ensure compliance.
- Evaluate all hardware, firmware, and software for impact on the security of the information systems; direct and ensure their modification if

requirements are not met; and authorize their purchase and use within the corporation and applicable subcontractor locations.

- Establish and administer the technical security countermeasures program to support the corporate requirements.
- Establish and administer a security test and evaluation program to ensure that all of corporate's and applicable subcontractors' information systems/ networks are operating in accordance with their contracts.
- Identify, evaluate, and authorize for use all information systems and other hardware within the corporation and at applicable subcontractor locations to ensure compliance with red/black engineering where proprietary and other sensitive information is processed.
- Direct the use of, and monitor, the corporate's information systems access control software systems; analyze all systems' security infractions/ violations and report the results to management and human resources personnel for review and appropriate action.
- Identify information systems business practices and security violations/ infractions; conduct inquiries; assess potential damage; direct and monitor corporate management's corrective action; and implement/recommend corrective/preventive action.
- Establish and direct a corporate-wide telecommunications security working group.
- Develop, implement, and administer a risk assessment program; provide analyses to management; modify corporate and subcontractor requirements accordingly to ensure a lowest-cost cyber security program.
- Establish and administer a cyber security awareness program for all corporate information systems users, to include customers and subcontractor users, and ensure they are cognizant of information systems threats and of security policies and procedures necessary for the protection of information systems.
- Direct and coordinate a corporate-wide information systems emergency/ disaster recovery/contingency planning program to ensure the rapid recovery of information systems in the event of an emergency or disaster.
- Direct the development, acquisition, implementation, and administration of the cyber security's software systems.
- Represent the corporation on all cyber security matters with customers, government agencies, suppliers, and other outside entities.
- Provide advice, guidance, and assistance to management relative to cyber security matters.
- Perform common management accountabilities in accordance with corporate's management policies and procedures.

SUMMARY[3]

The role of today's cyber security officer has evolved over time and will continue to evolve. The cyber security officer profession offers many challenges to anyone who wants to match wits with global hackers, criminals, terrorists, and other miscreants. In a business environment such as that of a global corporation, the cyber security officer has specific responsibilities. As a cyber security officer, you should understand the following:

- The cyber security officer position is a leadership position within a company.
- The recently hired cyber security officer must know what is expected of the company's new cyber security officer and should have a clear understanding of those expectations before taking the position.
- The three primary responsibilities of a cyber security officer are: (1) managing people, (2) managing the cyber security program, and (3) managing cyber security processes.
- The cyber security officer must set forth clear goals and objectives.
- The cyber security officer in the leadership role must be a company leader, team leader, and personal leader.
- The cyber security officer must provide cyber security service and support using team concepts.
- The cyber security officer should develop vision, mission, and quality statements as guides to developing a successful cyber security program.
- The cyber security officer should strive to administer a cyber security program in which all the major cyber security functions are under the responsibility of the cyber security officer.

---

[3] Much of the information in this chapter provides details that could be used to fill in the details of the cyber security officer's portfolio.

CHAPTER 7

The Cyber Security Program's Strategic, Tactical, and Annual Plans

Though this be madness, yet there is method in't

William Shakespeare[1]

Contents

Chapter Objective

The objective of this chapter is to establish the strategic, tactical, and annual plans for the cyber security organization. These plans will also set the direction for corporate's cyber security program while integrating the cyber security plans into corporate's plans, thus indicating that the cyber security program is an integral part of the corporation.

---

[1] William Shakespeare (1564–1616), English poet and playwright. Polonius, *Hamlet* (1601), Act 2, Scene 2.

119

INTRODUCTION

The saying "Ya gotta have a plan" definitely applies to successfully accomplishing the duties and responsibilities of a cyber security officer. Without strategic, tactical, and annual plans, the officer would be spending all of every day running from crisis to crisis and haphazardly trying to protect information and information systems for the corporation. In addition, these plans are the cost-effective method of providing a secure information environment for the corporation.

There will always be crises to contend with; however, even most crises can be planned for so that when they occur, an emergency plan can be implemented. The plan will provide at least guidance and an outline of what to do—not only what to do, but when and how to do it rapidly and effectively. Let's face it: Most crises can be identified, and we are already accustomed to doing so through our disaster recovery and contingency planning for such events as fires, typhoons, and earthquakes. We should do the same for other events that would be classified as an emergency, such as, but of course not limited to, the following:

- Web-site attack and defacement,
- Denial-of-service attack,
- Worm or virus attack, and
- Other malicious attacks or accidents.

As a professional cyber security officer, when you learn of a new type of attack, check your emergency contingency plans and determine whether the latest type of attack would be addressed by one of those plans. If so, great! If not, then it's time to develop another plan or update a current plan. By the way, as you should already know:

- These plans must be developed with input from various departments such as auditors, legal, and IT in a project team environment;
- They must be kept current; and
- They must be tested often to ensure that the identified emergency response team is trained and can operate effectively and efficiently.

As with the cyber security program, all plans should be placed online with read access for all employees. It will also be easier to keep the plans current, and through the intranet Website or through e-mail, everyone can be notified of changes to the plans. The cyber security officer should also have a project to ensure that information and systems protection policies and procedures are kept online for read access by all employees. The cyber security officer should consider, as much as possible, having a paperless cyber security program and cyber security organization.

At the corporate level, all information and systems protection plans are considered subsets of the cyber security program, as are all projects that are used to build the secure information environment.

CORPORATE'S CYBER SECURITY STRATEGIC PLAN

To be successful, the cyber security officer must have a cyber security strategic plan). That plan should be integrated, or at least compatible, with corporate's strategic business plan. It is this plan that sets the long-term direction, goals, and objectives for information protection as stated in the cyber security program, vision, mission, and quality statements.

Let's look at an example of a possible strategic business plan of a corporation.

The corporate strategic business plan sets forth the following information:

- The expected annual earnings for the next 7 years;
- The market-share percentage goals on an annual basis;
- The future process modernization projects based on expected technology changes of faster, cheaper, and more powerful computers, telecommunications systems, and robotics;
- Corporate expansion goals; and
- Corporate's acquisition of some current subcontractor and competitive companies.

The cyber security strategic business plan is the basic document on which to build the corporate cyber security program with the goal of building a comprehensive information protection environment at lowest cost and least impact to the company.

When developing the plan, the cyber security officer must ensure that the following basic cyber security principles are included, either specifically or in principle (since it is part of the cyber security strategy):

- Minimize the probability of a cyber security vulnerability,
- Minimize the damage if a vulnerability is exploited, and
- Provide a method to recover efficiently and effectively from the damage.

Let's assume that the corporate strategic business plan called for a mature cyber security program within the next seven years that:

- Can protect corporate's information while allowing access to its networks by its international and national customers, subcontractors, and suppliers and

- Can support the integration of new hardware, software, networks, etc., while maintaining the required level of cyber security without affecting schedules or costs.

The Cyber Security Strategic Plan Objective

The objectives of the plan are to:
- Minimize risks to systems and information,
- Minimize impact on costs,
- Minimize impact on schedules,
- Assist in meeting contractual requirements,
- Assist in meeting noncontractual requirements,
- Build a comprehensive systems security environment,
- Respond flexibly to changing needs,
- Support multiple customers' information protection needs,
- Incorporate new technologies as soon as needed,
- Assist in attracting new customers, and
- Maximize the use of available resources.

Cyber Security Strategic Plan and Team Concepts, Communication, and Coordination

To have a successful cyber security program, the strategy calls for one that also deals with the office politics aspect of the corporate environment. A key element, which was stated earlier in this book, is to remember that the information and information systems belong to corporate, and not to the cyber security officer. Therefore, cooperation and coordination are a must!

Many functional organizations have an interest in the cyber security strategic plan and other cyber security program-related plans; therefore, the plans should be discussed with other team members such as the auditors, security personnel, human resources personnel, legal personnel, and others deemed appropriate.

The plan should also be discussed with and input requested from key members of the user community and corporate managers. After all, what you do affects what they do! It is a great way to get communication and interaction going. This will lead to a better plan and one that has broad-based support.

Their input and their understanding of what the cyber security officer is trying to accomplish will assist in ensuring corporate-wide support for the cyber security program. For only with this kind of communication and interaction, can the cyber security officer's cyber security program succeed.

Cyber Security Strategic Planning Considerations

The planning considerations must include the following:

- Good business practices,
- Quality management,
- Innovative ideas,
- Cyber security vision statement,
- Cyber security mission statement,
- Cyber security quality statement, and
- Providing channels for open communication with others such as the auditors, systems personnel, security personnel, users, and management.

All these factors must be considered when developing a cyber security program strategy and documenting that strategy in the cyber security program.

The corporate process flow of plans begins with the corporate strategic business plan through the corporate annual business plan. Each plan's goals and objectives must be able to support one another: top–down and bottom–up.

Once this process is understood, the next step is to map the cyber security strategic plan into the corporate strategic business plan goals and objectives.

Mapping Corporate's Cyber Security Strategic Plan to the Corporate Strategic Business Plan

Corporate's strategy identified the annual earnings for the next seven years as well as market-share percentage goals. This clearly highlights the need for a cyber security program that will be cost-effective.

As was previously mentioned, cyber security is a "parasite" on the profits of corporate if it cannot be shown to be a value-added function (one that is needed to support the bottom line). Therefore, the cyber security program strategy must be efficient (cheap) and effective (good). If that can be accomplished, the cyber security program will be in a position to support the corporate strategy relative to earnings and market share.

Mapping these points in a flowchart or similar management tool can help the cyber security officer visualize a strategy prior to documenting that strategy in the cyber security strategic plan. The mapping will also assist the cyber security officer in focusing on the strategies that support the corporate strategies.[2]

---

[2] For those readers who are inclined to argue the technical definitions of terms, I concede that the definition of terms varies between corporations and those used here may not fit nicely into the definitions used by the corporation or government agency of the reader. However, the reader should not lose sight of the process being discussed. That is the important aspect of this chapter.

Writing the Cyber Security Strategic Plan

Writing the plan will come much more easily once the mapping is completed. Once that is accomplished, the cyber security officer will write the plan following the standard corporate format for plan writing.

The corporate format was determined to be as follows:

1. Executive summary
2. Table of contents
3. Introduction
4. Vision statement
5. Mission statement
6. Quality statement
7. Cyber security strategic goals
8. How the cyber security strategies support corporate strategies
9. Mapping charts
10. Conclusion

CORPORATE'S CYBER SECURITY TACTICAL PLAN

A tactical plan is a short-range plan (a three-year plan) that supports the corporate cyber security program and cyber security functional goals and objectives. The cyber security tactical plan should:

- Identify and define, in more detail, the vision of a comprehensive cyber security environment, as stated in the cyber security strategic plan;
- Identify and define the current corporate cyber security environment; and
- Identify the process to be used to determine the differences between the two.

Once that is accomplished, the cyber security officer can identify projects to progress from the current corporate cyber security environment to where it should be, as stated in the cyber security strategic plan. In the corporate tactical plan, it is also important to keep in mind:

- The company's business direction,
- The customers' direction, and
- The direction of technology.

Once these are established, the individual projects can be identified and implemented, beginning with the cyber security annual plan.

The corporate tactical business plan stated (again, using an example of a corporate plan), "In addition, it is expected to be able to integrate new hardware, software, networks, etc., with *minimum* impact on schedules or costs." Therefore, it will be necessary to establish a project with the objective of developing a process to accomplish that goal.

The cyber security officer must then also consider that the corporate cyber security program must contain processes to reevaluate the mechanisms used to protect information so that it is protected only for the period required. Therefore, a project must be established to accomplish that goal.

The corporate tactical business plan also called for the *completion* of a cyber security program that can protect corporate's information while allowing access to its networks by its international and national customers, subcontractors, and suppliers. Therefore, another project that must be developed is one that can accomplish this goal.

Writing the Cyber Security Tactical Plan

Writing the plan should be somewhat easier based on the experience gained in mapping the goals for the cyber security strategic plan and the corporate plans. Once that is accomplished, the cyber security officer will write the plan following the standard corporate format for plan writing.

The corporate format for the cyber security plan was determined to be as follows:

1. Executive summary
2. Table of contents
3. Introduction
4. Cyber security strategic goals
5. How the cyber security tactical plan supports the cyber security strategic plan
6. How the cyber security tactics support corporate tactics
7. Mapping charts (use an organization or flowchart if pictorial representation will help the reader under the approach used
8. Conclusion

CYBER SECURITY ANNUAL PLAN

The cyber security officer must also develop a cyber security annual plan to support the corporation's strategic business plan, cyber security strategic plan, and the corporate and cyber security tactical plans. The plan must include goals, objectives, and projects that will support the goals and objectives of corporate's annual business plan.

Corporate's cyber security annual plan is to be used to identify and implement projects to accomplish the goals and objectives as stated in all the other plans.

Remember, the cyber security program requires the following:

- Project management techniques,
- Gantt charts (schedule),
- Identified beginning date for each project,
- Identified ending date for each project,
- An objective for each project,
- Cost tracking and budget, and
- Identification of the responsible project lead.

Cyber Security Annual Plan Projects

The initial and major project of the cyber security officer's annual plan is to begin to identify the current corporate and cyber security environment. To gain an understanding of the current corporate environment, culture, and philosophy, the following projects are to be established:

1. Project title: Corporate Cyber Security Organization
   a. *Project lead*: Cyber security officer
   b. *Objective*: Establish a cyber security program to support organization
   c. *Start date*: January 1, 2016
   d. *End date*: July 1, 2016
2. Project title: Cyber Security Program Policies and Procedures Review
   a. *Project lead*: Cyber security officer
   b. *Objective*: Identify and review all cyber security program-related corporate documentation, and establish a process to ensure integration, applicability, and currency
   c. *Start date*: February 1, 2016
   d. *End date*: April 1, 2016
3. Project title: Cyber Security Team
   a. *Project lead*: Cyber security officer
   b. *Objective*: Establish a corporate cyber security program working group to assist in establishing and supporting a cyber security program
   c. *Start date*: January 1, 2016
   d. *End date*: February 1, 2016
4. Project title: Corporate Proprietary Process Protection
   a. *Project lead*: Cyber security organization systems security engineer
   b. *Objective*: Identification, assessment, and protection of corporate proprietary processes

    c. *Start date*: April 15, 2016

    d. *End date*: September 1, 2016

5. Project title: Cyber Security Organizational Functions

    a. *Project lead*: Cyber security officer

    b. *Objective*: Identify and establish cyber security organizational functions and their associated processes and work instructions

    c. *Start date*: January 15, 2016

    d. *End date*: July 1, 2016

6. Project title: Cyber Security Support to IT Changes

    a. *Project lead*: Cyber security organization systems security engineer

    b. *Objective*: Establish a process to provide service and support to integrate cyber security policies, procedures, and processes as changes are made in the IT environment

    c. *Start date*: March 15, 2016

    d. *End date*: October 1, 2016

Mapping the Cyber Security Annual Plan to the Corporate Annual Business Plan

As was previously shown, mapping the cyber security program and the cyber security annual plan to the corporate annual business plan can be easily accomplished. However, in this case, the corporate annual plan objectives were not indicated or used to map the corporate plan.[3]

Writing the Cyber Security Annual Plan

As noted earlier, writing of the plans must follow the corporate format. The cyber security annual plan is no exception, and the following format is required:

1. Executive summary

2. Table of contents

3. Introduction

4. Cyber security annual goals

5. Cyber security projects

6. How the cyber security projects support corporate's annual plan goals

7. Mapping charts

8. Conclusion

---

[3] The reader probably understands this process by now and can easily use this mapping method.

QUESTIONS TO CONSIDER

Based on what you have read, consider the following questions and how you would reply to them:
- Does your company have plans that can be considered strategic, tactical, or annual, for example, long-range or short-range plans?
- Have you read them?
- If not, how do you know you are providing adequate service and support to the company?
- Do you have strategic, tactical, and annual plans that support the company's business plans?
- If so, are they current?
- How do you know?
- Do you have a process in place to keep them current?
- If not, why not?
- If you do have such plans, do you have a process in place and flow-charted to show how the plans, your information and systems protection functions, projects, risk management strategy, cost–benefit philosophy, and such are integrated into your cyber security program that supports the company's plans?
- If not, why not?

SUMMARY

Planning is a vitally important and cost-effective way to establish a cost-effective and quality corporate cyber security environment. It will help focus on tasks that will effectively and efficiently meet the planning goals and objectives of a cyber security program. As part of that planning, the cyber security officer should consider the following points:
- The corporate cyber security strategic, tactical, and annual plans must be mapped and integrated into the corporate strategic, tactical, and annual business plans.
- The cyber security program-related plans must incorporate the cyber security vision, mission, and quality statements and their philosophies and concepts.
- The cyber security program-related plans must identify strategies, goals, objectives, and projects that support one another and the corporate plans.
- By mapping the goals of the corporate plans with those of the cyber security program-related plans, the required information fusion can take place and can be graphically represented.

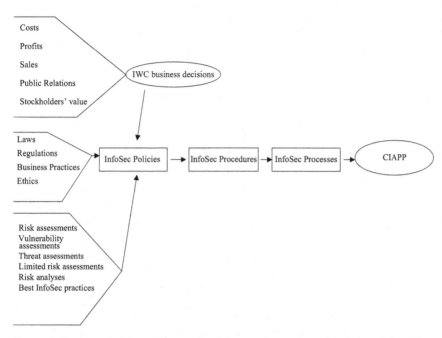

Figure 1 Depicts mapping of the goals of the corporate plan with those of the cyber security program where IWC stands for a generic corporation International Widget Corporation and CIAAP is the corporate information assurance annual plan.

- Mapping will make it easier for the cyber security officer to write the applicable cyber security plans.
- The cyber security annual plan generally consists of projects that are the building blocks of the cyber security program following the strategies and tactics of the corporate and other cyber security program plans. Figure 1 provides an example of mapping showing the relationship of plans. What, if anything, is lacking?

CHAPTER 8

Establishing a Cyber Security Program and Organization

We trained hard, but it seemed every time we were beginning to form up into teams, we would be reorganized. I was to learn later in life that we tend to meet any new situation by reorganizing

Petronius Arbiter[1]

Contents

Chapter Objective

The objective of this chapter is to describe how to establish a corporate cyber security program and its associated organization. A "what-if" approach is used in which a corporate security officer is shown to act in a certain way based on what is required of him or her by corporation in which that person is employed, using a fictional corporate environment.

[1] Petronius Arbiter (27–66), Roman satirist. *Satyricon* (first century) as quoted in Microsoft's *Encarta World*.

INTRODUCTION

The corporation's information and information systems are some of their most vital assets. These valuable assets must be consistently protected by all the corporation employees, contracted personnel, associate companies, subcontractors, and, in fact, everyone who has authorized access to these assets. They must be protected regardless of the information environment, whether through faxes, telephones, cellular phones, local area networks, Internet e-mails, hard copies, scanners, personal digital assistants (PDAs)—any device that processes, transmits, displays, or stores the corporation's sensitive information. What is meant by *sensitive* is all information that has been determined to require protection. That determination is based on basic, common business sense—for example, a marketing plan for next year's product must be protected, and it doesn't take a risk assessment to determine that. Some information must also be protected because there are laws that make that information protection a requirement—for example, private information about employees.

To provide that consistent protection, those individuals who have authorized access to the information and information systems must therefore do the following:

• Be provided with guidance,
• Understand how to apply information asset protection,
• Understand why such information asset protection is required, and
• Understand the corporation policy regarding that protection.

The corporation's executive management had decided that a policy document was needed. So, the corporation's cyber security officer was hired primarily to fulfill that requirement as stated in the corporate plans, such as the corporation strategic business plan.

CORPORATE CYBER SECURITY PROGRAM[2]

The cyber security officer knew that to successfully protect the corporation's information-related assets there must be formal guidelines and directions provided to the corporation's employees. There must also be some formal processes that are used to ensure that the corporation's information

[2] Some of the information from this section was modified from Dr. Gerald L. Kovacich's book coauthored with Edward P. Halibozek, *The Manager's Handbook for Corporate Security: Establishing and Managing a Successful Information Assets Protection Program,* published by Butterworth–Heinemann, 2003; now pending publication of a second edition.

assets were protected effectively and efficiently—in other words, "cheap and good." It would be obvious to the corporation's management and the cyber security officer that to do otherwise would cause employees to protect these information-related assets as they saw fit, or not protect them at all. Such was almost the case now, and it is hoped that the cyber security officer would know there was an urgent need to quickly establish a cyber security program.

The cyber security program would be developed taking into consideration or incorporating the following:

- Reasons for the cyber security program;
- The corporation's vision, mission, and quality statements;
- Information and systems legal, ethical, and best business practices;
- The corporation's strategic, tactical, and annual business plans;
- Information and systems protection strategic, tactical, and annual business plans;
- The corporation's overall information assets protection plans, policies, and procedures as directed by the corporate security office;
- Cyber security vision, mission, and quality statements;
- Current cyber security program-related policies;
- Current cyber security program-related procedures; and
- Other topics as deemed appropriate once the cyber security officer and the cyber security project team have established the baseline.

The cyber security program cannot be developed in a vacuum if it is to work. The input of others is a necessity: The cyber security program, if not done correctly, may have an adverse impact on the business of the corporation. Remember that the cyber security officer's cyber security functional organization must be a service- and support-driven organization. As part of that endeavor, the cyber security program must support the corporation's business plans. It then follows that the plans call for certain actions to protect the corporation's vital information and information systems assets.

Remember what is being discussed here are the plans, processes, policies, and procedures (P^4) that are established, implemented, and maintained as applying to all the corporation departments (P^4 because as each of the "P's" is added to the others, protection baseline increases exponentially). This should not be confused with the cyber security officer's cyber security organization's plans, policies, and procedures, such as work instructions and processes that apply strictly within that cyber security organization.

As the cyber security officer, one of your first tasks is to obtain a copy of the corporation cyber security program that was to be established by the prior cyber security officer. You may find that:

1. There is no such document,
2. The current one is not really current at all and needs updating, or
3. To your shock and amazement, the corporation cyber security program is current and an excellent document.

Of the three options, which would you prefer and why? Actually, there are benefits to all of the options, but they are listed in our preferred order. Does it seem strange that one would not opt for option 3? The one you choose will probably be based on where you are coming from and where you are going (your education and experience). OK, no more riddles.

Option 1 has some benefits. If there is no such document as the corporation cyber security program by any name, one can "do it right the first time" and develop one that meets the needs of the corporation using your own tried and true methods. However, the less experience you have, the more difficult it will be to do it right the first time. If you are new to the corporation cyber security officer position, it may be doubly difficult and a real problem. No, not a problem, because you are now in a high management position. These are not called problems. They are called *challenges*.

Having a corporate cyber security program that has been approved by those who must approve it (executive management) has some benefits, of course. "Approve it?" you say. "Why does anyone have to approve it? I am the cyber security officer, the security professional, the expert in the business. I know what I am doing. I don't need any nonsecurity people out there playing amateur information systems security expert." Great! That may have worked in the past, maybe in the times of the hunter–gatherers—but not now.

Here's the issue: As the cyber security officer, you are going to establish a cyber security program that will affect everyone and everything in the corporation in one form or another, since information systems permeate all levels of the corporation and the corporation cannot function without them. You are new to the corporation and really don't have a good handle on how information assets protection policies and procedures affect the corporation business of making widgets. You may have a great way to protect a certain, sensitive corporation information-related asset, but find that if it were implemented it would slow down production. That is not a good idea in the competitive, fast-paced, global marketplace in which the corporation competes for business. That may get you a warning first, but then you'll be fired (as was the case of the last cyber security officer?); or it may increase costs in other ways (slowing down production is a cost matter also).

Option 2 also has some very good advantages, especially for the cyber security officer who has less experience in the profession and/or less experience at the corporation. The advantage is that you have a framework on which to build, essentially changing it to how you envision the final baseline. However, as with option 1, some caution is advised. Option 2 allows you, as the new cyber security officer, the opportunity to see what executive management has authorized to date. In other words, you know how much "protection" the executive management of the corporation will allow at what expense to productivity, costs, etc.

This is important also because if you increase security, you must provide sound, convincing *business* reasons that should happen. In this cause, you have an edge because of the previous loss of the corporation information assets, which caused the firing of the former cyber security officer. In addition, the chief executive officer (CEO) is supportive in that the strategic business plan and the tactical business plan both have cyber security program goals, and those plans had to be approved by the CEO prior to implementation. Thus, the cyber security program already has high visibility and at least some executive management support. However, that honeymoon may not last long if you require protection mechanisms that aren't backed by sound business sense.

Option 3 is great if you are new to the cyber security officer position and/or lack confidence or experience in cyber security program development. However, caution is also needed here, because information assets were lost and the former cyber security officer was fired. You must get answers for the following questions:

- Did the information assets protection processes as set forth in the cyber security program leave a vulnerability that allowed the threat agent to take advantage of it?
- Was the cyber security program not the issue—did someone or some group fail to follow proper procedures?
- Was the cyber security officer just not the right person for the job at the corporation? (If this is the case, find out why so you don't make the same mistake, assuming you want to work for the corporation for more than a year or two.)

As the new cyber security officer, you should find the answers to these questions and then determine how the cyber security program can be enhanced to mitigate future attacks. The benefit of a current cyber security program is that it has received the concurrence of executive management—but remember, it may be a bad plan. After all, what does executive management know of cyber security program matters except what the cyber security officer tells them, aside from the "common sense" knowledge?

Let us assume that no corporation cyber security program is in existence. So, the cyber security officer must start from the beginning. Actually, that is not entirely true. As an experienced cyber security officer, the corporation cyber security officer has brought knowledge and experience to the corporation cyber security officer position. In addition, there are always some sort of information and information systems protection policies and guidelines available. It may be just a matter of gathering them all together for analysis as part of establishing the cyber security program baseline.

In addition, the cyber security officer has swapped and collected cyber security program plans from other cyber security professionals over the years that may prove useful. Several words of caution:

- Never take another's cyber security program (or any documents) without the approval of his or her appropriate corporate authority. Such plans may be considered and marked as corporate–confidential, corporate–private, corporate–proprietary, or the like. There is an ethics issue here.

- Furthermore, the other cyber security programs may be outdated or may not meet the needs of the corporation, perhaps because of technology changes, a different corporate culture, or a different corporate environment.

Using formal project management techniques, the cyber security officer decides to establish a cyber security program project team and selects a project lead, leads the team, or has the group select their own project lead. If the cyber security officer's cyber security organization has one or more specialists in information assets protection policies and procedures, then one of those specialists would be the natural one to head up the project team. Other team members should include those within the cyber security organization who are responsible for each of the functions of the cyber security organization.

These team members would not be used full time on the project, but would represent the cyber security functions and provide input as deemed appropriate by the cyber security program project team leader. The cyber security officer decided to use only specialists from the cyber security organization at this time to speed up the draft of the baseline cyber security program's primary document—that which contains the requirements and P^4. To do otherwise—to add auditors, information technology (IT) staff, human relations specialists, legal staff, etc.—would invariably cause too much time to be taken in discussing such matters as policies being too restrictive or not restrictive enough, leading to a slowdown or committee paralysis. The cyber security officer determined that coordination would be done upon establishment of the initial draft document.

Let's now assume there is a plan in place with outdated portions. The cyber security officer, who has already read the document and does not agree with some of the requirements in it and who sees other requirements that are obviously lacking, should first meet with the specialist currently responsible for the cyber security program and that person's manager (the assumption is that there are some cyber security staff already employed and that someone in the current cyber security organization has responsibility for the cyber security program—or equivalent plan or program). The main purpose of the meeting would be to determine why it is not current and discuss the rationale for all the requirements stated in the document. It may be that some portions were deleted because of executive management objections. These must be identified, because it is of little use to update the cyber security program if it is to meet resistance and rejection when it is briefed to and coordinated with executive management.

If the cyber security officer determines that there was resistance and disapproval of some aspects of the cyber security program, then the cyber security officer should look at that issue first. The approach the cyber security officer will use is to establish another cyber security project team, which will conduct a limited risk assessment related to the identified issues: management's rejection of some much-needed information assets protection requirements. The risk assessment is limited to a specific objective: determining the risks to a specific asset, the costs of mitigating that risk, or the rationale for the requirement. It is also limited in time. For each of these issues in which different information assets and departments have been involved, such as manufacturing and marketing, a separate, limited risk assessment will be conducted.

The results of the limited risk assessments will then be provided as part of a formal briefing to the vice president of that particular department, and a copy of the report will be given to the corporate information officer (CIO). The copy to the CIO (the cyber security officer's boss) will be given just to ensure that the CIO is in the communications loop and because a copy will be available for use when briefing the CEO and the executive management team on the new cyber security program and its changes. The limited assessment will be part of the backup documentation for the briefing. The cyber security officer reasons that a copy to the CEO would not be a good idea at this time, because then the cyber security officer would have to explain what it is and why the CEO has it.

The CEO does not currently understand how the new cyber security officer operates, and now is no time to take away from the priority cyber security program project management to provide a "for your information" report to the CEO. Some cyber security officers may think that such things help the cyber security officer gain visibility and show the "great" things that the cyber security officer and cyber security staff are accomplishing. However, it may have the opposite affect, as the CEO would ask questions:

- Why do I have this?
- What is it?
- What am I to do with it?
- Do I have to make a decision now based on it?

What is your reply as the cyber security officer? "Oh, I just thought you would enjoy reading it because I know you are not that busy; you don't have better things to do; my stuff is so much more important than what you do to run the corporation; and no, you don't have any action items that come from this. I just want to show you what a great job I'm doing." That *will* work in getting you recognized—but for all the wrong reasons and in the wrong way.

The limited risk assessment will state the risks, the mitigation factors, and the estimated costs of the increased protection of that particular asset or set of information assets. If the vice president of that department, who is also the person immediately responsible for the protection of that information asset or assets, does not concur with the increased protection, then the vice president must formally accept the risks in writing on the last page of the report and send it back to the cyber security officer.

The acceptance of risk statement reads as follows: *I have reviewed the findings of the limited risk assessment conducted by members of the corporation cyber security staff. I understand the potential loss of, or damage to, the corporation information assets under my care that may occur if additional protective processes are not put in place. I accept that risk.*

You will probably find that most people will be unwilling to sign such a document or will try to delay signing and hope the issue is forgotten. The cyber security officer can never let that happen. To resolve that issue, a reply of concurrence or nonconcurrence will be set forth in the document with a suspension date. If no reply is forthcoming by that date, the report states that additional safeguards will be put into effect no later than a specific date because of the failure of the action person to sign the document. A nonreply is taken as a concurrence.

Often the executive will try to find a way out of the dilemma and "negotiations" will take place in which various options will be examined, other than those already stated in the report. The cyber security officer cannot say no to such a request: To do so would allow the executive to say that the cyber security officer was not being cooperative, was not a team player, had a "take it or leave it" attitude. At the same time, this negotiation cannot go on indefinitely. If a roadblock is reached, then the executive and the cyber security officer should agree that the matter be discussed at a meeting with the CIO and/or CEO.

The corporation CIO would probably be wondering if there was some other way out of it. The CIO thinks: "Here this cyber security officer hasn't even been in the job a month, and already I'm getting involved in conflicts." The CIO does not like becoming involved in conflicts.

As a side note, no matter what final decision is made, the cyber security officer's performance review and probably merit raise may be affected because the cyber security officer was not able to resolve the issue (even though the fault was that of others). The cyber security officer could have resolved the issue by just allowing the other vice presidents or managers to have it their way. However, the cyber security officer knows that also contributed to the previous cyber security officer being fired. It is a no-win situation, but that's life as a cyber security officer. For the cyber security officer to do otherwise is unprofessional and an ethics issue.

The Corporate Cyber Security Program—Requirements

In developing a cyber security program, one must first look at the requirements that drive the formation of policies, which lead to procedures, which turn into processes to be followed by all those having authorized access to the corporation information and information systems assets.

Requirements, also known as cyber security *drivers,* are those laws, regulations, common business practices, ethics, and the like on which the policies are based. The policies are needed to comply with the requirements; the procedures are required to implement the policy; and the processes are steps that are followed to support the procedures.

The Corporate Cyber Security Program—Information Assets Protection Policies

When discussing information assets protection policy, we define it as a codified set of principles that are directive in nature and that provide the baseline for the protection of corporate information assets.

> *It is always the best policy to speak the truth, unless, of course, you are an exceptionally good liar.*
>
> **Jerome K. Jerome**

The corporate information assets protection policies are a series of policies that deal with the protection of various information assets categories within the corporation. These policies make up a major portion of the cyber security program, as they are the protection "rules." They are the first building blocks of the corporation information assets protection environment. Information assets protection policies are the foundation for a cyber security program. It is crucial that they:

- Cover all information assets that must be protected,
- Cover all aspects of information assets protection,
- Do not have any loopholes that could contribute to vulnerabilities,
- Be clearly written,
- Be concise,
- Take into account the costs of protection,
- Take into account the benefits of protection,
- Take into account the associated risks to the information assets,
- Are coordinated with executive management and others as applicable,
- Are concurred in by executive management and others as applicable,
- Are *actively* supported by executive management and all employees, and
- Include a process to ensure that they are kept current at all times.

One cannot state these requirements too strongly. They are the key to a successful cyber security program. If it is not stated in writing, it does not exist. After the information assets protection policies are established and approved in accordance with the corporation requirements (executive management approval for all policies that affect the entire the corporation), the information contained in the policies must be given to all corporate employees. This will be done through the corporation cyber security program education and awareness training program.

A key process that the cyber security officer must establish is one that will maintain all information assets protection policies in a current state. Because this is a crucial function, the cyber security officer has assigned one staff member full time to ensure that the policies are current at all times and ensure that when changes are considered, they are properly coordinated, and the information is dispensed to all employees as soon as possible. After all, the changes may just be procedural, or they may mitigate a risk to some valuable corporation information assets.

The cyber security officer's focal point for information assets protection policies is the central cyber security person to collect information that adversely affects the protection of information and information systems. That adverse information is analyzed by the focal point, with help from others as needed, to determine if policies must be added or modified to help mitigate the adverse effects—vulnerabilities—identified. If so, such changes are done based on a cost–benefits approach to mitigating the identified vulnerabilities.

For the position of an information assets protection policy specialist, the cyber security officer has chosen a person already employed by Human Resources (HR). This was done after interviews and looking at the experience of the cyber security staff. None of the cyber security staff were qualified or interested in such a position: The cyber security staff saw it as being a "nontechie paper shuffler" job. The cyber security officer purposely looked for a qualified employee within the corporation, since that person would already be familiar with the corporation culture and processes—basically, how things were done at the corporation.

The cyber security officer was able to get this new position approved by the HR Department and rated at a sufficiently high position level to attract the best candidates. The cyber security officer's rationale was to rate all new positions at as high a level as possible, so the cyber security officer could attract the best candidates in the corporation or outside the corporation. Such a position would be seen as a promotion by many in the corporation. This was not an easy task, but the cyber security officer had experience in working with HR specialists. The task was not as difficult as it might have been—and once had been for the cyber security officer.

The person hired had worked in an HR office and whose duties included writing HR policy and procedures documents, coordinating document approvals, and maintaining the corporation documentation library. The individual responded to a corporation "vacant position" announcement that was available to all employees through the online HR network.

The job description for the *Cyber Security Specialist* was developed by the cyber security officer based on past experience. The person was not actively recruited within HR, as this violated the corporation policy—people cannot actively try to "steal" employees from one another. As well as violating corporate policy, it is unethical.

One person who responded to the vacancy announcement had two years of experience at the corporation and had a bachelor's degree in journalism, but no cyber security or information assets protection experience. The cyber security officer wanted someone who could write and coordinate policies and procedures as the first priority and could secondarily learn about cyber security-related matters. The incentive was that the position was a promotion from the person's previously held position, and the person would be the lead in this function, rather than "just another employee" in the HR organization.[3]

At the corporation, the cyber security officer developed an administrative document architecture in which there was an overall information assets protection policy document followed by the other assets protection policy documents. The corporation overall policy document (Information Assets Protection Policy Document 500-1, also known as IAPPD 500-1) begins with a letter from the corporation CEO to show employees that this program was supported by the CEO:

To: All Corporation Employees

Subject: Protecting the Corporation's Information Assets to Maintain Our Competitive Edge through a Corporate Cyber Security Program

We are a leading international corporation in the manufacturing and sales of widgets. Today, we compete around the world in the global marketplace of fierce competition. To maintain a leadership position and grow, we depend first and foremost on all of you and provide you the resources to help you do your jobs to the best of your ability. You are vital to our success.

It is the policy of the corporation to protect all our vital assets that are the key to our success, and among these are our information-related assets. These include information, automated manufacturing tools, technology, information- and systems-driven processes, hardware, software, and firmware that we all rely upon to be successful.

---

[3] You may wonder why we go into such detail as to who is hired to do what or how it is done at the corporation. The reason is to provide, as nearly as possible, real-world experiences to the reader. Such information helps the reader by providing information that can be applied in real corporations; it also develops an overall knowledge of establishing and managing a corporate information assets protection program. In this case, a cyber security officer may look for someone to write policies by first looking for someone who knows security, when in fact it is more important to hire someone who can write policy. What to write will come from many sources. The policy specialist will not operate in a vacuum. How to write in clear and concise terms without ambiguities is the key.

You and these other vital corporation information assets must be able to operate in a safe environment, and our resources must be protected from loss, compromise, or other adverse effects that affect our ability to compete in the marketplace.

It is also corporation policy to depend on all of you to do your part to protect these valuable information-related assets in these volatile times. The protection of our information assets can be accomplished only through an effective and efficient cyber security program. We have begun an aggressive effort to build such a program.

This directive is the road map to our corporate cyber security program and the continued success of the corporation. In order for the cyber security program to be successful, you must give it your full support. Your support is vital to ensure that the corporation continues to grow and maintain its leadership role in the widget industry.

(Signed by the corporation President and CEO)

It is crucial that the CEO lead the way in the support of the protection of the corporation information assets. To get the preceding statement published, the cyber security officer relied on the policy cyber security staff member to draft a statement for the CEO to sign. The cyber security officer reasoned that it is always better to write a draft for someone to ensure that what is published meets the needs of the cyber security program and the corporation. The statement was drafted after reviewing numerous other documents and speeches made by the CEO to ensure that the words and format used were consistent with what the CEO normally signed.

The draft was edited by the cyber security officer and then coordinated by the cyber security officer with the Director of Corporate Security, since this had to do with the corporation assets. The Director of Security had no issues with the policy and in fact was happy that the cyber security officer was aggressively moving forward on this matter. In addition, the Director of Security believed that the cyber security officer pushing forward would eventually benefit the Security Department. Furthermore, if the cyber security officer ran into trouble with executive management, the Director could see how far the cyber security officer was able to go in meeting the information assets protection objectives. He likened the cyber security officer to a lead scout going through the corporation's executive management minefield. It would help the Director to politically choose his ground. After all, the Director was "old school." He didn't care much for computers, and he had no problem letting the cyber security officer take on the cyber security matters while the Director concentrated on more "mundane" security matters while awaiting his time for retirement in another four or five years.

Because the draft was going to the CEO, it was also reviewed and edited by the cyber security officer's boss, the CIO. It was then sent to the CEO's public relations staff and legal staff for editing and subsequently presented to the CEO by the cyber security officer accompanied by the CIO, who was always concerned when the cyber security officer was involved in anything that brought CEO visibility to any aspects of the CIO's department.

The cyber security officer accomplished another objective toward building a cyber security program for the corporation. The letter signed by the CEO was just one part of it. The cyber security officer also got support from the CEO to aggressively attack the vulnerabilities problems, because the CEO did not object to the assessment approach briefed by the cyber security officer as part of the cyber security program philosophy. That "hidden agenda" was used to initiate a more proactive effort that the Director of Audits and the cyber security officer had agreed to prior to the cyber security officer's meeting with the CEO. This tacit approval allowed the cyber security officer to establish a more proactive and aggressive cyber security program. All this may seem a little devious but not unethical—or is it? Do the results outweigh the tactics used to gain those results? You be the judge.

The cyber security policy document had a coordination note attached that showed all those who had seen the document (CEOs rarely sign anything relating to corporate business without input from the staff). If the cyber security officer had just made an appointment with the CEO and asked for concurrence on the document, the cyber security officer would undoubtedly be asked if the CIO had seen it, had it been coordinated with his (cyber security officer's) staff, etc. The cyber security officer would have said no, wasting the CEO's time and the cyber security officer's time. The CEO would never sign off on the document without CEO staff input. The whole incident would make the cyber security officer look foolish and unprofessional, and perhaps feel a little insecure, as though the CEO did not trust the cyber security officer.

One key factor is missing here. Do you know what it is? Would the CEO have signed the document without seeing the draft policy directive, IAPPD 500-1? The answer is probably yes. This is because the cyber security officer ensured that the letter was written without alluding to or identifying any "attached policy document" or any other document, for that matter. Why is this important? It is important because this document is timeless and can be used as a stand-alone document. The cyber security officer thought that it could also be attached to any information assets protection policy directive and would help enforce the policy directive because anyone would assume that the CEO's signed document is supporting the policy directive to which it is attached.

The fact is, it is probably true that the CEO would support the policy directive: That directive could not have been published and implemented without following the corporation directive publishing process. This process, as stated in the corporation directive HRD 5-17, includes directions as to proper coordination with applicable departments that would be affected by the directive.

The next day, the cyber security officer happened to be in discussion with the cyber security policy specialist around the coffeepot. They discussed the CEO's approval of the document, and the cyber security officer thanked the specialist for a great job.[4] The specialist said "Thanks" and also said, "You know, of course, that it is corporation policy that letters, regardless of who signs them, have no more than a 90-day life span? That policy was put in place because many executives and other managers were writing policy 'letters' to circumvent the coordination process for directives. So, these policy letters proliferated at the corporation. No one knew what was current and what wasn't, and many failed to follow the letters because 'they didn't work for that person' (the person who signed the letters). So, the letters were ignored. The last thing that the corporation needed was a bunch of letter policies flowing around and being ignored. That left the entire corporation atmosphere full of conflicts, some chaos, and an attitude of flouting any rules that one didn't like. In fact, that contributed to our loss of information assets, the firing of managers, including your predecessor. So, you don't want to end up starting that mess all over again. Do you?"

The cyber security officer didn't know that and was glad that the right person had been hired for the information assets protection policy specialist position. It's funny how things sometimes work out better than expected. An "cyber security techie" in that position would probably not have known that valuable piece of information.

The cyber security officer thought about what the information assets protection policy specialist had said. The cyber security officer wanted to keep to a minimum any objections to the information assets policy directives.

So, the cyber security officer directed that a copy of the CEO's signed document be attached to any information assets protection policy

---

[4] It is easy to take for granted the work of the staff. As a cyber security officer you should be sensitive to that and never forget to say thanks once in a while. It doesn't take a lot of effort, and it pays great dividends. Just like you, employees like to know they are appreciated.

document the cyber security officer was trying to get through the coordination process, published, and implemented. The cyber security officer also included a note on the coordination sheet that stated: *The attached document is an implementation document to meet the corporation information assets protection program requirements as stated in the CEO's document.* The cyber security officer was very satisfied with this approach and also directed that the CEO's letter be changed to a formal directive and so instructed the cyber security policy specialist. That directive, the cyber security officer reasoned, should not require any coordination because the CEO had already signed it. This was the case, and the CEO's letter became the corporation's IAPPD 500-1. Therefore, all other policy directives flowed from that overall directive—the CEO's memo-directive.

The cyber security officer directed that a project, with the cyber security policy specialist as the project lead, be established and implemented. The objective was to bring all information assets protection policy directives up to date. This would require all the corporation policy directives related to information assets protection to be reviewed, updated, coordinated, republished, and placed online, and that all briefings, training, and other processes be updated accordingly. The cyber security officer also directed that the project lead should prioritize the directives according to the following schedule:

• Directives that did not currently exist but must be developed to address the protection of various information assets and
• Directives that were the most outdated (continuing to those that were the least outdated).

The cyber security officer reasoned that outdated directives were better than no information assets policy directives, because where some were needed and did not exist, the information assets were more vulnerable. Although the missing directives would take the longest to get implemented, they were the most important. The cyber security officer also directed the information assets protection policy project team, with the policy specialist as the project lead, to do as much as possible in parallel. Those requiring the least amount of work could be done faster, and every updated directive was another victory in the war to protect corporate information assets.

War? The choice of words was used in all seriousness. The cyber security officer and the staff must get on a "war footing" and not treat their professional duties as some 9-to-5 job. Corporate information assets are being attacked from inside and outside the corporation, from within the home nation-state, and by competitors and nation-states from around the world on a 24/7 basis. This corporation was no exception, and in fact because of its leadership role in the widget industry, it was probably more at risk than some other the corporations.

The cyber security officer directed that all policy directives be limited to specific issues. The cyber security officer reasoned that to develop one large policy directive that covered all aspects of the corporation's information assets protection needs was not a good idea. Do you agree? Before answering, think about it from an employee's perspective. The employee has a job do to as a specialist in a chosen profession. Employees are not, nor do they want to be, cyber security specialists. To assist them in at least complying with the cyber security program, the "KISS" principle (keep it simple, stupid) should always be applied.

An employee who wants to do the right thing and comply with all the corporation directives and information assets protection directives is part of the group. Let's say the employee works in a marketing group. If there were just one large policy document, the employee would look at this monster and might be intimated by its size. The employee does not need to know about many of the information assets' protection requirements—for example, those that pertain to the manufacturing environment. Yes, one could do keyword searches if the documents are online, but in all probability, pertinent information would be scattered throughout the document. With the capability of putting documents online and maintaining them online, it is easy in today's word processing environment to just cut and paste applicable portions of other information assets protection documents that apply to more multiple information environments.

Many employees have lost patience trying to read through such large— and boring—documents. Let's face it, even cyber security professionals get bored reading cyber security documents. Ironically, some cyber security personnel never read the entire series of cyber security-related documents unless they have to, or unless someone embarrasses them by pointing out that they (cyber security personnel) are violating their own cyber security rules!

Topic-oriented information assets protection policy documents can be developed, coordinated, and implemented faster. In addition, employees can easily determine which directive to search for guidance without reading volumes. Also, one large directive would be almost constantly in a state of change because of various aspects requiring changes at different times.

The cyber security officer directed that, as a minimum, individual information assets policy directives were to be established to provide guidance for the protection of the following corporate information assets[5]:

- Overall information assets protection (CEO's signed letter);
- Information valuation, marking, storing, distribution, and destruction;
- Information processed, displayed, stored, and transmitted by information systems on the corporation's intranet;
- The corporation's telecommunications systems and voice mail;
- Cellular phones, PDAs, and pagers;
- Fax machines;
- Teleconferencing;
- Printers and scanners;
- Automated manufacturing;
- E-mail;
- Vital, automated records; and
- Violations of information assets protection policies, procedures, and processes.

The Corporate Cyber Security Program Requirements and Policy Directive

The corporation cyber security program directives followed the standard format for the corporation policies and included the following:

1. *Introduction,* which included some history of the need for cyber security at the corporation;
2. *Purpose,* which described why the document existed;
3. *Scope,* which defined the breadth of the Directive;
4. *Responsibilities,* which defined and identified the responsibilities at all levels, including executive management, organizational managers, systems custodians, IT personnel, and users. The Directive also included the requirements for customers', subcontractors', and vendors' access to the corporation systems and information.
5. *Requirements,* which included the requirements for:
   a. Identifying the value of the information;
   b. Access to the corporation systems;
   c. Access to specific applications and files;
   d. Audit trails and their review;

---

[5] Of course, this list is just a sample, as the topics would be based on the corporation, the corporate culture, and the methods used for publishing and implementing directives within each corporation.

    e. Reporting responsibilities and action to be taken in the event of an indication of a possible violation;

    f. Minimum protection for the hardware, firmware, and software[6]; and

    g. Cyber security procedures at the corporation department and lower levels.

Physical Security and Cyber Security Program Policy

The physical security functions for the most part fall under the Security Department. It was agreed by the Director of Security and the cyber security officer that the physical security program, as it related to cyber security, was to remain under the purview of the Security Department; however, those aspects related to cyber security would be coordinated with the cyber security officer or his or her designated representative.

The technical countermeasures program relating to emanations of systems' signals or covert signals that may be placed in the corporation's sensitive processing areas had been initially placed under the purview of the cyber security officer; however, the Director of Security apparently became concerned because the systems permeate the corporation, which appeared to give the cyber security officer a great deal of authority.

The cyber security officer's authority, which the Director equated to *power*, over physical security as it related to systems facilities was relinquished by the cyber security officer. The cyber security officer's rationale was:

- It showed the executive management and the Director of Security that the cyber security officer was interested in getting the job done right and not who had the authority to do it;
- This move, coupled with the cyber security procedures responsibility placed on the corporate management, gave clear indications to everyone that the cyber security officer was interested in getting the job done in a cooperative effort in which cyber security responsibilities belonged to everyone in a true team effort; and
- It took a heavy responsibility off the shoulders of the cyber security officer. The cyber security officer was no longer responsible for the physical security aspects; thus, the cyber security officer's attention could

---

[6] The physical security aspects of the requirements would have been coordinated with the applicable Security Department managers, since they have the responsibility for the physical security of the corporation assets. The cyber security officer's rationale was that physical security should be addressed in this document, because it is a basic protection process. The Director of Security agreed and approved that process.

be directed to more technical aspects of the cyber security program—those more enjoyable to the cyber security officer.

The agreement reached by the cyber security officer and Director of Security was for the Security Department to be responsible for:

- Control of physical access to information systems throughout the corporation;
- Physical access control badge readers to areas containing sensitive information-processing activities;
- Physical disconnects of all systems-processing information so sensitive that the information could not be processed outside specified areas;
- Review, analyses, and action related to physical access control audit trails; and
- Control of physical access of all visitors, vendors, subcontractors, customers, and maintenance personnel and the escorting of such personnel into sensitive information-processing areas.

The Corporation Cyber Security Program—Cyber Security Procedures

Over the years, the cyber security officer has had experience in several the corporations. The cyber security officer learned that the best way to provide an updated cyber security program is to begin at the highest level and work down. This form of information assets protection evaluation, analysis, and improvement is based on the fact that information assets protection is driven *and must be supported* from the top down. Therefore, the cyber security officer began with the overall corporation assets protection requirements (drivers), followed by the information assets protection policies. Once they were in place, those related procedures that were already in place were analyzed and projects established to update them and develop new ones where needed.

Each information assets protection policy requires compliance by those identified in the policy directives. Each of these directives requires one or more procedures to be established so that there is a standard method used to support and implement the policies, including their spirit and intent. The information assets protection directives previously discussed require procedures to be established to comply with those directives. For example, what procedures should be used to determine the classification to be given a piece of information: corporation–trade secret, corporation–sensitive, corporation–proprietary? Some procedures may be written for everyone in the corporation to follow, while various departments may write others based on their unique information environments.

There are various opinions as to how best to go about developing procedures. One continues to get to a more detailed level as one goes from requirements (drivers) to policies to procedures. The main issue is this: If the cyber security officer establishes a specific procedure to comply with a specific policy, which in turn assists in meeting the corporation goals as stated in the corporate strategic business plan, tactical business plan, and annual business plan, the procedures may not be practical in one or two of the corporation's departments. The department head may so state and may ask for a waiver saying that they can still comply if they have a different procedure that takes into account their unique working information environment. There may be more than one department with similar complaints. So, how does the cyber security officer ensure that people are following proper information assets protection procedures to comply with the information assets protection policies?

The cyber security officer has found that the best way to do this at the corporation is to require that the individual departments establish, implement, and maintain their own set of information assets protection procedures that comply with the policies. This has several benefits:

- Having each department write its own procedures helps enforce the philosophy that information assets protection is everyone's responsibility.
- There will be fewer complaints and requests for waivers because one or more of the corporation's departments cannot comply with the procedures as written by the cyber security officer's staff. This benefits the cyber security officer, as tracking waivers may turn into a nightmare—who has what waivers, why, and for how long.
- The departments can develop procedures that meet their unique conditions and because of that, the procedures should be more cost-effective.
- The cyber security officer and his or her staff will save time and effort in writing and maintaining information assets protection procedures. To be blunt—it's the departments' problem. However, the cyber security officer has offered to make cyber security staff available to answer questions and to provide advice as to what should be in the documents. This was done in the spirit of providing service and support to the corporation employees. The liaison contact for the cyber security officer would of course be the cyber security policy specialist.

The question then arose as to how the cyber security officer could be sure that the procedures written by each department meet the spirit and intent of the policies. Two methods were identified:

- The cyber security staff, as part of their risk management processes, would conduct limited risk assessment surveys, and as part of those surveys, the procedures would be reviewed. The limited risk assessments would indicate how well the procedures in place help protect the corporation information assets under the control of each department or suborganization.

- The corporation's audit staff would compare the procedures with the policies during their routine audits. The Director of Audits agreed to conduct such reviews, since that department is responsible for auditing compliance with federal, state, and local laws and regulations and the corporation's policies and procedures anyway. It also helped that since the cyber security officer's arrival, the cyber security officer and the Director of Audits met and agreed to monthly meetings to share information of mutual concern. The cyber security officer learned long ago that cyber security personnel have very few true supporters in helping them to get the job done, but auditors were one of them.

Procedures, along with their related processes, are the heart of a cyber security program because they provide the step-by-step approach for employees as to how to do their work and also ensure the protection of corporate information assets. And if the departments write their own procedures, they become actively involved as valuable team members in the process of protecting the corporation's valuable information assets.

CYBER SECURITY OFFICER THOUGHT PROCESS IN ESTABLISHING THE CYBER SECURITY ORGANIZATION

The cyber security officer also knew that a staff of cyber security specialists would be required because of the large size and geographical locations of the corporation systems and associated facilities. What the cyber security officer had to determine was how many specialists and what types were needed and how the cyber security officer's organization should be structured. Although there was a group of cyber security specialists that made up the corporation's cyber security organization that the cyber security officer inherited, they were disorganized and had been sort of "thrown together" by the previous cyber security officer, who was not employed long enough to get around to properly organizing the group.

The corporation cyber security officer must, in parallel to establishing a cyber security program baseline, also begin the task of establishing a cyber security program-related organization. The cyber security officer decided that the sole purpose of the organization was to lead and support the cyber security program. Therefore, the cyber security officer intended to provide an "umbilical cord" between the cyber security program and the cyber security officer's organization. After all, without some form of cyber security program, no cyber security organization would be necessary. In doing so, the cyber security officer needed to understand:

* The limits of authority,
* The amount of budget available, and
* The impact of establishing a cyber security program on the corporation—the culture change.

The cyber security officer also had to determine how to find qualified people who could build and maintain a cost-effective cyber security program. The staff must also be able to develop into a cyber security team in which everyone acts and is treated as a professional. The corporation cyber security officer wanted a group of cyber security professionals who were very talented, yet could leave their egos at the door when they came to work (not an easy task for very talented people).

The cyber security officer also had to consider that building an *empire* and a massive, bureaucratic organization would not only give the wrong impression to the corporation management, but would also be costly. Furthermore, the cyber security officer had to build an efficient and effective cyber security organization, as required by the corporation and as stated in the numerous plans. After all, wasn't that one of the implied conditions of employment?

Building a bureaucracy leads to cumbersome processes, which lead to slow decision cycles, which cause the cyber security program to have an adverse impact on costs and schedules, which leads to a cyber security program that does not provide the services and support needed by the company. This snowballing effect, once started, would be difficult to stop. And if stopped, it would require twice as long to rebuild the service and support reputation of the cyber security officer, the cyber security staff, and the cyber security program.

In developing the cyber security program organization, the cyber security officer also had to bear in mind all that was discussed with the corporate management and what was promised. These included:

* The corporation's history, business, and competitive environment;
* Mission, vision, and quality statements;
* The corporation and cyber security program plans; and
* The need for developing a cyber security program as quickly as possible, for the work will not wait until the cyber security officer is fully prepared.

Determining the Need for Cyber Security Subordinate Organizations

The cyber security officer must determine whether subordinate cyber security organizations are needed. If so, a functional work breakdown structure must be developed to determine how many subordinate organizations are needed and what functions should be integrated into what subordinate organizations.

The corporation's cyber security officer reviewed the cyber security officer's charter and cyber security program focus previously agreed to by the cyber security officer and executive management. That charter included the following cyber security program functions:

- Requirements, policies, procedures, and plans;
- Hardware, firmware, and software cyber security evaluations;
- Technical security countermeasures (function subsequently transferred to the Security Department);
- Cyber security tests and evaluations;
- Information system processing approvals;
- Access control;
- Noncompliance inquiries;
- Telecommunications security;
- Risk management;
- Awareness and training; and
- Disaster recovery/contingency planning.

The cyber security officer analyzed the plans, functions, number of systems, and number of users and determined that two subordinate organizations would be needed to provide the minimum cyber security program professional services and support.

Actually, the cyber security officer thought of dividing the functions into three organizations, but the need for one of those was borderline. Also, having three suborganizations might give the wrong impression to others in the corporation (one must always remember perceptions and appearances when building a cyber security program and organization). It would also provide another level of administrative overhead burden that would not be cost-effective. The cyber security officer reasoned that the two subordinate organizations would suffice for now; the organizations could be reevaluated at the end of the first year's operation.

The cyber security officer decided to brief the CIO (the boss) on the plan. The CIO thought it was reasonable, but wondered how the cyber security officer would handle the off-site locations in the United States, Europe, and Asia.

As with any good plan, nothing ever runs completely as expected. Being an honest and straightforward cyber security officer, the only logical comeback was "Huh?" The CIO went on to explain that their global locations are manufacturing sites making final or subassemblies of the widgets and shipping them to the main plant or global customers, as applicable.

The cyber security officer asked the CIO how other organizations handled the off-site. The CIO explained that they have smaller, satellite offices to provide the service and support needed at that location. The cyber security officer determined that before deciding on the need for a satellite office, the problem should be further evaluated. The cyber security officer explained to the CIO that the evaluation would be conducted within a week and a decision made at that time.

The cyber security officer subsequently determined that to provide quality services and support to the off-site locations, small cyber security organizations with dedicated staff should be in place at all facilities. This would replace the current staff, who, as an additional duty assigned by on-site facility executive managers, had to serve as part-time cyber security persons. This decision was based on several considerations:

- Conversations with managers of other organizations who had satellite offices at the off-site location, relative to how they handled the problem;
- Conversations with managers of other organizations who did *not* have satellite offices at the off-site location, as to how they handled the service and support requirements;
- Conversations with off-site facility executive managers;
- An analysis of the off-site locations' information systems configurations and processing;
- Information flow processes; and
- The cyber security program needs of each location.

Based on the analysis, the cyber security officer determined that cyber security program satellite offices were indeed necessary, but some functions could be supported from the corporate office, such as risk management, policy development, and requirements.

The cyber security officer informed the CIO of the decision and the basis for the decision, emphasizing its cost-effectiveness. The CIO agreed based on the business logic shown by the cyber security officer, the minimal number of cyber security staff needed, and what the CIO sensed as the cyber security officer's strong commitment to the cyber security program using a lowest cost/minimum risk approach.

> *The number of people in any working group tends to increase regardless of the amount of work to be done*
>
> **Cyril Northcote Parkinson**[7]

Developing the Cyber Security Program Organization Structure

Based on the cyber security officer's analyses, the cyber security officer established the cyber security program organization—at least on paper.

The cyber security officer found that establishing the cyber security program organization to date had been the easy part. Now came the bureaucracy of coordinating and gaining approval of the cyber security program organization from the designated organizations, such as organizational planning, HR, and facilities, as well as completing their and other organizations' forms.[8]

A word of caution to the cyber security officer: Some *service and support* organizations are more interested in proper completion of the administrative bureaucracy than in helping their internal customers. Just grin and bear it. You can't change it, except over time, and now is not the time. The priority is getting the cyber security program and the cyber security organization off the ground. Concentrate on that priority.

Developing the Cyber Security Program Subordinate Organizations

The cyber security officer determined that the subordinate organizations must also have charters that identify the cyber security program functions that are to be performed by the staff of those organizations. The cyber security officer further determined that to recruit managers for the subordinate organizations was premature. The cyber security officer reasoned that what was needed first was professional cyber security personnel who could begin the actual program work. The cyber security officer would manage all the organizations until such time as the workload and cost-effectiveness considerations determined that a subordinate manager or managers were needed.

---

[7] Cyril Northcote Parkinson (1909–1993), British political scientist, historian, and writer. Parkinson's Law (1958), as quoted in Microsoft's *Encarta World*.

[8] Since each corporation has a somewhat different *forms bureaucracy,* no attempt will be made here to complete any forms. Those readers who have to make any changes in an organization can appreciate the maze the cyber security officer must now go through.

Based on the work to be performed, and the analyses discussed above, the cyber security officer developed the charters for the subordinate organizations. In the interim, the cyber security officer used a matrix management approach with the off-site facility managers who were responsible to the CIO for overall information and information systems management.

Responsibilities of Cyber Security Program Subordinate Organizations

Cyber Security Program Access Control and Compliance

The cyber security officer is the acting manager of the cyber security program Access Control and Compliance subordinate organization.

The following is the summary of the position:

Provide the management and direction and conduct analyses required to protect information processed on the corporation's information systems from unauthorized access, disclosure, misuse, modification, manipulation, or destruction, as well as implementing and maintaining appropriate information and information systems access controls; conduct noncompliance inquiries; and maintain violations tracking systems.[9]

Detailed accountabilities include:

1. Implement, administer, and maintain user access control systems by providing controls, processes, and procedures to prevent the unauthorized access, modification, disclosure, misuse, manipulation, or destruction of the corporation's information.

2. Monitor user access control systems to provide for the identification, inquiry, and reporting of access control violations. Analyze system access control violation data and trends to determine potential systems' security weaknesses and report to management.

3. Conduct inquiries into cyber security program violations/incidents and related cyber security program business practices, corporation policies, and procedures. Identify the exposures/compromises created, and recommend to management corrective and preventive actions.

4. Direct, monitor, and guide the cyber security program activities of the corporation's access control support groups and systems to ensure adequate implementation of access control systems in meeting cyber security program requirements.

[9] The cyber security officer decided that the priority of the cyber security program was the systems and information at their facilities. The sticky problem of dealing with cyber security program issues, such as subcontractors and customers, would have to wait. The cyber security officer reasoned that if it had a successful, professional program, it would be easier to gain the cooperation of those outside the corporation.

5. Establish and manage an information systems defensive system, including firewalls and related intrusion detection systems.
6. Provide advice on and assistance with the interpretation and implementation of cyber security program policies and procedures, contractual cyber security program requirements, and related documents.

Cyber Security Program Policy and Risk Management

The cyber security officer is the acting manager of the cyber security program Policy and Risk Management subordinate organization.

The following is the summary of the position:

Provide the management and direction and develop, implement, and maintain cyber security program policies and procedures, awareness, disaster recovery and contingency planning, cyber security program system life cycle processes, cyber security tests and evaluations, risk management, and cyber security program technical security and related programs to protect the corporation systems and information.

Detailed accountabilities include:

1. Identify all cyber security program requirements needed and develop the corporate policies and procedures necessary to ensure conformance to those requirements.
2. Evaluate all hardware, software, and firmware to ensure conformance to cyber security program policies and procedures, recommend modifications when not in conformance, and approve them when in conformance.
3. Establish and administer a cyber security tests and evaluations program to ensure compliance with systems' security documentation and applicable cyber security program requirements.
4. Establish, implement, and maintain a cyber security technical program to identify all electronic threats and mitigate those threats in a cost-effective manner.
5. Establish and maintain a cyber security awareness program to ensure that the corporation management and users are cognizant of cyber security program policies, procedures, and requirements for the protection of systems and information and their related threats.
6. Develop, implement, and administer a risk management program to identify and assess threats, vulnerabilities, and risks associated with the information for which the corporation has responsibility and recommend cost-effective modifications to the cyber security program, systems, and processes.

7. Establish and maintain a disaster recovery/contingency planning program that will mitigate cyber security program, corporation information, and systems' losses and ensure the successful recovery of the information and systems with minimal impact on the corporation.

Off-Site Cyber Security Program Organizations

The cyber security officer is also the acting manager of the off-site cyber security program subordinate organizations. However, the cyber security officer has determined that it will be necessary to appoint a person as a supervisor to manage the day-to-day operations of the off-site cyber security program. At the same time, there are not enough personnel, as stated by HR, to appoint a manager at each off-site location. However, the supervisor has authority to make decisions related to that activity, with several exceptions. The supervisor cannot counsel the cyber security program staff, evaluate their performance (except to provide input to the cyber security program manager), make new cyber security program policy, or manage budgets.

The following is the summary of the position:

Implement, maintain, and administer a cyber security program for the corporate resources at the off-site location and take the actions necessary to ensure compliance with the cyber security program requirements, policies, and procedures to protect the corporation's information from compromise, destruction, and/or unauthorized manipulation.[10]

Detailed accountabilities include:

1. Implement and administer the corporation's plans, policies, and procedures necessary to ensure compliance with stated the corporation's cyber security program requirements for the protection of all information processed, stored, and/or transmitted on the corporation's information systems.

2. Administer a cyber security tests and evaluations program to ensure that all the corporation's information systems are operated in accordance with appropriate cyber security program requirements and contract specifications.

3. Administer and monitor the local use of the corporation's information systems access control software systems, analyze all infractions/violations, and document and report the results of questionable user activity for cyber security program inquiries.

---

[10] Because of its off-site location, this position requires cyber security program functions to be performed that are similar to or the same as most functions noted for the entire cyber security program organization.

4. Identify information systems' business practice irregularities and security violations/infractions; conduct detailed inquiries; assess potential damage; monitor the corporation management's corrective action; and recommend preventive measures to preclude recurrences.

5. Administer a cyber security education and training awareness program for all the corporate managers and users of the corporation's information systems to ensure they are cognizant of information systems' threats and are aware of the cyber security program policies/procedures necessary for the protection of information and information systems.

6. Represent the cyber security program manager relative to all applicable corporation cyber security program matters as they apply to personnel, resources, and operations at the off-site location.

7. Provide advice, guidance, and assistance to management, system users, and systems' custodians relative to cyber security program matters.

8. Perform other functions as designated or delegated by the cyber security program manager.

Cyber Security Job Descriptions

After establishing and gaining final approval for the cyber security organization, and while trying to begin establishing a formal, centralized cyber security program, the cyber security officer determined it was now time to begin hiring some cyber security professionals.

However, before that could be accomplished, and in accordance with the corporation organizational development and HR requirements, a cyber security job family first had to be established. After all, the corporation, being a high-tech, modern corporation, requires that employees be assigned to career families to support their career development program as directed by the HR Department. And, unfortunately, it seems that cyber security functions have never been a formal part of the corporation. Therefore, there are no job families that seem to meet the needs of the cyber security program functions.

The cyber security officer and the HR representative discussed the matter and agreed that the cyber security officer would write the cyber security functional job family descriptions. The cyber security officer was told that they must be generic, so they are flexible enough to support several cyber security job functions within each level of the job family. The HR representative advised the cyber security officer that this is necessary to ensure the flexibility needed for recruiting, hiring, and subsequent career development of the cyber security professionals. Also, it would streamline the process and ensure that the number of cyber security job family position descriptions could be kept to a minimum, thus also decreasing bureaucracy and paperwork.

At the conclusion of the meeting, the HR representative provided the cyber security officer with the job descriptions for the security, auditor, and IT job family. Also provided were several forms that had to be completed when submitting the cyber security job family descriptions, as well as forms to be used for documenting each job family description by grade level.

Armed with the challenges of this new onslaught of bureaucratic paper, and bidding adieu to the smiling HR representative, the cyber security officer headed back to the office to begin the task of writing the corporation's cyber security job family as sample descriptions (while wondering when there would be time to do *real* cyber security program work).

After reviewing the provided job descriptions and reading the paperwork needed to make this all happen, the cyber security officer wrote and provided the HR representative with the function descriptions of the cyber security job family! After several iterations and compromises, and approvals through a chain of organizational staffs, the job family was approved.

Cyber Security Job Family Functional Descriptions

The following detailed cyber security job family functional descriptions were developed and approved by the applicable corporation departments:

1. Systems Security Administrator

Position summary: Provide all technical administrative support for the cyber security organization.

Duties and responsibilities:

a. Filing.

b. Typing reports and other word processing projects.

c. Developing related spreadsheets, databases, and text/graphic presentations.

Qualifications: High school diploma, 1 year of security administration or 2 years of clerical experience. Must type at least 60 words per minute.

2. System Security Analyst Associate

Position summary: Assist and support cyber security staff in ensuring all applicable corporation cyber security program requirements are met.

Duties and responsibilities

a. Support the implementation and administration of cyber security software systems.

b. Provide advice, guidance, and assistance to system users relative to cyber security program matters.

c. Identify current cyber security program and cyber security functional processes and assist in the development of automated tools to support those functions.

d. Assist in the analysis of manual cyber security program and cyber security functions and provide input to recommendations and reports of the analyses to the cyber security officer.

e. Maintain, modify, and enhance automated cyber security functional systems of cyber security tests and evaluations, risk assessments, software/hardware evaluations, access control, and other related systems.

f. Collect, compile, and generate cyber security program functional informational reports and briefing packages for presentation to customers and management.

g. Perform other functions as assigned by the cyber security officer and cyber security management.

Position requires being assigned to perform duties in one or more of the following areas:

- *Access control*—Maintain basic user access control systems by providing processes and procedures to prevent unauthorized access or the destruction of information.

- *Access control/technical access control software*—Assist access control support groups and systems by providing software tools and guidance to ensure adequate implementation of access control systems in meeting cyber security program requirements, as well as defensive systems such as firewalls and related intrusion detection systems.

- *Access control/violations analysis*—Monitor the use of the corporation access control software systems; identify all cyber security systems infractions/violations; document and report the results of questionable user and system activity for cyber security program inquiries.

- *Cyber security tests and evaluation/cyber security program systems documentation*—Conduct cyber security tests and evaluations on stand-alone (non-networked) systems to ensure that the systems are processing in accordance with applicable cyber security program-approved procedures.

Qualifications: This position normally requires a bachelor's degree in a cyber security-related profession.

3. Systems Security Analyst

Position summary: Identify, schedule, administer, and perform assigned technical cyber security analysis functions to ensure all applicable requirements are met.

Duties and responsibilities

a. Represent cyber security program to other organizations on select cyber security program-related matters.

b. Provide advice, guidance, and assistance to managers, system users, and system custodians relative to cyber security program matters.

c. Provide general advice and assistance in the interpretation of cyber security program requirements.

d. Identify all cyber security program requirements necessary for the protection of all information processed, stored, and/or transmitted by the information systems; develop and implement plans, policies, and procedures necessary to ensure compliance.

e. Identify current cyber security program functional processes and develop automated tools to support those functions.

f. Analyze manual cyber security program functions and provide recommendations and reports of the analyses to cyber security management.

g. Maintain, modify, and enhance automated cyber security program functional systems of cyber security tests and evaluations, risk assessments, software/hardware evaluations, access control, and other related systems.

h. Collect, compile, and generate cyber security program function informational reports and briefing packages for presentation to customers and management.

i. Perform other functions as assigned by cyber security management.

Position requires being assigned to perform duties in the following areas:

- *Access control/technical access control software*—Administer and maintain user access control systems by providing controls, processes, and procedures to prevent the unauthorized access, modification, disclosure, misuse, manipulation, or destruction of the corporation's information, as well as defensive systems such as firewalls and related intrusion detection systems.

- *Access control/violations analysis*—Administer and monitor the use of the corporation's access control software systems; analyze all systems cyber security program infractions/violations; document and report the results of questionable user and system activity for cyber security program inquiries.

- *Noncompliance inquiry*—Identify and analyze cyber security program business practice irregularities and cyber security program violations/infractions; conduct detailed inquiries; assess potential damage; monitor corrective action; and recommend preventive, cost-effective measures to preclude recurrences.

- *Risk assessment*—Perform limited risk assessments of cyber security program systems and processes; determine their threats, vulnerabilities, and risks; and recommend cost-effective risk mitigation solutions.
- *Cyber security tests and evaluation/cyber security program system documentation*—Schedule and conduct cyber security program tests and evaluations on stand-alone (nonnetworked) systems to ensure that the systems are processing in accordance with applicable cyber security program-approved procedures.

Qualifications: This classification normally requires a bachelor's degree in a cyber security-related profession and at least 2 years of practical experience.

4. System Security Analyst Senior

Position summary: Identify, evaluate, conduct, schedule, and lead technical cyber security analysis functions to ensure that all applicable corporation cyber security program requirements are met.

Duties and responsibilities

a. Provide technical analysis of cyber security program requirements necessary for the protection of all information processed, stored, and/or transmitted by systems; interpret those requirements; and translate, implement, and administer division plans, policies, and procedures necessary to ensure compliance.

b. Represent cyber security program on security matters with other entities as assigned.

c. Provide advice, guidance, and assistance to senior management, system managers, and system users and custodians relative to cyber security program matters.

d. Perform other functions as assigned by cyber security management.

Position requires being assigned to perform duties in the following areas:

- *Access control/technical access control software*—Implement, administer, and maintain systems' user access control systems through the use of controls, processes, and procedures to prevent their unauthorized access, modification, disclosure, misuse, manipulation, and/or destruction, as well as defensive systems such as firewalls and related intrusion detection systems.
- *Access control/violations analysis*—Coordinate, administer, and monitor the use of systems' access control systems; analyze systems security infractions/violations employing statistical and trend analyses and report the results.

- *Cyber security program awareness*—Prepare, schedule, and present cyber security program awareness briefings to systems managers, custodians, and users. Act as focal point for dissemination of cyber security program information through all forms of media.
- *Disaster recovery*—Coordinate and ensure compliance with system disaster recovery/contingency plans to ensure the rapid recovery of systems in the event of an emergency or disaster.
- *Hardware and software cyber security program evaluations*—Evaluate all hardware, firmware, and software for impact on the cyber security program of the systems; monitor and ensure their modification if requirements are not met; and authorize their purchase and use within the corporation.
- *Noncompliance inquiry*—Identify and conduct technical analyses of cyber security program business practices and violations/infractions; plan, coordinate, and conduct detailed inquiries; assess potential damage; and develop and implement corrective action plans.
- *Risk assessments*—Conduct limited cyber security technical risk assessments; prepare reports of the results for presentation to management.
- *Cyber security tests and evaluations/cyber security program documentation*—Schedule and conduct cyber security tests and evaluations to ensure that all the applicable systems are operating in accordance with cyber security program requirements.
- *Technical countermeasures*—Conduct technical surveys and determine necessary countermeasures related to physical information leakage; conduct sound attenuation tests to ensure that information processing systems do not emanate information beyond the corporation's zone of control.

Qualifications: This classification normally requires a bachelor's degree in a cyber security-related profession and 4 years of practical, related experience.

5. System Security Analyst Specialist

Position summary: Act as technical cyber security program advisor, focal point, and lead to ensure all cyber security program functions are meeting the corporation requirements, as well as developing and administering applicable programs.

Duties and responsibilities:

a. Act as technical advisor for cyber security program requirements necessary for the protection of all information processed, stored, and/or transmitted by systems; interpret those requirements; and translate, document, implement, and administer the corporation cyber security program plans, policies, and procedures necessary to ensure compliance.

b. Represent cyber security program on security matters with other entities as assigned.

c. Provide advice, guidance, and assistance to senior management, IT managers, system users, and system custodians relative to cyber security program matters.

d. Perform other functions as assigned by cyber security management.

Position requires being assigned to perform duties in a combination of the following areas:

- *Access control/technical access control software*—Implement, administer, and maintain systems' user access control systems through the use of controls, processes, and procedures to prevent their unauthorized access, modification, disclosure, misuse, manipulation, and/or destruction, as well as defensive systems such as firewalls and related intrusion detection systems.

- *Cyber security program awareness*—Prepare, schedule, and present cyber security program awareness briefings to system managers, custodians, and users. Act as focal point for dissemination of cyber security program information through all forms of media.

- *Disaster recovery*—Coordinate and ensure compliance with system disaster recovery/contingency plans to ensure the rapid recovery of systems in the event of an emergency or disaster.

- *Hardware and software cyber security program evaluations*—Evaluate all hardware, firmware, and software for impact on the cyber security program of the systems; monitor and ensure their modification if requirements are not met; and authorize their purchase and use within the corporation.

- *Risk assessments*—Conduct limited cyber security program technical risk assessments; prepare reports of the results for presentation to management.

- *Cyber security tests and evaluations/cyber security program documentation*—Schedule and conduct cyber security tests and evaluations to ensure that all the applicable systems are operating in accordance with cyber security program requirements.

- *Technical countermeasures*—Conduct technical surveys and determine necessary countermeasures related to physical information leakage; conduct sound attenuation tests to ensure that information processing systems do not emanate information beyond the corporation's zone of control.

Qualifications: This classification normally requires a bachelor's degree in a cyber security program-related profession and 6 years of cyber security program experience.

6. System Security Engineer

Position summary: Act as a technical systems management consultant, focal point, and project lead for cyber security program functions and programs developed to ensure the corporation's requirements are met.

Duties and responsibilities

a. Act as a lead in the identification of government, customers, and corporation cyber security program requirements necessary for the protection of information processed, stored, and/or transmitted by the corporation's systems; interpret those requirements; and develop, implement, and administer the corporation cyber security program plans, policies, and procedures necessary to ensure compliance.

b. Represent the cyber security program office, when applicable, on cyber security program matters as well as serving as the corporation's liaison with customers, government agencies, suppliers, and other outside entities.

c. Provide advice, guidance, and assistance to senior and executive management, the corporation's subcontractors, and government entities relative to cyber security program matters.

d. Provide technical consultation, guidance, and assistance to management, systems users, and cyber security program software systems by providing controls, processes, and procedures.

e. Establish, direct, coordinate, and maintain a disaster recovery/contingency program for the corporation that will mitigate systems and information losses and ensure the successful recovery of the system and information with minimal impact on the corporation.

f. Act as lead for the technical evaluation and testing of hardware, firmware, and software for impact on the security of the systems; direct and ensure their modification if requirements are not met; authorize their purchase and use within the corporation and approve them when in conformance.

g. Develop or direct the development of original techniques, procedures, and utilities for conducting cyber security program risk assessments; schedule and conduct cyber security program risk assessments and report results to management.

h. Direct and/or lead others in conducting technical cyber security program countermeasure surveys to support cyber security program requirements and report findings.

i. Direct and administer cyber security tests and evaluations programs to ensure that the applicable systems are operating in accordance with cyber security program requirements.

j. Provide technical consultation and assistance in identifying, evaluating, and documenting use of systems and other related equipments to ensure compliance with communications requirements.

k. Investigate methods and procedures related to the cyber security program aspects of microcomputers, local area networks, mainframes, and their associated connectivity and communications.

l. Identify and participate in evaluation of microcomputer and local area network cyber security program implementations, including antivirus and disaster recovery/contingency planning functions.

m. Perform development and maintenance activities on cyber security program-related databases.

n. Recommend and obtain approval for procedural changes to effect cyber security program implementations with emphasis on lowest cost/minimum risk.

o. Lead and direct cyber security personnel in the conduct of systems cyber security program audits.

p. Participate in the development and promulgation of cyber security program information for general awareness.

q. Perform other functions as assigned by the cyber security manager.
Position requires being assigned to perform duties in the following area:

• *Supervisor, project leader*—Provide assistance, advice, guidance, and act as technical specialist relative to all cyber security technical functions.

Qualifications: This classification normally requires a bachelor's degree in a cyber security-related profession and a minimum of 10 years of cyber security program-related experience.

Recruiting Cyber Security Professionals

Once the cyber security officer had gotten the cyber security organizational structure and the cyber security job family functional descriptions both approved, the next task was to begin recruiting and hiring qualified cyber security professionals.

Hold it! Not so fast! The cyber security officer must first determine the following:

• How many cyber security professionals are needed?
• What functions will they perform?
• How many are needed in each function?

- How many are needed in what pay code?
- How many should be recruited for the off-site location?
- Does the off-site location or main plant have the highest priority?

The cyber security officer must plan for the gradual hiring of personnel to meet the cyber security program and cyber security organizational needs based on a prioritized listing of functions. Obviously, a mixture of personnel should be considered. One or two high-level personnel should be hired to begin establishing the basic cyber security program and cyber security processes. Personnel who meet the qualifications of a system security engineer should be hired immediately. At least two should be hired. One would be the project lead to begin the process of establishing the formal functions of one of the cyber security subordinate organizations and the other would do the same for the other cyber security organization. At the same time, the access control function positions should be filled, as they represent the key cyber security program mechanism of access control.

Functions such as risk management, noncompliance inquiry, and the awareness program could come later. The rationale used by the cyber security officer for this decision was that cyber security program policies had not been established, so there was nothing on which to base noncompliance inquiries or an awareness program. The next position to be filled, after the two systems security engineers and access control personnel, was the position of the emergency planning, disaster recovery planning, and contingency planning specialist.

The cyber security officer reasoned that while access controls were being tightened up and analyzed, the engineers were beginning to build the process for each function, with much of the access control process development being done with the assistance of the access control administrators. In the event of a disaster, the systems must be up and operational in as short a time period as possible. This is crucial to the well-being of the corporation.

Unfortunately, the type of individual the cyber security officer would ideally want to employ is not usually readily available. In addition, the corporation's policy is one of "promote from within" whenever possible. So, although a *more* qualified individual may be available from outside the corporation, the cyber security officer may have to transfer a less qualified individual currently employed within the corporation, because that person does meet the minimum requirements for the position—at least as interpreted by the HR personnel.

The cyber security officer soon began to realize that compromise and coordination were a *must* if there was to be even a slight chance of succeeding in building the corporation cyber security program. Based on a self-evaluation, the cyber security officer decided to find as many people as possible within the corporation who were willing to transfer and who met the minimum requirements for a cyber security program position. The cyber security officer soon learned why the job descriptions approved through the HR Department include words such as "normally" and "equivalent." The cyber security officer naively thought that those words would assist in bringing in cyber security professionals. It never entered the cyber security officer's mind that others could also use the position descriptions to help recruit personnel—some who just barely would meet the minimum requirements!

For the cyber security officer who is trying to quickly build a cyber security program and cyber security organization, the compromises on staff selection may help or they may hurt. In either case, it is important to begin the hiring process quickly.

Identifying In-House Cyber Security Candidates

Those individuals within the corporation organizations who have been providing access control in either a full- or a part-time position for their department's local area networks may be good access control candidates.

The IT Department may also be a place to "recruit" (make personnel aware of the positions available) cyber security candidates. The audit and cyber security organizations may also provide places to find cyber security candidates.

A word of caution to the cyber security officer: Most managers do not take kindly to recruiting of their employees, as it means they will be short-handed until they can find replacements. In addition, the cyber security officer should beware of individuals whom the managers recommend. These may just be the people that the manager has been trying to find some way to get rid of for some time!

The cyber security officer has enough problems building a cyber security program, establishing and managing a cyber security organization, handling the day-to-day cyber security program problems, attending endless meetings, trying to hire a professional cyber security program staff, and having to transfer personnel who don't meet the cyber security officer's expectations to then be saddled with an employee recommended by another manager who turns out to be a "difficult" employee.

A difficult employee will occupy more of the cyber security officer's time than three other staff members combined. It seemed that the corporation IT Department had a penchant for this. So, *beware of geeks bearing gifts!*

Identifying Outside Cyber Security Candidates

There are many sources that can be used to recruit talented cyber security professionals, many limited only by imagination and budget (especially budget!). Regardless of how or where you recruit, the recruitment must be coordinated with the HR staff.

To recruit cyber security personnel, the Controller must validate and approve (on another form, of course) that there is budget set aside for the cyber security organization to hire staff.

Then once that hurdle is jumped, the HR personnel must validate that you have completed the necessary form describing the position you want to hire against, the minimum qualifications, and the pay range for that position. Luckily, all the cyber security officer has to do in this case is basically transcribe the general position description onto the new HR form used for recruiting candidates and advertising the position.

Just as the corporation cyber security officer thought that the door was now flung wide open to recruit cyber security professionals, one of the HR personnel walked up to the cyber security officer and mentioned how boring the HR job was, and that it would be nice to transfer to another, more exciting organization—and the cyber security job seemed to be a very exciting one. Experience? Well, of course the person is proficient is *using* a computer! Another often-found problem is the manager or staff member who has a cousin just graduating from college who would be perfect for the cyber security position.

The cyber security officer soon began to realize that building and managing an outstanding, state-of-the-art cyber security program and a cyber security organization staffed by talented cyber security professionals might become more of a dream than a reality.

Once the cyber security officer was able to fend off these and similar charges, the recruitment effort within and outside the corporation could start in earnest! Among the ways to recruit cyber security professionals are through:
- Local advertisement in trade journals, newspapers, etc.,
- Hiring a consulting firm to find the right people,
- Passing the word among colleagues,
- Asking cyber security associations to pass the word, and
- Using the Internet to advertise the position.

With a few cyber security personnel on board, the cyber security officer could begin to work on the cyber security program and also begin work on developing the baseline processes and functions with the cyber security organization.

QUESTIONS TO CONSIDER

Based on what you have read, consider the following questions and how you would reply to them:

- Do you have a formal, that is, documented cyber security program?
- If not, why not?
- What would you consider as the benefits of such a plan?
- What would you consider as the negatives of such a plan?
- Have you ever briefed executive management on cyber security-related matters?
- Do you identify the costs of staffing and providing cyber security functions using a cost–benefit risk management process?
- If you were to develop a cyber security program for the corporation, what would you do differently from what was stated in this chapter?
- If you could build and manage a cyber security organization for the corporation, how would the structure compare to the one cited in this chapter, and why?
- How would you manage the off-site locations—for example, would you manage them from the corporate office, or ask some off-site manager to matrix manage the staff for you?
- What other job descriptions would you add to the ones provided?
- What other duties and responsibilities would you add to the job descriptions provided in this chapter?
- Do you know how to successfully work with HR staff to meet their requirements and also effectively and efficiently get your objectives accomplished?

SUMMARY

Once plans were in place, the cyber security officer could begin to develop a cyber security organization to support the cyber security program. To do so, the cyber security officer must understand the following:

- Establishing an effective and efficient cyber security organization and program requires a detailed analysis and integration of all the information that has been learned through the entire process of becoming a cyber security officer at the corporation.
- Determining the need for cyber security subordinate organizations requires detailed analysis of the corporation's environment and an understanding of how to successfully apply resource allocation techniques to the cyber security functions.

- Once the need for cyber security subordinate organizations is determined, the cyber security officer must determine what functions go in what organizations.
- Establishing a formal cyber security organization and cyber security job family requires cooperation with HR organizations and others; patience and understanding are mandatory.
- A cyber security officer who establishes a new organization for a corporation will be compelled to live within a less than ideal corporate world in which forms and bureaucracies rule the day. To survive, the cyber security officer must understand how to use those processes efficiently and effectively to succeed.
- In most corporations, currently employed personnel who desire a cyber security position, and who meet the minimum cyber security requirements, must be hired before hiring an individual from the outside.
- Recruiting qualified cyber security professionals can be accomplished only through a widespread recruitment effort, using many marketing media; and successful advertisement is sometimes a matter of how much recruitment budget is available.

CHAPTER 9

Determining and Establishing Cyber Security Functions

Work is necessary for man. Man invented the alarm clock

Pablo Picasso[1]

Contents

---

[1] Attributed to Pablo Picasso (1881–1973), Spanish painter and sculptor. Microsoft's *Encarta Dictionary*.

Chapter Objective

We began this section of the book with an overview of the duties and responsibilities of the cyber security officer and then discussed establishing a cyber security program and the related cyber security plans and organization. We will continue the trend to narrow the focus: This chapter describes a process to determine what cyber security functions are needed to successfully establish a cyber security program and related organization, as well as how to incorporate those functions into the cyber security organization's day-to-day level-of-effort work.

INTRODUCTION

There are many different ways to configure a cyber security organization, and there are many ways to configure the cyber security functions that are part of that organization. Many cyber security officers begin establishing a cyber security organization, or "inherit" one, without looking at the need for the various functions and from where that need was derived. As stated earlier, all functions should be derived from one or more of the following requirements (drivers):

- Laws,
- Regulations,
- Best business practices,
- Best cyber security practices,
- Ethics,
- Privacy needs, and
- Corporate policies.

When developing or reorganizing a cyber security program, one can consider one of three basic structures as they relate to the cyber security program organization that the cyber security officer will manage and lead. The three basic options are:

- Centralized cyber security program organization under the cyber security officer,
- Decentralized organization throughout the corporation, or
- A combination of the two.

One of the major factors in deciding what philosophy and approach to take is the culture of the corporation, as well as the charter of the cyber security officer spelling out the cyber security officer's duties and responsibilities. The cyber security officer must remember that the more centralized the organization, the more problems and work for the cyber security officer and staff. The old adage "If you want it done right, do it yourself" may work for some, but as a cyber security officer, that approach will bring you more stress than usual. In addition, you will definitely age exponentially. Developing and maintaining a protected information environment for the corporation require the support and active involvement of all employees. Sometimes a cyber security officer forgets that and tries to take on the entire protection matter instead of leading a corporate team effort. Such an approach leads to more problems than solutions for developing and maintaining a protected information environment.

So, what should you do? The best approach seems to be a combination. For example, this corporate cyber security officer decided that the overall information and information systems protection logically should be centralized under the cyber security officer and cyber security program staff. After all, they have the experience and know-how to lead this effort. However, at the same time, why get burdened with trying to write and maintain current cyber security program procedures that must be implemented by the departments to comply with those cyber security program policies? So, procedures written for compliance, as previously stated, will be the responsibility of the corporate departments. Their adequacy will be determined through audits, cyber security program tests and evaluations, noncompliance inquiries, and the like.

In addition, the corporate departments will be responsible for developing, implementing, and maintaining the processes that are an integral part of the procedures needed to comply with the cyber security program.

PROCESSES

The cyber security officer must also develop procedures, functions, and processes to comply with the cyber security program policies, as an organizational manager. In addition, the cyber security officer must lead the effort to develop functions that the cyber security program organization will perform to lead and support the corporate cyber security program.

This cyber security officer decided that the best approach is through the drivers' (cyber security program–cyber security program requirements) baseline. So, based on the drivers, one is then able to develop a "needs" statement or statements. These can be set forth in various ways, such as the vision, mission, and quality statements, and incorporated into plans, for example, strategic, tactical, and annual, as previously discussed. Regardless of how and in what form you state these needs for the cyber security program, they must support corporate plans, policies, objectives, and goals and must also eventually be tied to action items.

These action items are then analyzed and are implemented—for example, established as cyber security program functions that are then incorporated into the cyber security officer's cyber security program organization as its charter of responsibilities and accountabilities, as stated in the previous chapter. One step to look at is the process. A process is basically "a series of actions directed toward a particular aim."[2] After the drivers and needs are identified, the cyber security officer must establish a process for meeting the identified requirements. The process is basically the details of how a function is to be performed.

The action items should be part of a formal project management program in which, as stated earlier, you, as the cyber security officer, determine that there is a need for some sort of cyber security program action that will take time and must be incorporated into the cyber security program organization. Remember, the project plans have:

• Objectives to accomplish,
• Beginning and ending dates,
• Tasks identified and assigned,
• Personnel assigned to tasks,
• Budget allocated, and
• Time allocated for completing those tasks.

There are many cyber security program-related functions; however, at this corporation, the cyber security officer determined that the functions identified in the cyber security officer's charter were the main functions that were driven by or related to the baseline cyber security program. Therefore, they are the basic functions that should be established, and a flow process description should be developed relative to how the functions should be performed. For example[3]:

• Cyber security program requirements identification;
• Cyber security program plans, policies, processes, and procedures;
• Awareness education and training;
• Access control;

---

[2] *Encarta World English Dictionary*, ©1999, Microsoft Corporation. All rights reserved. Developed for Microsoft by Bloomsbury Publishing Plc.
[3] Others can be added, but these basic examples give the reader a good idea of what is needed.

- Evaluation of hardware, firmware, and software for impact on the security of the information systems;
- Security tests and evaluations;
- Noncompliance inquiries;
- Risk management; and
- Disaster recovery/contingency planning.

VALUING INFORMATION

Before addressing the cyber security program functions, the cyber security officer determined that to provide an effective cyber security program with the least impact to cost and schedule, it is important to establish a process to determine the value of information.

The cyber security officer's reasoning was that no information should be protected any more than is necessary. The rationale used by the cyber security officer was as follows:

The value of information is time dependent. In other words, information has value for only a certain period of time. Information relative to a new, unique corporate widget must be highly protected, and that includes the electronic drawings, diagrams, processes, etc. However, once the new widget is announced to the public, complete with photographs of the widget, selling price, etc., much of the protected information no longer needs protection.

That information, which once required protection to maintain the secrecy of this new widget, can now be eliminated. This will save money for the corporation because cyber security program costs are a *parasite on the profits* of the corporation. Those costs must be reduced or eliminated as soon as possible. It is the task of the cyber security officer and staff to continuously look for methods to accomplish this objective.

How to Determine the Value of Corporate Information

Determining the value of the corporation's information is a very important task, but one that is seldom done with any systematic, logical approach by a company. However, the cyber security officer believed that to provide the program the corporation required, this task should be undertaken.

The consequences of not properly classifying the information could lead to overprotection, which is costly, or underprotection, which could lead to the loss of that information and thus of profits.

To determine the value of information, the cyber security officer must first understand what is meant by *information* and what is meant by *value*.

The cyber security officer must also know how to properly categorize and classify the information, and what guidelines are set forth by government agencies or businesses for determining the value and protection requirements of that information. In addition, how the information owners perceive the information and its value is crucial to classifying[4] it.

Why Is Determining Information Value Important?

If the information has value, it must be protected; protection is expensive. One should protect only that information which requires protection, only in the manner necessary based on the value of that information, and only for the period required.

The Value of Information

One might ask, "Does all the information of a company or government agency have value?" If you, as the corporate cyber security officer, were asked that question, what would be your response? The follow-on question would be "What information does *not* have value?" Is it that information which the receiver of the information determines has no value? When the originator of the information says so? Who determines whether information has value?

These are questions that the cyber security officer must ask—and answer—before trying to establish a process to set a value to any information. As you read through this material, think about the information where you work, how it is protected, why it is protected, etc.

The cyber security officer knows that a centralized approach would not work for valuing information, as every piece of information must be analyzed according to a specific criterion, identified according to a certain protective category, such as corporate-sensitive, and then marked and protected accordingly. The cyber security officer knew that the best approach was to set the criteria and guidelines for the identification, marking, transmission, storage, and destruction of corporate information and have the information owners identify the information that they produce and, following the policy guidelines in the cyber security program, protect that information. Those criteria and requirements would be developed as part of the cyber security officer's project team, which would also include various department representatives, such as manufacturing, procurement, legal, security, finance, and planning.

---

[4] In the context used here, the term *classify* has nothing to do with classification as it relates to national security information, such as confidential, secret, and top secret.

The holder of the information may determine the value of the information. Each person places a value on the information in his or her possession. The information that is necessary to successfully complete a person's work is very valuable to that person; however, it may not be very valuable to anyone else. For example, to an accountant, the accounts payable records are very important, and without them, the accountants could not do their job. However, for the person manufacturing the company's product, that information has little or no value.

Ordinarily, the originator determines the value of the information, and that person categorizes or classifies that information, usually in accordance with the established guidelines.

Three Basic Categories of Information

Although there are no standard categories of information, most people agree that information can logically be categorized into three categories:

- Personal, private information;
- National security (both classified and unclassified) information (addressed in Chapter 12); and
- Business information.

Personal, private information is an individual matter, but also a matter for the government and businesses. People may want to keep private such information about themselves as their age, weight, address, cellular phone number, salary, and likes and dislikes.

At the same time, many countries have laws that protect information under some type of "privacy act." In businesses and government agencies, it is a matter of policy to safeguard certain information about employees, such as their ages, addresses, and salaries. Therefore, this requirement (cyber security program driver) must be considered in developing the information value and protection policy and guidelines.

Although the information is personal to the individual, others may require that information. At the same time, they have an obligation to protect that information because it is considered to have value.

Business information also requires protection based on its value. At this corporation, this information was sometimes categorized as follows:

- Corporate–confidential,
- Corporate–internal use only,
- Corporate–private,
- Corporate–sensitive,
- Corporate–proprietary, and
- Corporate trade secret.

The number of categories used will vary with each company; however, the fewer categories, the fewer problems in classifying information and also, possibly, the fewer problems in the granularity of protection required. Again, this is a cost-item consideration. The cyber security officer found that private, internal use only, and proprietary would meet the needs of the cyber security program.

This company information must be protected because it has value to the company. The degree of protection required is also dependent on the value of the information during a specific period of time.

Types of Valued Information

Generally, the types of information that have value to the business and that require protection include the following: All forms and types of financial, scientific, technical, economic, or engineering information, including, but not limited to, data, plans, tools, mechanisms, compounds, formulas, designs, prototypes, processes, procedures, programs, codes, or commercial strategies, whether tangible or intangible, and whether stored, compiled, or memorialized physically, electronically, graphically, photographically, or in writing.

Examples of information requiring protection may include research, proposals, plans, manufacturing processes, pricing, and product.

Determining Information Value

Based on an understanding of information, its value, and some practical and philosophical thoughts on the topic as stated above, the cyber security officer must have some sense of what must be considered when determining the value of information.

When determining the value of information, the cyber security officer must determine what it cost to produce that information. Also to be considered is the cost in terms of damages caused to the company if it were to be released outside protected channels. Additional consideration must be given to the cost of maintaining and protecting that information. How these processes are combined determines the value of the information. Again, don't forget to factor in the time element.

There are two basic assumptions to consider in determining the value of information: (1) All information costs some type of resource(s) to produce, for example, money, hours, or use of equipment; and (2) not all information can cause damage if released outside protected channels.

If the information costs to produce (and all information does) and no damage is done if it is released, you must consider, "Does it still have value?"

If it costs to produce the information, but it cannot cause damage if it is released outside protected channels, then why protect it?

The time factor is a key element in determining the value of information and cannot be overemphasized. Let's look at an example in which information is not time dependent—or is it? There is a company picnic to take place on May 22, 2016. What is the value of the information before, on, or after that date? Does the information have value? To whom? When?

If you're looking forward to the company's annual picnic, as is your family, the information as to when and where it is to take place has some value to you. Suppose you found out about it the day after it happened. Your family would be disappointed, they would be angry at you for not knowing, you would feel bad, etc. To the company, the information had "no value." However, the fact that the employee did not receive that information caused him or her to be disgruntled and blame the company for his or her latest family fight. Based on that, the employee decided to slow down his or her productivity for a week.

This is a simple illustration, but it indicates the value of information depending on who has and who does not have that information, as well as the time element. It also shows that what is thought to be information not worth a second thought may have repercussions costing more than the value of the information.

The following is another example: A new, secret, revolutionary widget built to compete in a very competitive marketplace is to enter the market on January 1, 2017. What is the value of that information on January 2, 2016?

Again, to stress the point, one must consider the cost to produce the information and the damage done if that information were released.

If it cost to produce and can cause damage if released, it must be protected. If it cost to produce, but cannot cause damage if released, then why protect it? At the same time, be sensitive to dissemination. Information, to have value, to be useful, must get to the right people at the right time.

Business Information Types and Examples

Types of *internal use only* information:
- Not generally known outside the company,
- Not generally known through product inspection,
- Possibly useful to a competitor, and
- Provides some business advantage over competitors.

Examples are the company telephone book, company policies and procedures, and company organizational charts.

Types of *private* information:
- Reveals technical or financial aspects of the company,
- Indicates the company's future direction,
- Describes portions of the company's business,
- Provides a competitive edge, and
- Identifies personal information of employees.

Examples are personnel medical records, salary information, cost data, short-term marketing plans, and dates for unannounced events.

Types of *sensitive* information:
- Provides significant competitive advantage,
- Could cause serious damage to the company, and
- Reveals long-term company direction.

Examples are critical company technologies, critical engineering processes, and critical cost data.

Questions to Ask When Determining Value

When determining the value of your information, you should, as a minimum, ask the following questions:
- How much does it cost to produce?
- How much does it cost to replace?
- What would happen if I no longer had that information?
- What would happen if my closest competitor had that information?
- Is protection of the information required by law, and if so, what would happen if I didn't protect it?

INTERNATIONAL WIDGET CORPORATION (IWC) CYBER SECURITY PROGRAM FUNCTIONS PROCESS DEVELOPMENT

The cyber security officer has learned that the development of a new cyber security program requires the establishment of cyber security program functions for that program. Establishing a process for each function, as the first task, will assist in ensuring that the functions will begin in a logical, systematic way that will lead to a cost-effective cyber security program.

Requirements Identification Function

As previously stated, the cyber security officer has determined that the driver for any cyber security program-related function is the requirements for that function. The requirements are the reason for the cyber security program. This need is further identified and defined and is subsequently met by the establishment of the cyber security program functions.

So, to begin the functions' process identification, it is important to understand where the requirement—where the need—comes from as seen from a slightly different perspective.[5] For this corporation, it is as follows:

- A need for a cyber security program as stated by executive management to protect the corporation's competitive edge, which is based on information systems and the information that they store, process, display, and transmit;
- Contractual requirements as specified in contracts with customers, such as protecting customers' information;
- Contractual requirements as specified in contracts with subcontractors, such as protecting subcontractors' information;
- Contractual requirements as specified in contracts with vendors, such as protecting vendors' information;
- Corporate's desire to protect its information and systems from unauthorized access by customers, subcontractors, and vendors; and
- Federal, state, and local laws that are applicable to the corporation, such as requirements to protect the privacy rights of individuals and corporations as they relate to the information stored, processed, and transmitted by IWC systems.

CYBER SECURITY OFFICER'S CYBER SECURITY PROGRAM FUNCTIONS

The cyber security officer has gone through the process previously noted to identify the baseline functions that are needed within the cyber security program organization to support the cyber security program, which as mentioned earlier supports business needs as stated in the strategic, tactical, and annual business plans. The following paragraphs identify, describe, and discuss some of the functions identified by the cyber security officer.

Awareness Program

The cyber security officer decided to concentrate, as a high priority, on the cyber security program Education Awareness and Training Program (EATP)

---

[5] You may find that this driver–requirement, cyber security program–cyber security program functions topic is redundant. Ideally, it is, and you are beginning to get it ingrained in your cyber security officer head that these are the basics that every cyber security officer should know and use as the baseline for leading and managing an information and systems protection program for a company or government agency. I hope that after reading this book, certain basic philosophies, such as the fact that the cyber security program is a parasite on the profits, will be made an automatic part of any cyber security type of program and cyber security program organization you will lead and manage.

as a major cyber security program organizational function and also as an integral part of the cyber security program. The EATP was needed to make the users aware of the need, as well as their responsibility, to protect information and systems, as well as to gain the users' support in the protection of information and systems.

The cyber security officer reasoned that once the policies of the cyber security program were developed and published, the employees must be made aware of them and also why they were necessary. For only with the full support and cooperation of the employees, could a successful cyber security program be established and maintained.

The awareness program process was broken into two major parts:
- Awareness briefings and
- Continuing awareness material.

Awareness Briefings

The awareness briefings included information relative to the need for information and systems protection, the impact of protecting and not protecting the systems and information, and an explanation of the cyber security program.

The cyber security officer reasoned that the awareness material and briefings, when given as a general briefing, could be used only for new employees. The general briefings failed to provide the specific information required by various groups of systems users. Thus, the awareness briefings were tailored to specific audiences as follows:
- All new hires, whether or not they used a system, the rationale being that they all handle information and come in contact with computer and telecommunication systems in one form or another;
- Managers;
- System users;
- Information Technology Department personnel;
- Engineers;
- Manufacturers;
- Accounting and Finance personnel;
- Procurement personnel;
- Human Resources personnel;
- Security and Audit personnel; and
- The system security custodians (those who would be given day-to-day responsibility to ensure that the systems and information were protected in accordance with the cyber security program policy and procedures).

A process was established to identify these personnel, input their profile information into a database, and, using a standard format, track their awareness briefing attendance at both their initial briefings and their annual rebriefings. That information would also be used to provide them, through the IWC mail system, with awareness material.

Continuing Awareness Material

The cyber security officer, in concert with the Human Resources and Training staffs, decided that ensuring that employees were aware of their cyber security program responsibilities would require constant reminders. After all, information and systems protection is not the major function of most employees. However, a way must be found to remind the employees that it is a *part* of their function.

It was decided that awareness material could be cost-effectively provided to the employees. This was accomplished by providing cyber security program material to the employees through:

- Annual calendars,
- Posters,
- Labels for systems and disks,
- Articles published in the corporate publications such as the weekly newsletter, and
- Log-on notices and system broadcast messages, especially of cyber security program changes.

Although this EATP baseline was not all-inclusive, the cyber security officer believed that it was a good start that could be analyzed for cost-effective improvements at the end of the calendar year.

ACCESS CONTROL AND ACCESS CONTROL SYSTEMS

The cyber security officer determined that the access control and access control systems ranked as a high priority in establishing processes for the control of access to systems, as well as the access to the information stored, processed, and transmitted by those systems. Therefore, access controls were divided into two sections:

- Access to systems and
- Access to the information on the systems.

The cyber security officer reasoned that each department created and used the corporate systems and their information. Therefore, they should be responsible for controlling access to those systems and information.

The major systems, such as the corporate-wide area network, were owned and operated by the IT Department, while individual systems and local area networks (LANs) were owned and operated by the individual departments.

As part of the cyber security program, the corporation, in coordination with other departments' managers, established a process for all employees who required access to the systems to perform their job functions. Such employees would have to obtain system access approval from their manager and from the manager or designated representative of that system and/or the information owner, such as for financial database access. The owners' approval was based on a justified need for access as stated by the employee's manager. If the system and/or information owners agreed, access was granted.

The cyber security officer had found, during the initial evaluation of the cyber security program of the corporation, that departments had logically grouped their information into categories. They had done so to control access to their own files. This made it easy for the security officer, because the managers of the departments agreed that once access to systems was granted by the system owners, access to the information on those systems should be approved by the owners of those groups of files, databases, etc.

Thus, the access control process included a justification by an employee's manager stating not only what systems, and why, the employee needed access to, but also what information he or she required access to in order to perform his or her job.

For the most part, this was an easy and logical process. For example, in the Accounting Department, personnel generally had access to the groups of files and databases based on their job functions—accounts payable, accounts receivable, etc.

This access control process helped maintain an audit trail of who approved access to whom and for what purposes. It also helped provide a separation of functions that is a vital component of any cyber security program. For example, an accounts payable person should not also be the accounts receivable person and the invoice processing person. Such a system would allow one person too much control over a process that can be—and has been—used for committing fraud.

The benefits of the foregoing process to the cyber security officer were that it documented an informal process that for the most part had been in place, and it also placed cyber security program responsibilities for systems and information access exactly where it belonged, with the identified owners of the systems and information.

In one instance, a cyber security officer found that one manager did not want to take responsibility for a LAN in the department, and since others outside the department used the information, the manager did not want to take ownership of the information. The manager thought the IT Department should be the owner—after all, they were responsible for the maintenance of the system.

The cyber security officer in this case asked the manager if the cyber security officer could then be responsible as the owner of the systems and the information. The manager quickly agreed. The cyber security officer then told the manager that since it was now owned by the cyber security program organization, access to the systems and information would be denied to all those not in the cyber security program organization.

The manager objected, stating that the personnel in his organization needed access to those systems and their information to perform their job functions. After further discussion, the organizational manager agreed that his organization would appear to be the logical owners and subsequently accepted that responsibility.

Access Control Systems

The cyber security officer, in coordination with the IT, Security, and Audit Departments, determined that the access control systems (hardware and software) belonged to the same departments and organizations identified as the system owners. However, the cyber security program personnel would establish the detailed procedures for the access control systems and the auditors would evaluate compliance with those procedures.

The system owners agreed to this process and also to appointing a primary and alternate system custodian who would be responsible for ensuring that the cyber security program policies and procedures were followed by all those who used the systems. In addition, the custodian would review the system audit trails, which were mandatory on all corporate systems.[6]

EVALUATION OF ALL HARDWARE, FIRMWARE, AND SOFTWARE

All new hardware, firmware, and software should be evaluated for its impact on the security of information and systems. This was determined to be necessary in a joint agreement between the cyber security officer and the IT Department personnel, auditors, and security personnel.

---

[6] At first, the audit trails requirements were to be applied only to those systems processing sensitive information; however, it was quickly discovered that all the systems, because of their networking, fell under that category. Management agreed that the additional cost of such a requirement was beneficial based on the risk of loss of that information to internal or external threats.

To perform this function with minimal impact on cost and installation schedules, it was determined that a baseline checklist would be developed and that this checklist would be completed by the suppliers of the product, in concert with the cyber security program staff. Any items that adversely affected the cyber security program would be evaluated based on a risk assessment, using the approved risk management and reporting process.

The process included completion of the baseline cyber security program checklist and a technical evaluation by cyber security program personnel in concert with IT personnel. If the item (hardware, software, etc.) was considered *risk-acceptable,* it was approved for purchase.

If the item was not risk-acceptable, the risk management process identified countermeasures. Although this process generally approves the purchase of almost all items, some items might have an unacceptable level of risk, but would still be accepted because of their value to the company. In those instances, special audit trails could be created to monitor the use of the item. In any case, the cyber security officer understood that it is always better at least to know that a system is vulnerable than not to know the vulnerability existed until it was too late.

The cyber security officer identified the several potential processes relative to new, modified, or upgraded systems' hardware, software, and firmware implementation in which the protection of information and information systems could be subject to increased vulnerabilities. The cyber security officer decided to form a project team to evaluate these and other processes. The project team would include the cyber security officer's staff specialist as the project lead, as well as IT representatives, department representatives, a procurement representative, a contracts representative, and a legal representative. These representatives were chosen for the following reasons:

- IT: They are responsible for the major systems, such as intranets and Internet interfaces.
- Departments: They are responsible for their own stand-alone systems, such as microcomputers, and for their own LANs that are not connected outside the department.
- Procurement: They are responsible for ordering the hardware, software, and firmware.
- Contracts: They, based on cyber security officer coordination, include cyber security program-related specifications and clauses in the corporate contracts, such as software from a vendor certified free of malicious codes. Furthermore, if a product is vulnerable or increases the systems'

vulnerabilities, the contract may call for the vendor to patch the software or provide the source code for programmers to patch the code.

- Legal: They are responsible for ensuring that all issues related to contracts and procurement matters mandating cyber security program criteria are stated in such a way as to ensure their enforcement through legal means.

RISK MANAGEMENT PROGRAM

The objective of the risk management program is to *maximize security and minimize cost through risk management.*

What Is Risk Management?

Because it is the baseline for all of the cyber security officer's decisions relative to information and systems protection, the cyber security officer decided to formalize the function of risk management as an integral part of the cyber security program and the cyber security program organization.

The cyber security officer knew that for corporate employees, especially management, to understand the philosophy behind how cyber security program-related decisions were made, they should have some basic grasp of the risk management philosophy. Thus, the cyber security officer directed that this topic be an integral part of the cyber security program and EATP. The cyber security officer knew that to understand the risk management methodology, one must first understand what risk management means. The cyber security officer defined risk management as the total process of identifying, controlling, and eliminating or minimizing uncertain events that may affect system resources. It includes risk assessments; risk analyses, including cost–benefit analyses; target selection; implementation and testing; security evaluation of safeguards; and overall cyber security program review.

The cyber security officer established the objective of the risk management process as follows: *to provide the best protection of systems and the information they store, process, display, and/or transmit at the lowest cost consistent with the value of the systems and the information.*

Risk Management Process

Remember that the cyber security program is a corporate program made up of professionals who provide service and support to their company. Therefore, the risk management process must be based on the needs of customers.

Also, the cyber security officer wanted to be sure that the risk management concepts, program, and processes were informally and formally used in all aspects of the cyber security program, including when and how to do awareness briefings and the impact of information systems security policies and procedures on the employees.

The following steps should be considered in the cyber security officer's process:

1. Management interest: Identify areas that are of major interest to executive management and customers; approach from a business point of view. So, the process should begin with interviews of your internal customers to determine what areas of the cyber security program are adversely affecting their operations the most. Then, target those areas first as the starting point for the risk management program.
2. Identify specific targets: Software applications, hardware, telecommunications, electronic media storage, etc.
3. Identify input sources: Users, system administrators, auditors, security officers, technical journals, technical bulletins, risk assessment application programs, etc.
4. Identify potential threats: Internal and external, natural or human-made.
5. Identify vulnerabilities: Through interviews, experience, history, testing.
6. Identify risks: Match threats to vulnerabilities with existing countermeasures, verify, and validate.
7. Assess risks: Acceptable or not acceptable, identify residual risk, and then certify the process and gain approval. If the risks are not acceptable, then:
   * Identify countermeasures,
   * Identify each countermeasure's costs, and
   * Compare countermeasures, risks, and costs to mitigated risks.

Recommendations to Management

When the risk assessment is completed, the cyber security officer must make recommendations to management. Remember in making recommendations to think from a business point of view: cost, benefits, profits, public relations, etc.

Risk Management Reports

A briefing that includes a formal, written report is the vehicle to bring the risks to management's attention. The report should include areas identified that need improvement, areas that are performing well, and recommended actions for improvement, including costs and benefits.

Remember that it is management's decision to either accept the risk or mitigate the risk and how much to spend to do so. The cyber security officer is the specialist, the in-house consultant. It is management's responsibility to decide what to do. They may follow your recommendations, ignore them, or take some other action. In any case, the cyber security officer has provided the service and support required.

If the decision is made that no action will be taken, there is still a benefit to conducting the analyses. The cyber security officer now has a better understanding of the environment, as well as an understanding of some of the vulnerabilities. This information will still help in managing a cyber security program. The cyber security officer has developed a risk management process to be used as an overall baseline for implementation as part of the risk management philosophy of the corporation.

SECURITY TESTS AND EVALUATIONS PROGRAM

The cyber security officer saw the need for a security tests and evaluations program (ST&E) once the cyber security program processes of awareness, access control, and risk management were implemented.

The ST&E was developed to incorporate testing and evaluating of the total cyber security program processes, environments, hardware, software, and firmware as a proactive method to support risk assessments and the evaluation of the systems' components.

The cyber security officer believed that the auditors' compliance audits were more of a checklist process of ensuring compliance with the corporate cyber security program policies and procedures. What was needed, the cyber security officer reasoned, was a way to actually test cyber security program processes, systems, etc., to determine whether they were meeting the cyber security program needs of the corporation—regardless of whether they complied with the cyber security program policies and procedures.

For example, the ST&E would include periodically obtaining a user ID on a system with various access privileges. The cyber security program staff member using that identification would violate that system and attempt to gain unauthorized access to various files, databases, and systems. That information was analyzed in concert with a comparison of the system's audit trails, thus profiling the cyber security program of a system or network. Also, the ST&E would include a review of records and prior audit trail documents to help establish the "cyber security program environment" being tested and evaluated.

NONCOMPLIANCE INQUIRIES

Noncompliance inquiries (NCIs) were identified as a cyber security officer responsibility and the process was developed by the cyber security program staff and coordinated with the audit and security management. The NCI process was as follows:

- Receive allegations of noncompliance by auditors, security personnel, managers, users, and generally anyone else.
- The allegation was evaluated and, if not considered acceptable, filed.[7]
- If the allegation was substantiated, an inquiry was conducted. The inquiry included interviews, technical reviews, document reviews, etc.
- The information gathered was analyzed, collated, and provided in a formal report to management with copies to appropriate departments such as security and human resources.
- The report was protected for reasons of privacy and also included recommendations and trend analyses to mitigate future occurrences.

CONTINGENCY AND EMERGENCY PLANNING AND DISASTER RECOVERY PROGRAM

A contingency and emergency planning and disaster recovery (CEP-DR) program is one of the least difficult programs to establish and yet always seems to be a difficult task. With the change in information systems' environments and configurations—client–server, LAN, distributed processing, etc.—this problem may be getting worse.

Prior to discussing CEP-DR, it is important to understand why it is needed. It is really a very important aspect of a cyber security program and may even be its most vital part.

The cyber security officer must remember that the purpose of the cyber security program is to:

- Minimize the probability of a security vulnerability,
- Minimize the damage if a vulnerability is exploited, and
- *Provide a method to recover efficiently and effectively from the damage.*

What Is It?

Contingency planning is making a plan for responding to emergencies, running backup operations, and recovering after a disaster. It addresses what

---

[7] The cyber security officer was sensitive to privacy issues and did not want to initiate an inquiry without substantiated information, since someone may have a grudge against another and use the process to harass him or her.

action will be taken to return to normal operations. Emergencies requiring action would include such natural events as floods and earthquakes, as well as human-caused acts such as fires or hacker attacks causing denial of services.

Disaster recovery is the restoration of the information systems, facility, or other related assets following a significant disruption of services.

Why Do It?

Primarily users often ask the question, why is a CEP-DR program necessary? Everyone associated with using, protecting, and maintaining information systems and the information that they store, process, and/or transmit must understand the need for such a program:

- To assist in protecting vital information,
- To minimize adverse impact on productivity, and
- To support the business staying in business!

How Do You Do It?

Each CEP-DR program is unique to the environment, culture, and philosophy of each business or government agency. However, the basic program, regardless of business or agency, requires the development and maintenance of a CEP-DR plan. It must be periodically tested, problems identified and corrected, and processes changed to minimize the chances of adverse events happening again.

The CEP-DR Planning System

The corporation's CEP-DR plan must be written based on the standard format used by the corporation. The following generic format is offered for consideration:

1. *Purpose*: State the reason for the plan and its objective. This should be specific enough that it is clear to all who read it why it has been written.
2. *Scope*: State the scope and applicability of the plan. Does it include all systems, all locations, subcontractors?
3. *Assumptions*: State the priorities, the support promised, and the incidents to be included and excluded. For example, if your area does not have typhoons, will you assume that typhoons, as a potential disaster threat, will not be considered?
4. *Responsibilities*: State who is to be responsible for taking what actions. This should be stated clearly so everyone knows who is responsible for what. Consider a generic breakdown such as managers, systems

administrators, and users. Also, specific authority and responsibility should be listed by a person's title and not necessarily by that person's name. This approach will save time in updating the plan because of personnel changes.

5. *Strategy*: Discuss backup requirements and how often they should be accomplished based on classification of information; state how you will recover, etc.

6. *Personnel*: Maintain an accurate, complete, and current list of key CEP-DR personnel, including addresses, phone numbers, page numbers, and cellular phone numbers. Be sure to establish an emergency prioritized, notification listing and a listing of response team members and how to contact them in an emergency.

7. *Information*: Maintain an on-site inventory listing and an off-site inventory listing; identify the rotation process to ensure a history and current inventory of files. Identify vital information. This information must come from the owner of that information and must be classified according to its importance, based on approved guidelines.

8. *Hardware*: Maintain an inventory listing, including supplier's name, serial number, and property identification number; ensure that emergency replacement contracts are in place; maintain hard copies of applicable documents on and off site.

9. *Software*: Identify and maintain backup operating systems and application systems software. This should include original software and at least one backup copy of each. Be sure to identify the version numbers, etc. In this way, you can compare what is listed in the plan with what is actually installed. It would not be a unique event if software backups were not kept current and compatible with the hardware. If this is the case, the systems might not be able to work together to process, store, and transmit much-needed information.

10. *Documentation*: All-important documentation should be identified, listed, inventoried, and maintained current in both on- and off-site locations.

11. *Telecommunications*: The identification and maintenance of telecommunications hardware and software listings are vital if you are operating in any type of network environment. Many systems today cannot operate in a stand-alone configuration; thus, the telecommunications lines, backups, schematics, etc., are of vital importance to getting back in operation within the time period required. As with other documentation, their identification, listing, etc., should be maintained at multiple

on- and off-site locations. Be sure to identify all emergency requirements and all alternative communication methods.

12. *Supplies*: Supplies are often forgotten when establishing a CEP-DR
plan, as they often take a back seat to hardware and software. However,
listing and maintenance of vital supplies are required, including the
name, address, telephone numbers, and contract information concerning suppliers. Be sure to store sufficient quantities at appropriate locations on and off site. If you don't think this is an important matter, try
using a printer when its toner cartridge has dried out or is empty!.

Physical supplies for consideration should include plastic tarps to
protect systems from water damage in the event of a fire in which
sprinkler systems are activated

13. *Transportation and equipment*: If you have a disaster or emergency requiring the use of a backup facility or obtaining backup copies of software,
etc., you obviously must have transportation and the applicable equipment (e.g., a dolly for hauling heavy items) to do the job. Therefore,
you must plan for such things. List emergency transportation needs and
sources, how you will obtain emergency transportation and equipment,
and which routes and alternate routes to take to the off-site location.
Be sure to include maps in the vehicles and also in the plan. Be sure
there are fully charged, hand-held fire extinguishers available that will
work on various types of fires, such as electrical, paper, or chemical.

14. *Processing locations*: Many businesses and agencies sign contractual agreements to ensure that they have an appropriate off-site location to be used
in the event their facility is not capable of supporting their activities.

Ensure that emergency processing agreements are in place that will
provide you with priority service and support in the event of an emergency or disaster. Even then, you may have a difficult time using the facility
if it is a massive disaster and others have also contracted for the facility.

Be sure to periodically use the facility to ensure that you can process, store, and/or transmit information at that location. Don't forget to
identify on-site locations that can be used or converted for use if the
disaster is less than total.

15. *Utilities*: Identify on-site and off-site emergency power needs and locations. Don't forget that these requirements change as facilities, equipment, and hardware change. Battery power and uninterruptable power
might not be able to carry the load or might be too old to even work.
They must be periodically tested. As with the printer cartridge supplies,
systems without power are useless. In addition to power, don't forget

the air conditioning requirements. It would be important to know how long a system can process without air conditioning based on certain temperature and humidity readings.

16. *Documentation:* Identify all related documentation; store it in multiple on- and off-site locations, and be sure to include the CEP-DR plan.
17. *Other:* Miscellaneous items not covered above.

Test the Plan

Only through testing can the cyber security officer determine that a plan will work when required. Therefore, it must be periodically tested. It need not be tested all at once, because that would probably cause a loss of productivity by the employees, which would not be cost-effective.

It is best to test the plan in increments, relying on all the pieces to fit together when all parts have been tested. Regardless of when and how you test the plan, which is a management decision, it must be tested. Probably the best way to determine how and what to test, and in what order, is to prioritize testing based on prioritized assets.

When testing, the scenarios used should be as realistic as possible. This should include emergency response, testing backup applications and systems, and recovery operations.

Through testing, document the problems and vulnerabilities identified. Determine why they occurred and establish formal projects to fix each problem. Additionally, make whatever cost-effective process changes are necessary to ensure that the same problem would not happen again or that the chance of it happening is minimized.

The cyber security officer evaluated the corporate organizational structure relative to the corporation. After coordination with the Director of Security, a process was developed to integrate the cyber security officer and staff into the current CEP-DR process.

QUESTIONS TO CONSIDER

Based on what you have read, consider the following questions and how you would reply to them:
- Do you believe that the basic requirements—drivers—discussed in this chapter are valid?
- Can you think of others that you would use as a cyber security officer?
- After the requirements are identified, in what order would you prioritize policies, procedures, plans, processes, functions, and processes?

- Why did you decide to prioritize each in the order noted?
- Do you have a process in place for valuing company information?
- If not, how do you know what to protect in a cost-effective manner?
- If you have such a process in place, is it current?
- Is it working?
- How do you know it is working cost-effectively?
- What are the functions that you as a cyber security officer believe are required to be a part of your cyber security program organization?
- Which ones are optional, and why?
- Which ones would never be authorized by management to be part of your cyber security program responsibilities?
- Do you use a formal, documented risk management philosophy?
- If not, how do you cost-effectively make cyber security program decisions?
- If so, is that philosophy shared with the employees so they can understand why certain cyber security program decisions are made?
- Are you an integral part of the company's CEP-DR processes?
- If not, should you be?
- If so, are you involved in testing the CEP-DR plans?
- After an emergency or disaster, are you involved in verifying and validating that all the security hardware, software, and firmware are operating in accordance with the cyber security program and security specifications?
- If not, how would you know they were even turned back on by IT personnel after the systems went offline and were brought back online again?

SUMMARY

It is crucial for a cyber security officer who is new to the corporation to evaluate the current cyber security program organizational structure, the staff, and their experience and education and ensure the organization is cost-effectively structured. The cyber security officer should consider the following points:

- Establishing the proper cyber security program functions in the right priority order is vital to establishing the cyber security program organization and cyber security program baseline.
- The cyber security program functional processes should generally follow the function descriptions noted in the cyber security officer's charter of responsibilities.

- Establishing a process to determine the categories of information identified by the general value of that information would assist in the development of a cost-effective cyber security program.
- Functions and processes should be developed based on requirements such as laws and regulations.
- Flowcharts should be developed to help visualize the linkage between requirements; plans; vision, mission, and quality statements; policies; processes; and functions.

CHAPTER 10

Establishing a Metrics Management System

Don't work harder—work smarter

Ken Blanchard

Contents

Chapter Objective

This chapter is designed to provide basic guidance necessary for the development of a metrics methodology to understand what, why, when, and how a cyber security program can be measured. Using a fictitious corporation and functions that were previously described, a metrics system will be developed. The chapter includes a discussion of how to use the metrics to brief management, justify budget, and use trend analyses to develop a more efficient and effective cyber security program.

The Information Systems Security Officer's Guide

INTRODUCTION

Some of the most common complaints cyber security officers make are that management doesn't support them and—as the famous comedian Rodney Dangerfield is known for saying—"I get no respect." Another complaint is that the costs and benefits of a cyber security program cannot be measured.

As for the first two, you get support, because you are being paid—and these days, more often than not, quite handsomely—and you have a budget that could have been part of corporate profits. Furthermore, respect is earned. Besides, if you want to be popular, you are definitely in the wrong profession.

One often hears management ask:

- "What is all this security costing me?"
- "Is it working?"
- "Can it be done at less cost?"
- "Why isn't it working?"

That last question often comes right after a successful denial-of-service attack or some other attack on the corporate systems or Web sites. Of course, many cyber security officers respond by saying that it can't be measured. That is often said out of the cyber security officer's ignorance of processes to measure costs or because the cyber security officer is too lazy to track costs.

The more difficult question to answer is, "What are the measurable benefits of a cyber security program and the functions that provide support under the cyber security program?" Of course, one could always use the well-worn statement, "It can be measured only as a success or failure depending on whether or not there have been successful attacks against our systems." The truth is that many attacks go unnoticed, unreported by the users or information technology (IT) people. Furthermore, separating attacks from "accidents" (human error) is usually not easy; however, metrics can help in the analyses.

What Is a Metric?

To begin to understand how to use metrics to support management of a cyber security program, it is important to understand what is meant by "metrics." For our purposes, a metric is defined as *a standard of measurement using quantitative, statistical, and/or mathematical analyses.*

What Is a Cyber Security Program Metric?

A cyber security program metric is the application of quantitative, statistical, and/or mathematical analyses to measure cyber security program functional trends and workload—in other words, tracking what each function is doing in terms of level of effort (LOE), costs, and productivity.

There are two basic ways of tracking costs and benefits. One is by using metrics relative to the day-to-day, routine operations of each cyber security program function. These metrics are called LOE and are the basic functions noted in the cyber security officer's charter of responsibilities and accountabilities. Examples would be daily analyses of audit trail records of a firewall, granting users access to systems, and conducting noncompliance inquiries. In more financial terms, these are the recurring costs.

The other way of tracking costs and benefits is through formal project plans. In other words, if the tasks being performed are not the normal LOE tasks, then they fall under projects. Remember that functions are never-ending daily work, while projects have a beginning and ending date with a specific objective. In more financial terms, these are the nonrecurring costs.

So, to efficiently and effectively develop a metrics management program, it is important to establish that philosophy and way of doing business. Everything that a cyber security officer and staff do can be identified as fitting into one of these two categories: LOE or project.

What Is Cyber Security Program Metrics Management?

Cyber security program metrics management is the managing of a cyber security program and related functions through the use of metrics. It can be used where managerial tasks must be supported for such purposes as backing the cyber security officer's position on budget matters, justifying the cost-effectiveness of decisions, or determining the impact of downsizing on providing cyber security program service and support to customers.

The primary process to collect metrics is as follows:

- Identify each cyber security program function[1];
- Determine what drives that function, such as labor (number of people or hours used), policies, procedures, and systems; and
- Establish a metrics collection process. The collection process may be as simple as filling out a log for later summarization and analysis. The use of a spreadsheet that can automatically incorporate cyber security program statistics into graphs is the preferred method. This will make it easier for the cyber security officer to use the metrics for supporting management decisions, briefings, etc.

The decision to establish a process to collect statistics relative to a particular cyber security program function should be made by answering the following questions:

- Why should these statistics be collected?
- What specific statistics will be collected?

[1] It is assumed each function costs time, money, and use of equipment to perform.

- How will these statistics be collected?
- When will these statistics be collected?
- Who will collect these statistics?
- Where (at what point in the function's process) will these statistics be collected?

By answering these questions for each proposed metric, the cyber security officer can better analyze whether a metrics collection process should be established for a particular function. This thought process will be useful in helping explain it to the cyber security program staff or management, if necessary. It will also help the cyber security officer decide whether he or she should continue maintaining that metric after a specific period of time. Since the corporate cyber security officer had begun with an analysis of cyber security program requirements (drivers) that led to the identification of a cyber security officer charter that led to the identification of cyber security program functions with process flowcharts, the task of developing metrics will be much easier. That is because each step noted in the cyber security program functions' flowcharts can be a point of quantifying and qualifying costs of performing each specific function.

All metrics should be reviewed, evaluated, and reconsidered for continuation at the end of each year, or sooner—when a requirement changes, a function may also change. Remember that although the collection of the metrics information will help the cyber security officer better manage the cyber security program duties and responsibilities, a resource cost is incurred in the collection and maintenance of these metrics. These resources include:

- People who collect, input, process, print, and maintain the metrics for you;
- Time to collect, analyze, and disseminate the information; and
- The hardware and software used to support that effort.

When using these metrics charts for management briefings, one must remember that the chart format and colors are sometimes dictated by management; however, which type of chart is best for analysis or presentation to management is probably up to the cyber security officer.

The cyber security officer should experiment with various types of line, bar, and pie charts. The charts should be kept simple and easy to understand. Remember the old saying, "A picture is worth a thousand words." The charts should need very little verbal explanation.

If the cyber security officer will use the charts for briefings, the briefing should comment only on the various trends. The reason for this is to clearly and concisely present the material and not get bogged down in details, which detract from the objective of the charts.

One way to determine whether the message of the charts is clear is to have someone look at each chart and describe what it tells him or her. If it is what the chart is supposed to portray, then no changes are needed. If not, the cyber security officer should then ask the viewer what the chart does seem to represent and what leads him or her to that conclusion. The cyber security officer must then go back to the chart and rework it until the message is clear and is exactly what the cyber security officer wants the chart to show. Each chart should have only one specific objective, and the cyber security officer should be able to state that objective in one sentence, such as "This chart's objective is to show that cyber security program support to corporate is being maintained without additional budget although the workload has increased 13%."

The following paragraphs identify some basic examples of cyber security program metrics that can be collected to assist a cyber security officer in managing a cyber security program and briefing the management on the program and the program's organization. By the way, when establishing a briefing to management in which the metrics charts will be used, a similar chart can be used to start off the briefing. That chart tracks the requirements (drivers) that can be traced to each function. One may also want to provide more detailed charts tracking specific requirements to specific functions.

Of course, as the cyber security officer, you would want to get more specific and track to a more detailed level of granularity. In fact, the cyber security program staff responsible for leading a specific function should be tasked with developing this chart or charts. That way, the staff will know exactly why they are doing what they do. The next step would be for them to track their workflow, analyze it, and find more efficient ways to do the job. At the same time they would also look at current costs and cost savings as more efficient ways are found to successfully accomplish their jobs.

The cyber security officer must remember that metrics are a tool to support many of the cyber security officer's decisions and actions; however, they are not perfect. Therefore, the cyber security officer must make some assumptions relative to the statistical data to be collected. That's fine. The cyber security officer must remember that metrics are not rocket science, only a tool to help the cyber security officer take better-informed actions and make better-informed decisions. So, the cyber security officer should never get carried away with the hunt for "perfect statistics," or become so involved in metrics data collection that "paralysis by analysis" takes place.[2]

The spreadsheets and graphs used for metrics management can become very complicated, with links to other spreadsheets, elaborate three-dimensional graphics, etc. That may work for some, but the cyber security officer should consider the KISS (keep it simple, stupid) principle when collecting and maintaining metrics. This is especially true if the cyber security officer is just getting started and has no or very little experience with metrics. One may find that the project leads who are developing an "automated statistical collection" application are expending more hours developing the application—which never seems to work quite right—than it would take to manually collect and calculate the statistical information.

It is also important, from a managerial viewpoint, that all charts, statistics, and spreadsheets be done in a standard format. This is necessary so that they can be ready at all times for reviews and briefings to upper management. This standard is indicative of a professional organization and one that is operating as a focused team.

Cyber security officers who are new to the cyber security officer position, or management in general, may think that this is somewhat ridiculous. After all, what difference does it make as long as the information is as accurate as possible and provides the necessary information? This may be correct, but in the business environment, standards, consistency, and indications of teaming are always a concern of management. Your charts are indicative of those things.

The cyber security officer has a hard enough job getting and maintaining management support. The job should not be made more difficult than it has to be.

Another negative impact of nonconformance of format will be that the attendees will discuss the charts and not the information on them. Once "nonconformance to briefing charts standards" is discussed, management has already formed a negative bias. Thus, anything presented will make it more difficult to get the point across, gain the decision desired, and meet the established objective of the briefing.

It is better just to follow the established standards than to argue their validity. It is better to save energy for arguing for those things that are more important. After all, one can't win, and the cyber security officer does not want to be seen as "a non-team player" more than necessary.

---

[2] Dr. Gerald L. Kovacich has used approximately 47 metrics charts at various times to assist in managing several large cyber security programs and cyber security program organizations.

Of course the number, type, collection methods, etc., that the cyber security officer will use will be dependent on the environment and the cyber security officer's ability to cost-effectively collect and maintain the metrics.

METRICS 1: CYBER SECURITY PROGRAM LEVEL OF EFFORT DRIVERS—NUMBER OF USERS

There are two basic cyber security program LOE drivers within an organization, that is, those things that cause the cyber security program workload to be what it is, increasing or decreasing. The two basic drivers are:

- The number of systems that fall under the purview of the cyber security program and cyber security officer's overall responsibility for protection and
- The number of users of those systems.

A question that must be asked is: Why are these metrics worth tracking? They are worth tracking because they drive the cyber security program workload—the LOE—which means they drive the number of hours that the cyber security program staff must expend in meeting their cyber security program responsibilities relative to those systems and users.

As the number of users on the corporate networks changes or the number of systems changes, so does the workload; therefore, so does the number of staff required and the amount of budget required—time to do the job. For example, assume that the corporation is downsizing—a common occurrence that cyber security officers will eventually face in their cyber security program careers. If the cyber security officer knows that the corporation will downsize its workforce by 10%, and assuming that the workforce all use computers, which is not unusual in today's corporations, the workload should also decrease about 10%. This may cause the cyber security officer to also downsize (lay off staff) by approximately 10%.

However, the downsizing, whether it is more or less than the corporate average, should be based on the related cyber security program workload. The cyber security program drivers are metrics that can help the cyber security officer determine the impact of the corporation's downsizing on the cyber security program and its organization. The metrics associated with that effort can also justify downsizing decisions to corporate management— to include possibly downsizing by 5 or 12% instead of 10%. For example, more layoffs may mean more cyber security program-related infractions, which means an increase in noncompliance inquiries and thus an increase in the workload. Massive layoffs would also mean more work for those who are responsible for deaccessing employees from the systems prior to employment terminations. The metrics can show this work increase and make a case to management for not laying off cyber security program staff until after the other major layoffs have occurred.

Charting Level of Effort through Number of System Users

As a cyber security officer, you decided that it would be a good idea to use the driver's metric that is used for tracking the number of system users. You have gone through the analytical process to make that decision based on answering the why, what, how, when, who, and where questions.

Why Should These Statistics Be Collected?

The driver's metric that tracks the number of system users for which the cyber security officer has cyber security program responsibility is used to assist in detailing the needed head-count budget for supporting those users. As an example, the following functions are charted based on the number of corporate system users:

- Access control violations,
- Noncompliance inquiries, and
- Awareness briefings.

What Specific Statistics Will Be Collected?

- Total users by location and systems and
- Total systems by location and type.

How Will These Statistics Be Collected?

- The total number of users will be determined by totaling the number of user IDs on each network system and adding to it the number of stand-alone systems. It is assumed that each stand-alone system has only one user.
- Stand-alone microcomputers and networked systems (which will count as one system) will be identified and totaled using the approved system documentation on file within the cyber security program organization on the approved systems database. At the corporation, all systems processing sensitive information falling within the categories previously identified at the corporation for identifying information by its value must be approved by the cyber security officer (or designated cyber security program staff members). Therefore, data collection is available through the cyber security program's records.

When Will These Statistics Be Collected?

The statistics will be compiled on the first business day of each month and incorporated into Metrics 1, cyber security program drivers, graph maintained on the cyber security program department's administrative microcomputer.

Who Will Collect These Statistics?

The statistics will be collected, inputted, and maintained by the project leaders responsible for each cyber security program function, such as system accesses and system approvals.

Where (at What Point in the Function's Process) Will These Statistics Be Collected?

The collection of statistics will be based on the information available and on file in the cyber security program organization through close of business on the last business day of the month.

Of course, the number of system users affects all cyber security program functions. Follow-on charts would show the workload relative to the other cyber security program functions that are affected. Bold fonts are used to highlight important facts that the cyber security officer wants to emphasize—management's eyes are naturally drawn to bold fonts.

Significance of the System Users Chart

The number of system users is also a driver of cyber security program workload because the cyber security program functions' LOE and some projects are based on the number of users. They include the following:

- The cyber security program staff provides access controls for users;
- The number of noncompliance inquiries will probably increase based on the increased number of users;
- The number of noncompliance inquiries may actually increase when the corporation downsizes because of more hostility among the employees (a metrics chart showing caseload may help in defending cyber security officer staff from more drastic layoffs than may have been required by management);
- The time to review audit trail records will increase as a result of more activity because of more users; and
- The number of awareness briefings and processing of additional awareness material will increase as a result of an increase in users.

Remember that as a cyber security officer you are also a cyber security program "salesperson" and must effectively advertise and market information and systems protection to corporation's personnel. A chart can be used by the cyber security officer for the following:

- Justify the need for more budget and other resources;
- Indicate that the cyber security program is operating more efficiently, because the budget and other resources have not increased although the number of systems has increased; and
- Help justify why budget and other resources cannot be decreased.

When deciding to develop metrics charts to track workload, efficiency, costs, etc., of that function, always start at the highest level and then develop charts at lower levels (in more detail) that support the overall chart. This is done for several purposes. The cyber security officer may have limited time to brief a specific audience, and if it is an executive management briefing, the time will be shorter, as usually their attention span is short when it comes to cyber security program matters. So, the "top-down" approach will probably work best. If you have time to brief in more detail, the charts are available. If executive management has a question relative to some level of detail, then the other charts can be used to support the cyber security officer statements and/or position in reply to the question of the audience.

Granting Users Access to Systems

A major cyber security program service and support function is to add new users to systems and to provide them new access privileges as directed by their management and information owners.

As part of that service and support effort, the cyber security officer wants to ensure that these users are given access as quickly as possible, because without their access or new access privileges, the users cannot perform their jobs.

If users cannot gain expeditious access, then the cyber security program is costing the corporation in terms of lost productivity of employees or even possibly lost revenue in other forms.

The cyber security officer, in coordination with the cyber security program staff responsible for the access control function, evaluated the access control process and determined that users should be given access within 24h of receipt of a request from management.

The cyber security officer decided to track this process because of its high visibility. Nothing can damage the reputation of the cyber security officer and staff faster than a hostile manager whose employees cannot get systems access to be able to do their work, leading, for example, to increased costs due to lost department productivity caused by the slowness of accessing employees to systems. To develop a metrics chart, one should first create a flowchart of the function.

> *Anything worth doing does not have to be done perfectly—at first.*
>
> **Ken Blanchard**

EXAMPLES OF OTHER METRICS CHARTS

There are numerous metrics charts that can be developed to support the various needs of the cyber security officer and the cyber security program. The cyber security officer may also use this information when budget cuts are required. The chart can be shown to management and modified to show what would happen if the staff were cut by one person, two people, etc. In other words, the average users' initial access to systems in terms of turnaround time would increase. Management may or may not want to live with those consequences. The cost can be quantified by taking the average hourly wage of the employee, identifying how much productivity time is lost with access coming within one business day, and comparing that to time lost if access, because an access control person has been laid off, takes two business days.

For example, an employee earns $15 an hour. The employee shows up at the desk of an access controller at the start of the business day, 8.00am. That employee is authorized system access by 8.00am the next day. This loss of at least 8 h of productivity at $15 an hour would be the normal cost of the cyber security program function of access control, or $120 per employee. However, if the access was not authorized until the day after, the cost per employee would be $240.

The chart can show the cyber security officer where staff cuts can be made and still meet the expected goals. The cyber security officer can also use this information when deciding to reallocate resources (transfer a person) to another function for which the goals are not being met and the fastest way to meet the goals is to add head count. A word of caution here—adding or decreasing head count is usually considered a fast, simple solution. However, it is not always the answer.

> *Sometimes when the numbers look right the decision is still wrong!*
>
> **Ken Blanchard and Norman Vincent Peale**

Many project leaders and cyber security officers have found over the years that projects and LOE problems are not always solved by assigning more bodies to solving the problem. One should first look at the process and at systemic problems. This is usually a more cost-effective approach to solving these types of problems. For example, using the example of the newly hired employee getting first-time system access, suppose a way was found to cut that time down to 1 h. The costs saving would be from the normal $120 to $15, or a saving of $105 per new employee. Such charts can be used for management briefings and will show specifically how the cyber security officer and staff are lowering cyber security program costs, at least for that particular cyber security program function.

As with all metrics charts, a decision must also be made whether to collect the data monthly, quarterly, semiannually, annually, or somewhere in between. The time period will depend on several factors. These include, but are not limited to:
- What they will be used for, such as monthly or annual executive briefings;
- Budget justifications;
- Cyber security program staff functions resource allocations; and
- The objectives of each chart.

A subchart of this chart may be the average time spent, in hours, per type of inquiry. Once the time elements are known, they can be equated to productivity gains and losses, as well as budget, such as money, equipment, and staff.

Cyber Security Program Tests and Evaluations

The cyber security officer may decide to establish a process that will provide guidelines on the need, establishment, and implementation of metrics charts. The cyber security officer uses a cyber security program function to develop the process—the methodology—with the following results:
- The cyber security program will conduct security tests and evaluations (ST&E) as prescribed by the corporation's cyber security program policies and procedures.
- Results of the cyber security program ST&E will be charted.
- Each chart will be evaluated to determine whether a pattern/trend exists.
- Patterns/trends will be evaluated to determine how effectively a function is being performed.
- Results and recommendations will be presented, in accordance with cyber security program policies and procedures, to the applicable managers.

Another cyber security program function that provides opportunities for using metrics management techniques is the function of the cyber security program ST&E.

The cyber security officer may consider a reallocation of staff because of the increased workload. Also to be considered is whether to change the ST&E process. One consideration is to conduct fewer ST&E. If one does that, it would be important to monitor the number of noncompliance inquiries, as they may go up. For example, fewer ST&E may result in increased systems vulnerabilities, which may in turn lead to more successful attacks and thus to more noncompliance inquiries. Another factor the cyber security officer may consider is doing more ST&E using automated cyber security program software to replace some currently manual testing.

One can also consider providing training to department staff so they can do their own ST&E and provide reports to the cyber security officer. This is usually not a good idea, as the objectivity of the testing may be questionable. For example, they may find vulnerabilities but not report them, because they do not want to incur the costs in time and budget to mitigate the risks identified by these vulnerabilities. In addition, as far the corporation as a whole is concerned, one is only passing on the costs in terms of allocation of resources to conduct the ST&E to another department and not decreasing overall cyber security program costs.

Remember that the corporation is a global corporation with plants and offices on three continents. Since the cyber security officer has overall cyber security program and cyber security program functional responsibility for all locations, a process must be put in place for metrics management at all locations. The cyber security program–cyber security program functional leads at all the locations would provide the statistics and charts for their locations. These statistics would be indicators for establishing cyber security program functional resource allocations based on the "worst" locations.

The issue that will often come up when designing charts is what type of charts to use—bar, line, pie, etc. The choice should be to use the format that meets the chart's objective in the most concise and clear way.

Cyber Security Program Education and Awareness Training

The cyber security program's education and awareness training program (EATP) is one of the major baselines of the cyber security program. It follows that it is an integral part of the cyber security officer's cyber security program organization. It doesn't matter whether briefings, training, and such are given by a cyber security program staff member, the corporate training office, the Director of Security's security training personnel, Human Resources new-hire briefings, or a combination of any of these. It is a cyber security program, and therefore a cyber security program cost, and it should be metrics-managed.

Let's assume that to be somewhat cost-effective, the goal is to have at least 15 employees on average attend each briefing. That being the case, this metrics chart or another like it would show not only the number of briefings and the total attendees, but also the average number of attendees per briefing. In addition, a straight line could be included at 15 so that the average attendees per briefing can easily be compared against the goal of 15 employees per briefing.

If the goal was not being reached, as the cyber security officer, you might want to discuss the matter with your cyber security program leader for the EATP. Certainly if the goal is not being met, you can't, and obviously shouldn't, ignore it. There is nothing worse than setting a goal, metrics managing to attain that goal, and then ignoring it when it is not being met. Furthermore, as a cyber security officer you shouldn't just wait until the end of the year to attempt to correct the matter in a discussion with your EATP lead and then zap that person in his or her year-end performance evaluation.

Let us assume that employees must attend an annual briefing relative to the cyber security program and their duties and responsibilities. Assume that they prepare to attend the briefing and walk to the briefing room and that that takes 15 min. They attend a 1-h briefing and return to their place of work, for a total time of 90 min. At an average employment rate of $15 per hour, each employee's time (and lost productivity, since they are not performing the work for which they were hired) for the annual briefing is $22.50. Let's also suppose that the corporation employs 100,000 people worldwide and all of them must attend the annual briefing. That means that the annual briefing program, excluding the time the cyber security program specialist takes in preparing the updated material each year and other expenses, costs an astounding $2,250,000!

One can argue that the briefings are necessary, they save money in the long run because valuable corporation is protected, and all that. However, that does not change the fact that this is a rather costly program. In fact, there is no indication that the cost–benefits have ever been validated. Yet, every cyber security officer knows that employee awareness of the threats, vulnerabilities, and risks to information and information systems is an absolute necessity. So, what can be done to lower the cost of such a program?

Using the project team approach, the cyber security officer should establish a project team to look at the costs, benefits, and risks of not having an annual briefing and other methods for providing awareness to employees. Possibly the use of e-mails, online briefings, and other electronic means could eliminate the need for the employees to physically attend a briefing. Possibly briefings could be eliminated or online bulletins used.

Cost-Avoidance Metrics

As a cyber security officer, you may want to use the metrics management approach to be able to quantify the savings of some of your decisions. For example, when analyzing your budget and expenditures, you note that a major budget item is travel costs for your staff. This is logical, because staff, as well as you, must travel to the various corporate offices to conduct cyber security program tests and evaluations.

Again, using the project management approach, you lead a project team of yourself, staff members, and representatives from the contract office and the travel office. Your goal is to find ways to cut travel costs while still meeting all the cyber security program's and your charter's responsibilities. A representative from the contract office will advise the project team on contractual obligations and ways in which they can be met with less travel, but without violating the terms of the contracts. The travel office will give advice on ways to cut travel costs. For example, because many trips are known well in advance, flights and hotels can also be booked in advance.

Metrics Management and Downsizing

All cyber security officers at one time or another in their careers face the need to downsize—that is, lay off, fire, or terminate—cyber security program staff. However, if you are operating at peak efficiency and have not built any excess staff into meeting your charter responsibilities, you may be able to make a case for not terminating staff or for terminating fewer personnel.

Many managers, and cyber security officers are no exception, tend to forget that they are hired to do a job, and that job is not to build an "empire" or bureaucracy. The key to success is getting the job done efficiently and effectively—as we said before, good and cheap. In addition, the more staff members and the larger the budget you have, the more people problems you will have and the harder the financial people will try to take some of your budget. So you are constantly battling to maintain your large budget.

If, on the other hand, you have a small staff and a smaller budget, you have a better chance of protecting what you have, because it is the minimum needed to get the job done. That approach coupled with metrics management techniques and periodic briefings to executive management will help you continue to get the job done as you deem appropriate, even though other organizations are losing staff.

Let's look at some figures showing various ways of presenting information based on metrics management's data collection efforts:

Another chart that is important for briefing management is one that shows the LOE versus the hours available for the cyber security program staff. The difference between LOE and time available can be shown to be part of a briefing on work backlog or used to show the difference in overtime being worked. A subchart may show details on the amount of backlog and its impact on the cost of doing business. It can also show the overtime costs being paid and perhaps a comparison of that cost with the cost of hiring one or more additional staff. Seeing this comparison would help in making decisions as to which is cheaper, paying overtime or hiring more staff.

These charts must also be accompanied by others showing productivity and drivers of workload, as in some of the charts shown earlier. This is necessary because management will ask why you must do the things you do and why you must do them in the way you are doing them. This quest for productivity and efficiency gains will be a constant chore for the cyber security officer. It is a challenge, but one that can be supported by metrics charts.

Layoffs are a fact of life in business, and metrics charts can help the cyber security officer justify head count and work, as shown by some of these charts. The chart can show measurement in terms of head count or hours that are equivalent to head count.

Generally, when management decides to cut costs, they lay off employees as the easiest method. They also usually direct each manager to cut a certain percentage of staff, say, 20%. However, although this may be the easiest way, it is not the best way; sometimes it would be cheaper to keep some of the staff, because their loss causes delays costing millions of dollars worth of production, sales, etc. As we all know, executive management often takes a short-term, "what's in it for me now" approach to managing their parts of the business.

Metrics management can help the cyber security officer plead the case to not cut 20% of staff. One word of caution: The cyber security officer should do this objectively and based on providing effective and efficient service and support to the corporation's departments. It should never, ever be based on keeping a large staff and bureaucracy for the sake of status, power, ego, or other nonbusiness reasons.

The cyber security officer would include information relative to the impact of both the corporation's directed layoff numbers and those of the cyber security officer. This must be objectively done based on a business rationale. This information would include the following, identified as increasing the level of risks to information and information systems:

- *Contingency planning*: Contingency, emergency, and disaster recovery testing and plan updates will be delayed. The result will be anything from no impact to not being able to effectively and efficiently deal with an emergency.

- *Awareness program*: Employees may not be aware of their responsibilities, thus leaving the systems open to potential attack or an increase in the potential for the loss of sensitive information.

- *Access violations analyses*: There will be delays of between 48 and 72 h in the analyses of audit records. Thus, an attack against corporate systems would not be known for at least 48–72 h. During that period, information could be stolen. However, something like a denial-of-service attack would be known when it was successful. The opportunity to identify the initial attempts at these attacks over a period of time would be lost, and with it the chance to mount defenses before the attacks were successful. The result will be systems, possibly production systems, that are down for an unknown period of time.

- *Noncompliance inquiries*: The average time it would take to complete an inquiry would increase by more than 2 weeks. Thus, no action to adjudicate the alleged infraction would be possible until the report was delivered to management. Furthermore, the alleged infraction may have called for the revocation of system privileges of the employee or employees who are the subject of the inquiry. Thus, their ability to be productive employees during that time would be negated.

- *Access control*: It is assumed that the number of new employees hired would be drastically reduced, and that could mitigate some of the LOE expended by the access controllers. However, employees requiring changes in privilege would have those access changes delayed an additional 48–72 h from the present average of 8–12 h. This may adversely affect their productivity. To allow departments to do their own employees' privilege changes was evaluated under a previous project and found not to be realistic: The information to which the employees needed access did not belong to that department; most often it belonged to another information owner. These information owners did not want others to access their information without their approval. In addition, this change would just be transferring the costs and would not save the corporation any additional resources.

The foregoing is a small example of how metric management techniques can be used when the need for budget cuts occurs. The example provides some insight into how metric management techniques help mitigate the risks of budget and staff downsizing when such downsizing will hurt the cyber security program and the corporation. Metric management techniques can help the cyber security officer make a case to executive management. Furthermore, if the cyber security officer, supported by the metric management approach, has been periodically briefing management of the cyber security program and the cyber security officer's projects and LOE, the cyber security officer will have gained the confidence of management as a reliable manager who gets the job done as efficiently and effectively as possible.

PROJECT MANAGEMENT

As previously discussed, there are two basic types of work performed by the cyber security officer and staff: (1) LOE and (2) projects. We have discussed LOE and have provided some examples of process and metrics flowcharts relative to LOE.

It has been stated several times, but bears repeating: Projects are established when some tasks related to the cyber security program and/or its functions must be completed but they are not ongoing tasks. It is imperative that the cyber security officer be intimately familiar with and experienced in project management—as well as time management.

Remember that whether or not some task should be a project depends on whether it has the following:
- A stated objective (generally in one clear, concise, and complete sentence),
- A beginning date,
- An ending date,
- Specific tasks to be performed to successfully meet that objective,
- A project leader, and
- Specific personnel to complete each task and the time period in which the task will be completed.

Let's assume that the corporate information officer (CIO) sent a memo to the cyber security officer based on a conversation that the CIO had with the Director of IT. It seems that they had a meeting and during the meeting the discussion turned to IT projects related to their projects of upgrading systems, such as hardware, software, and their general maintenance. The cyber security program policy called for such upgrades and maintenance efforts to ensure that the information environment is maintained in compliance with the requirements set forth in the cyber security program. The Director stated that the IT staff didn't know if that was always the case when they made changes to systems. Consequently, the Director suggested that members of the cyber security officer's organization be part of the IT project teams with responsibility for determining whether the changes kept the corporation's information environment secure. The CIO agreed and sent the cyber security officer a letter to that effect. When the cyber security officer received the memo, the cyber security officer discussed the matter with the Senior Systems Security Engineer. It was decided that a project be developed to establish a process and function to comply with the request from the CIO and Director of IT.

As a cyber security officer, you should be able to identify several issues that the cyber security officer must resolve apart from initiating this project. First, the Director of IT and the cyber security officer should be working closely together, and by doing so, they could have dealt with this matter without involving their boss, the CIO. In addition, the fact that the CIO sent a memo to the cyber security officer, instead of calling or meeting personally with the cyber security officer, indicates that the communication and working relationship between the CIO and the cyber security officer must be improved. The cyber security officer must take action to immediately begin improving the communication and relationship with the Director and the CIO.

A project chart should include the following:
- *Subject*: The project name—Security Test and Evaluation Function Development
- *Responsibility*: The name of the project leader—John Doe, cyber security program Senior Systems Security Engineer.
- *Action Item*: What is to be accomplished—IT requires cyber security officer support to ensure that information and systems protection are integrated into IT systems' integration, maintenance, and update processes.

- *References*: What caused this project to be initiated—for example, "See memo to cyber security officer from CIO, dated November 2, 2002."
- *Objective(s)*: State the objective of the project—Maintain a secure information environment.
- *Risk/Status*: State the risk of not meeting the objective(s) of this project— Because of limited staffing and multiple customer projects being supported, this project may experience delays as higher priority LOE and projects take precedence.
- *Activity/Event*: State the tasks to be performed, such as "Meet with IT project leads."
- *Responsibility*: Identify the person responsible for each task. In this case, it is the Senior Systems Security Engineer, John Doe.
- *Calendar*: The calendar could be a year-long, monthly, quarterly, or 6-month calendar with vertical lines identifying individual weeks. Using the 6-month calendar, the project lead and assigned project team members would decide what tasks had to be accomplished to meet the objective. Arrows and diamonds, for example, identified in the legend, would be used to mark the beginning and ending dates of each task. The arrows are filled in when the task is started and when the task is completed; the diamonds are used to show deviations from the original dates.
- *Risk—Level*: In this space, each task is associated with the potential risk that it may be delayed or cost more than allocated in the budget for the task. Using "high," "medium," or "low" or "H", "M", or "L", the project lead, in concert with the person responsible for the task, assigns a level of risk.
- *Risk—Description*: A short description of the risk is stated in this block. If it requires a detailed explanation, that explanation is attached to the project plan. In this block the project lead, who is also responsible for ensuring that the project plan is updated weekly, states "See Attachment 1."
- *Issue Date*: The date the project begins and the chart initiated goes in this block.
- *Status Date*: The most current project chart date is placed here. This is important because anyone looking at the project chart will know how current the project chart is.

Other types of charts can also be developed to show project costs in terms of labor, materials, and the like. A good, automated project plan software program is well worth the costs for managing projects.

In the case of project charts, the cyber security officer can use them to brief management relative to the ongoing work of the cyber security program organization and states of the cyber security program. The cyber security officer receives weekly updates on Friday morning in a meeting with all the cyber security officer's project leaders, during which each project lead is given 5 min to explain the status of the project—for example, "The project is still on schedule" or "Task No. 2 will be delayed because the person assigned the task is out sick for a week; however, it is expected that the project completion date will not be delayed because of it."

The cyber security officer holds an expanded staff meeting the last Friday of each month. All assigned cyber security program personnel attend these meetings, which last 2–3 h. At these meetings, 1 h is taken for all project leads and cyber security program functional leads to brief the status of their LOE and projects to the entire staff. The cyber security officer does this so that everyone in the organization knows what is going on—a vital communications tool. Also during this time, other matters are briefed and discussed, such as the latest risk management techniques, conferences, and training available.

QUESTIONS TO CONSIDER

Based on what you have read, consider the following questions and how you would reply to them:

- Do you use formal metrics management techniques?
- If not, why not?
- If so, are they used to brief management?
- Are each of your cyber security program functions documented, not only in work instructions but also in process flowcharts?
- Do you use similar charts to document the cyber security program functional LOE?
- What other charts would you develop for each of the cyber security officer functions?
- Do you have at least one metrics chart to track the costs of each cyber security program function?
- How would you use metrics management charts to justify your budget requests?
- How would you use metrics management charts to justify the number of your staff?
- How many charts, by function and description, would you want to use as a cyber security officer?

SUMMARY

Metrics management techniques will provide a process for the cyber security officer to support cyber security program- and cyber security program-related decisions. The cyber security officer should understand the following points:

- Metrics management is an excellent method to track cyber security program functions related to LOE, costs, use of resources, etc.
- The information can be analyzed, and results of the analyses can be used to:
  Identify areas where efficiency improvements are necessary;
  Determine effectiveness of cyber security program functional goals;
  Provide input for performance reviews of the cyber security program staff (a more objective approach than subjective performance reviews of today's cyber security officers); and
  Indicate where cyber security program service and support to the corporation requires improvement, meets its goals, etc.

CHAPTER 11

Annual Reevaluation and Future Plans

Read not to contradict and confute, nor to believe and take for granted, nor to find talk and discourse, but to weigh and consider

Francis Bacon[1]

Contents

Chapter Objective

This chapter describes the process that can be used each year to determine the successes and failures of the cyber security program and organization and a methodology that can be used to correct the failures and to plan for the upcoming years.

INTRODUCTION

The information environment of the corporation is very dynamic and must be so for the corporation to successfully compete in the fast-paced widget business in the global marketplace. Consequently, the world of the cyber security officer must also be very dynamic. The cyber security officer must

---

[1] Francis Bacon (1561–1626), English philosopher, lawyer, and statesman. *Essays* "Of Studies" (1625)—*Encarta Book of Quotations*, © & (P) 1999, Microsoft Corporation. All rights reserved. Developed for Microsoft by Bloomsbury Publishing Plc.

223

constantly be looking at where the corporate business is going and modify the cyber security program and its organization accordingly. The cyber security officer cannot sit back and think that the cyber security program is in place, its organization is established, and everything is running smoothly—even when you think it is.

As the corporation's cyber security officer you must be working every day to provide effective and efficient service and support to the corporation in the future. You must project ahead and look at potential new threats to the corporation's information and systems and begin now to mitigate those future threats, such as cellular phones with installed digital cameras. The cyber security officer, like all cyber security officers, must establish proactive processes, as today's corporations depend too much on information and information systems to have those systems fail because the cyber security officer did not see the threat coming. *Today's cyber security officers must be proactive and not constantly reactive.* Proactive processes are prepared to mitigate threats before they can occur—and it is cheaper than being reactive.

The cyber security officer must also reevaluate the cyber security program and have processes in place to constantly update it. In addition, all cyber security program functions must be reevaluated and updated as the need arises, but at least annually. The cyber security officer should lead an annual year-end review and analysis of the cyber security program and cyber security program functions. This is done so that the cyber security officers can have some assurance that they are operating in the most effective and efficient way possible and needed changes are in place.

ONE-YEAR REVIEW

The corporation's fiscal year and calendar year both end on December 31. The cyber security officer decides that the beginning of the fourth quarter (October) is a good time to start planning for the coming year and begin evaluating the current year.

To plan for the coming year, the cyber security officer must first determine how successful the cyber security program and the cyber security program staff have been for the past year. Of interest would be:
- What was accomplished?
- What was planned but never completed, and why?
- What was planned but never started, and why?
- What was successful, and why?
- What wasn't successful, and why?

- What processes are current?
- What processes require updating?
- If a process was outdated, why was it not updated as needed?
- Is the cyber security program organization operating within budget?
- If not, why not?
- What budget is required for the coming year, as well as two or three years from now?
- If more budget is required, why?
- If more budget is needed, are there other measures that can be taken to minimize the need for a larger budget? (Remember that as a cyber security officer, you get paid for results and not the size of your cyber security program staff or the size of your budget.)

Level-of-Effort Activities

The cyber security officer tasked each cyber security program functional lead to form a project team with selected members of the cyber security program functional staff and evaluate the processes used for completing their assigned level-of-effort (LOE) function. Of course, if the cyber security program function was a one-person job, that person would conduct the review by him- or herself and ask for input as needed from other staff members and the cyber security officer. Remember that the LOE activities are those activities or functions that are the day-to-day cyber security program tasks performed by the cyber security program staff. These activities were those identified as the cyber security officer responsibilities previously discussed and included:

- Access control,
- Awareness program,
- Noncompliance inquiries, and
- Security tests and evaluations program, etc.
  This is to be accomplished by each functional team sitting down together to determine:
- What worked?
- What didn't work?
- Why it worked (process may be useful for other functions)?
- Why it didn't work?
- How much time they spent doing each task or subtask on average?
- How the job might be done better?
- How the processes might be changed, why, and what are the potential savings?

- Which forms, if any, should be modified or eliminated? and
- Other considerations.

The cyber security officer directed that any recommended changes be quantified in time and/or cost savings, as applicable. If the changes could not be quantified, the staff members would have a difficult time changing the process. The cyber security officer reasoned that, with few exceptions, process changes that did not save time or money were probably not worth making, as nonquantified changes cost money with usually no return value.

The cyber security officer directed that all members of each function support their functional lead in this endeavor and provide a briefing to be held the first week in November as part of the cyber security officer's expanded staff meeting, which all cyber security program staff attended. During that briefing, the functional processes would be discussed and modifications approved where necessary. If the modifications could not be accomplished within 30 days, a formal project plan would have to be developed and briefed at that November meeting.

Projects

During the first week of October, the cyber security officer will also begin the evaluation of the cyber security program for the past year. The cyber security officer, in concert with the cyber security program staff, will review the projects that were begun this year, as well as those projects that were begun last year and completed this year.

The cyber security officer will determine the following:

- Did each project accomplish its objective?
- Was the project completed in accordance with the project plan?
- For those projects not completed on time, what was the cause of not meeting the completion date?
- For those projects completed ahead of schedule, why were they completed ahead of schedule? (The cyber security officer wants this information because it may be due to poor project planning, which must be corrected, or it may be due to a unique approach that could be used on other projects.)
- What was the cost of each project?
- Were the projected benefits of the projects realized, and if not, why not?

The cyber security officer will, in concert with the cyber security program staff, analyze all the projects and, based on that evaluation, modify the process used for initiating, determining costs, determining resource allocations, and determining schedules for all new projects.

Also of importance is feedback from corporate employees: their evaluation of service and support provided to them by the cyber security officer and cyber security program staff. The employees' opinions as to what improvements can be made in the cyber security program to minimize costs and provide the necessary level of information environment protection are also important. The cyber security officer and staff will develop a survey to be sent out to all departments. The feedback received will also be incorporated into the year-end evaluation–analysis. Some cyber security officers may not want to take this survey approach, because they may be reluctant to receive criticism and complaints from non-cyber security program professionals about how the cyber security officer and cyber security program staff can better do their jobs. However, such feedback is important and should be welcomed and considered at all times.

Once the analysis is complete, the cyber security officer and staff members will determine what new projects will be required for the following year. Those projects, once identified, will be assigned to the applicable members of the staff, that is to the project leads. The staff members will then be given 30 days to complete a draft project plan. That plan will identify the specific objective to be accomplished, all tasks, milestones, resources required, etc.

During the staff meeting held during the first week of November, all the project leads will present their project plans to the cyber security officer and the staff. The project plans will be evaluated and discussed by the cyber security officer and the staff. Any recommended changes to the project plans will be cause for actions to be taken to change the plans as appropriate. In addition, the overall project plan process will be discussed and modified as needed.

It is the responsibility of the cyber security officer to ensure that adequate resources are allocated for the completion of the projects as planned. Where several members of the cyber security program staff are assigned to lead or support multiple projects, the cyber security officer will prioritize the projects and then allow the project lead and project support staff to work out the details. Where conflicts in work arise, the matter will be discussed with the cyber security officer, who will make the final decision based on the input of all those concerned and the proper allocation of resources.

This approach follows the management philosophy of having decisions made at the lowest possible level where the required information on which to base a decision is known. It also meets the cyber security officer's philosophy of trusting your professional cyber security program staff and treating them as part of the professional cyber security program team.

CYBER SECURITY PROGRAM STRATEGIC, TACTICAL, AND ANNUAL PLANS

Once the cyber security officer has been briefed on the above LOE and projects, the results will be mapped against the cyber security program strategic, tactical, and annual plans. The LOE and project results could be identified as some of the specific building blocks of each of the plans.

The cyber security program annual plan's goals should have been accomplished. If so, the cyber security officer then identifies the links between the successful accomplishment of those goals with the corporation's annual business plan and the cyber security program and also the strategic and tactical plans as appropriate.

If a direct link between the accomplishments of the cyber security program staff and the goals of the plan cannot be shown, the cyber security officer must question why the specific projects or LOE identified were ever done in the first place. There may be a very valid reason; however, this should always be questioned, as any resource allocations that cannot be directly linked back to the accomplishment of stated goals are probably misallocations. They are an added cost burden on the cyber security program budget as well as an additional overhead cost to the corporation.

LINKING CYBER SECURITY PROGRAM ACCOMPLISHMENTS TO CORPORATE GOALS

The cyber security officer believes that the initial reasons for the corporation's cyber security program and the corporation's reasons for establishing the cyber security officer position have not changed, but a reverification and validation would probably be a good idea. To be sure that the cyber security program and the cyber security officer's accomplishments are meeting their stated purpose, the cyber security officer decides on the following course of action:

- Using a link-analysis methodology, the cyber security officer maps all the LOE and project results to all applicable cyber security program and corporate plans and
- The cyber security officer develops a formal presentation to be given to the corporate executive management in which the cyber security program status is briefed (assuming that the cyber security officer's boss agrees).

If the cyber security officer does a link analysis, it may disclose that overall cyber security program goals, LOE, projects, and objectives were, with some minor setbacks and exceptions over the year, meeting the needs of the corporation.

Let's look at some possible scenarios: The cyber security officer discussed the matter with the corporate information officer (CIO). The CIO agreed that a briefing would be a good idea, especially since this was the end of the first year of the formal cyber security program under the cyber security officer. The executive management would want to know:

- What was accomplished,
- The cost of the cyber security program,
- The status of the overall protection of the corporation's information environment, and
- What else was needed to ensure a secure information environment.

The CIO provided several recommendations:

- The briefing should take no longer than 15 min and allow 15 min for questions;
- The cyber security officer should not use any technical jargon but speak in business terms of costs, benefits, and competitive advantage and give the management some sense of assurance that the information and systems are being protected as needed;
- The briefing charts should be clear, concise, and more of a graphical presentation than text—another reason for "management by metrics";
- The briefing should be given professionally and objectively; it should not be used as a soapbox for requesting additional resources or to show how great job the cyber security officer is doing;
- All briefing charts should be provided in a package for each member of the audience with supporting detailed charts; and
- At least 5 of the 15 min should be used to brief on next year's projects and goals, their costs, and how they would benefit the corporation.

The cyber security officer had not been prepared to present the new year's plans and projects as part of the briefing. However, it appeared that the necessary information would be available based on the previous briefings and discussions with the cyber security program staff.

The cyber security officer suggested a briefing to be held the first week of December. The CIO agreed to set it up. The cyber security officer's rationale for a meeting in December was that the cyber security program staff's LOE and project input would be available on or about the first week of November, and that would provide sufficient time to develop the briefing.

The cyber security officer wanted to ensure that the briefing accomplished its goals, and that could be jeopardized, not by the material, but by the manner and format used. The cyber security officer had heard of several briefers having their messages ignored because the format, fonts, colors, or whatever was used to present the facts was not liked by one or more of the executive management.

The cyber security officer knew that such trivia should not be a prime concern of executive management, but the cyber security officer also knew that such things did occur. To ensure that the cyber security program briefing was successful, the proper format would be the first item of business.

The cyber security officer stopped by the desks of several of the key executive managers' secretaries, who provided insight as to the correct format, font size, and color of slides to use. At the same time, the cyber security officer was given some valuable tips from several of the secretaries as to how to present the material in a manner that the executives preferred. (Note: Although throughout this book the cyber security officer actions are discussed, some may be delegated by the cyber security officer, such as this task to the cyber security officer secretary or administrative assistant.)

The cyber security officer long ago learned that the secretaries of the executive managers had great insight into what worked with their bosses and what didn't. The cyber security officer's respect for them and informal assistance to them over the year had made them close allies. Now, that friendship would be able to help ensure a successful briefing format.

As part of this briefing, the cyber security officer developed an annual report for each corporate department vice president based on the metrics charts used throughout most of the year. That annual report contained some narrative and analyses supported by metrics charts showing the status of each department's compliance with the cyber security program and the security of their information environment. It included an executive summary in the front of the report and recommendations for improvements that could be made in the future, as well as the benefits of the recommended improvement versus the potential costs and cost savings.

METRICS ANALYSIS

As part of the year-end review, the cyber security officer did a complete analysis of the metrics charts that had been developed and used throughout the first year of the cyber security program.

The cyber security officer noted that the charts had grown to more than 47 separate metrics charts. The cyber security officer was concerned that some of the charts had outlived their usefulness, while others continued to be of value, and possibly some new charts were needed.

The analysis of the metrics charts indicated that several of the charts had been necessary to track particular problem areas. However, some of the problems appeared to have been resolved and the metrics charts, for the previous 4 months, had supported that view.

Some metrics charts were developed and briefed periodically to management because some managers were interested in periodically knowing the amount of LOE being used to support some specific tasks. The cyber security officer decided to identify those charts to the managers who were interested in the information and gain their approval to eliminate those charts, as it appeared the information provided had met their needs. If not, it might be possible to provide that information to management on an annual or semiannual basis instead of the current monthly or quarterly report. The final decision should be made by the cyber security officer's customer[2].

The cyber security officer took all the metrics charts and identified them by their objectives—in other words, their purpose for being developed and used. Those would also be linked to specific areas that support the corporate cyber security program and cyber security program organizational plans. The cyber security officer wanted to be sure that the metrics used to help manage the cyber security program and its organization met the needs of the cyber security program, of management, and of the cyber security program organization.

The cyber security officer knew that metrics charts tend to increase and seem to sometimes take on a life of their own. The cyber security officer was concerned that the time it took to track specific LOEs and projects using metrics was sometimes not cost-effective. By identifying the charts against their purpose in a matrix, the cyber security officer found that it was easy to analyze the metrics charts and their purpose.

PLANNING FOR NEXT YEAR

The cyber security officer had received the input from the cyber security program staff at the November meetings. Based on that input, the cyber security officer was prepared to write next year's cyber security program annual plan and update the cyber security program strategic and tactical

[2] Depending on the working environment of the corporation, the customer may be internal, e.g. management, external, e.g. corporation's customer(s), or both.

plans. However, to accomplish those tasks, the corporate plans must be received. After all, the cyber security program plans had to support the corporate plans.

The cyber security officer knew that the draft of the corporate plans would not be available until January. Therefore, the cyber security officer drafted the cyber security program annual plan and updated the cyber security program strategic and tactical plans based on information gathered through discussions with various levels of management involved in developing the corporate annual plan and updating the tactical and strategic plans.

The cyber security officer implemented the cyber security program plans on January 1, without waiting for the draft corporate plans. The cyber security officer did so to begin the much-needed LOE modifications and projects that were time-dependent. If they were not started right after the first of the year, their schedules might have to be slipped. The cyber security officer could not afford to do that and took the risk that the information gathered to date was accurate and that any changes at the corporate level would cause only minor adjustments to the cyber security program schedules—if any.

As part of the cyber security officer and cyber security program staff year-end analyses, a flowchart was developed, which would be used for briefings and also would let cyber security program staff see how their jobs supported the corporation.

The cyber security officer and staff also took all their risk management reports for the year and evaluated what was accomplished to correct cyber security program deficiencies and determine what needed to be done in the coming year to correct other deficiencies. These then were linked through a vulnerabilities–projects flowchart to identify "Strategic Direction: Cyber Security Program Projects to Address Vulnerabilities."

After completion of all the executive management briefing charts, and one week prior to briefing executive management, the cyber security officer gave the briefing, with additional analysis of the cyber security program and cyber security program functional accomplishments, to the cyber security program staff. The one-week interval was to ensure that the briefing was accurate and that the charts said what needed to be said. The cyber security program staff could evaluate the briefing and provide an avenue for constructive criticism. After all, the cyber security officer wanted, as a side issue, to show executive management the outstanding job done by the cyber security program staff during the past year, without saying so. In other words, let the briefing speak for that.

The CIO was invited to attend the cyber security officer's "expanded staff meeting" so that the CIO would not have any surprises at the executive management briefing. In addition, the cyber security officer wanted the CIO to attend to say a few words after the briefing, thanking the cyber security program staff for their fine work over the past year. The cyber security officer believed that such visibility of cyber security program staff to executive management would also boost morale, as they would see that their hard work was appreciated.

Upon the completion of the successful briefing, the cyber security officer scheduled another expanded staff meeting to be held on a Friday before the holidays and scheduled to last all day. At that expanded staff meeting, the cyber security officer had a catered lunch brought in as a special measure of thanks to the cyber security program staff. After all, if the cyber security program staff was not successful, the cyber security officer could not be successful.

QUESTIONS TO CONSIDER

Based on what you have read, consider the following questions and, as a cyber security officer, how you would reply to them:

- Do you have a process in place to conduct a formal year-end analysis of your cyber security program and cyber security program functions?
- If not, why not?
- If so, does it include cost–benefit analyses?
- Do you provide a "state-of-the-cyber security program" report of the corporate information environment at year's end?
- If so, is it briefed to executive management?
- Are "subreports" provided to each department head addressing specifically the status of the protection of their information environment?
- Do you involve your cyber security program staff in the year-end reviews, analyses, and planning?
- Do you reward your cyber security program staff for a job well done at year's end—by more than words?
- How would you go about conducting and improving on the process described in this chapter?

SUMMARY

Evaluations and analyses of the entire cyber security program and cyber security program organization help maintain a proactive and current protected information environment. The cyber security officer should remember the following points:

- It is a good idea to evaluate the entire cyber security program and cyber security program functions on an annual basis.
- The evaluation should include all projects and LOEs.
- Changes should be made by which value is added in terms of cost decreases, productivity gains, or time savings.
- Executive management should receive a clear, concise, business-oriented briefing on the state of the cyber security program and the corporation's current protected information environment at least on an annual basis.
- Metrics charts should be evaluated at least annually and then eliminated or modified as necessary.
- Link-analysis methodologies are useful in determining the success of a cyber security program.

CHAPTER 12

High-Technology Crimes Investigative Support

It was a common saying of Myson that men ought not to investigate things from words, but words from things; for that things are not made for the sake of words, but words for things

Diogenes Laërtius[1]

Contents

Chapter Objective

This chapter discusses the duties and responsibilities of a cyber security officer when it comes to providing service and support for deterring high-technology crimes, conducting noncompliance inquiries, assisting with computer forensics support, and dealing with law enforcement. A fictional case study scenario will be used.

INTRODUCTION

Not long after the cyber security officer took over the job as the cyber security officer, a meeting was held between the cyber security officer and the Director of Security. At that time, an agreement was reached as to the cyber security officer's duties and responsibilities and those of the Director of Security. The Director of Security agreed that the cyber security officer's duties and responsibilities would conflict with those of the Security Department if the cyber security officer conducted any type of investigation. The Director

---

[1] Diogenes Laërtius (third century?), Greek historian and biographer. *Lives of the Philosophers* "Myson" (third century?)—*Encarta® Book of Quotations*, © & (P) 1999, Microsoft Corporation. All rights reserved. Developed for Microsoft by Bloomsbury Publishing Plc.

of Security and the cyber security officer reached a compromise and agreed that any infractions of the cyber security program could be looked at by the cyber security officer as long as they related to noncompliance with the cyber security program, such as violation of automated information protection.

They both agreed to the following:

- To differentiate between an investigation and the cyber security officer's inquiries by having the cyber security officer call that function "non-compliance inquiries" (NCIs) and focusing on the cyber security program infractions;
- An information copy of each NCI was to be forwarded to the Director of Security;
- The cyber security officer would provide technical and forensics support to the Security staff, when requested;
- The Director of Security was the corporate focal point for law enforcement liaison activities, and any need to contact a law enforcement agency must be approved by the Director of Security, as well as others such as the Public Relations staff and the legal staff;
- In the event of the cyber security officer or members of the cyber security officer's staff were contacted for any requests by outside agencies for investigative assistance, that request must be coordinated with the Director of Security and others at the corporation;
- The cyber security officer's staff would provide in-house computer forensics training to the Security staff twice a year;
- The Security staff would provide in-house training in assets protection and basic investigative techniques, such as how to conduct an interview, to the cyber security program staff twice a year; and
- The Security staff would provide the budget for computer forensics software to be used in support of Security investigations, on an as-needed basis.

After completion of the discussion with the cyber security officer, the Director of Security knew that the cyber security officer and the cyber security program organization under the corporate information officer (CIO) were where they should be. The complicated job and headaches of the cyber security officer relative to NCIs and the entire cyber security program matter were something that the Director did not want to be responsible for.

DUTIES AND RESPONSIBILITIES OF A CYBER SECURITY OFFICER IN DETERRING HIGH-TECHNOLOGY CRIMES

Although investigations at the corporation are the purview of the Security staff, the cyber security officer and the Director of Security both knew that many such investigations, or NCIs, are high-technology based, such as those involving microprocessors (computers). Therefore, the cyber security officer's staff would be active in supporting Security's anticrime program as part of Security's assets protection program for the corporation. They both knew that the entire corporate assets protection program would be best served, that is, more effectively and efficiently accomplished, if the cyber security officer and the cyber security program functions reported to the Director of Security instead of to the CIO.

However, at the corporation, as at many corporations, the Director of Security really did not want that responsibility, and politically, it was a difficult sell to executive management. Furthermore, the cyber security officer position, which now reports to the CIO, who reports to the corporate executive officer (CEO), would be downgraded, as the cyber security officer would report to the Director of Security, who reports to the Vice President of Human Resources, who reports to Corporate Office Executive Vice President, who reports to the CEO. The position would also mean less prestige, less money, and the inability to exercise management authority at a sufficiently high level.

However, the Director and the cyber security officer agreed that a high-technology crime prevention program should be established at the corporation as part of the corporation's total assets protection program, which was led by the Director of Security. Therefore, the Director and the cyber security officer decided to establish a project to provide such a program and ensure that it interfaced with the cyber security program. It was also agreed that a long-term goal would be to integrate the crime prevention, cyber security, and corporate physical assets protection policies into an overall cyber security program under the authority of both the Director and the cyber security officer using a matrix management approach.

The Director and the cyber security officer agreed that the cyber security officer's approach to the cyber security program and its related functions was adaptable to the development of a high-technology crime prevention program. After that initial baseline was developed by the cyber security officer, the Director would integrate antitheft, antifraud, and other crime-related policies, procedures, and processes into the program and baseline them as part of the corporate assets protection program under the authority of the Director of Security.

They both agreed that the basis on which to build the corporation high-technology crime prevention program (HTCPP) was the development of a comprehensive high-technology crime prevention environment at lowest cost and least impact to the corporation.

The Director and the cyber security officer decided to categorize HTCPP investigations and NCIs so that they could more easily be analyzed and placed in a common database for analyses such as trends or vulnerabilities of processes that allow such incidents to occur. The cyber security officer agreed that the cyber security officer's organization would maintain the database, but the Security staff would have input and read access. However, modifications, maintenance, upgrades, and deletions would be controlled by the cyber security officer to ensure that the integrity of the database was maintained. The initial categories agreed to by the Director and cyber security officer were:

- Violations of laws (required by law to be reported to a government investigative agency);
- Unauthorized access;
- Computer fraud;
- Actions against users;
- Actions against systems;
- Interruption of services;
- Tampering;
- Misuse of information;
- Theft of services;
- Other crimes in which computers were used, such as:
  Money laundering
  Copyright violations
  Intellectual property thefts
  Mail fraud
  Wire fraud
  Pornography
- Other crimes
- Violators:
  Internal
  External

It was further agreed that these categories would be expanded based on analyses of investigations and noncompliance inquiries conducted to date.

ASSISTING WITH COMPUTER FORENSICS SUPPORT

Businesses, public agencies, and individuals increasingly rely on a wide range of computers, often linked together into networks, to accomplish their missions. Because computers have become ubiquitous, they are often a highly productive source of evidence and intelligence that may be obtained by properly trained and equipped cyber security program and investigative professionals. Equipping the specialists to be able to competently search corporation systems is essential. In many cases, a suspect will use a computer to plan the crime, keep diaries or records of acts in furtherance of a conspiracy, or communicate with confederates about details via electronic mail. In other schemes the computer will play a more central role, perhaps serving as the vehicle for an unauthorized intrusion into a larger system from which valuable files or other information is downloaded or tampered.

Surprisingly, even many sophisticated criminals who are highly computer literate remain unaware of the many software utilities available that allow evidence to be scavenged from various storage media, including hard drives, random access memory, and other locations in the operating system environments such as file slack, swap, and temporary files. Therefore, every investigation of crimes and unauthorized activities should now assume that some effort will be invested in examining computers and computer records to locate relevant evidence that will prove or disprove allegations or suspicions of wrongdoing.

Whether computers are themselves used as the tool to commit other crimes or merely contain documents, files, or messages discussing the scheme or plans, computers can provide a wealth of useful information if properly exploited. A major barrier to obtaining this potentially valuable evidence is the relative lack of knowledge of many corporate and law enforcement investigators concerning high-technology—computer technology. This lack of familiarity and experience hampers the computer forensics specialists' ability to conduct effective searches. When the crime scene itself is a computer or a network, or when the evidence related to the illegal or unauthorized activities is stored on a computer, there is no substitute for the use of "computer forensics" to gather relevant evidence.

Webster's Dictionary defines forensics as "belonging to, used in, or suitable to courts of judicature or to public discussion and debate."[2] Thus, *computer forensics* is a term that we define as describing the application of legally sufficient methods and protocols and techniques to gather, analyze, and preserve computer information relevant to a matter under investigation. Operationally, computer forensics encompasses using appropriate software tools and protocols to efficiently search the contents of magnetic and other storage media and identify relevant evidence in files, fragments of files, and deleted files, as well as file slack and swap space.

[2] *Merriam–Webster's Collegiate Dictionary.* G&C Merriam Company, 1973.

The cyber security officer and cyber security program NCI specialist assigned as the Security support focal points provided a computer forensics awareness briefing to the corporation Security staff. The briefing gave an introduction to computer forensics and also discussed the support the cyber security officer staff would give the Security staff. The cyber security officer agreed to support the corporation Security staff by providing high-technology-related forensic services.

DEALING WITH LAW ENFORCEMENT

There is a great lack of communication between cyber security professionals and law enforcement agencies. Neither profession seems to know what the other does or how they can assist each other. The cyber security officer works primarily in the internal world of the corporation. Therefore, cyber security officers usually are ignorant of what investigations are being conducted by law enforcement agencies, even in the cities where the corporation has facilities.

This lack of communication means that the cyber security officer, and more often than not the Director of Security, is not aware of local high-technology crime investigations that law enforcement are conducting. Thus, the cyber security officer is unaware of some high-technology crime techniques that would be useful to know about when developing internal defenses and controls to protect the corporation against such attacks.

When to Call for Help—and Whom.

If you or one of your staff is conducting an NCI or supporting a Security staff member conducting an investigation, there is more than one person who can be of assistance. These include:

- Victims,
- Witnesses,
- Consultants,
- Vendors,
- Suspects, and
- Law enforcement officers.

What if a high-technology crime is perpetrated at the corporation and the law requires a law enforcement agency to be contacted? What if management decides that they want the perpetrator caught and prosecuted? They will file a complaint with the appropriate law enforcement agency, and the cyber security officer has an important role to play to support prosecution of the criminal. Therefore, the cyber security officer should be aware of the processes involved. Some of the things to consider are:

- Does the corporation have a company policy as to when or when not to call an outside law enforcement agency?
- Are Legal staff involved?
- Are Human Resources personnel involved?
- Are Public Relations personnel involved?
- Is budget available to support the investigation and prosecution?
- Is the question "Can the corporation stand the bad publicity?" considered in making the decision?
- Is executive management prepared for the required commitment?
- Is reporting required by law?
- If yes, should it be reported?
- If no, should it be reported?

When deciding whether to call law enforcement, one should also consider:

- Costs versus benefits,
- Extent of loss,
- Probability of identifying and successfully prosecuting the suspect,
- Potential lawsuits that will follow if someone is identified (whether or not he or she is successfully prosecuted), and
- Time in supporting the criminal justice process: investigation through prosecution.

There are some advantages to calling law enforcement, who can:

- Perform acts that are illegal if done by citizens,
- Obtain search warrants to recover property,
- Gain access to related information, and
- Protect victims under some instances.

Some of the disadvantages of calling law enforcement for help include:

- Control over the incident is lost,
- It is probably costly and time-consuming, and
- The company must be willing to cooperate in the prosecution, during which the case may receive high visibility from news media, stockholders, and others.

If you decide to call in a law enforcement agency, corporate management must also decide which one to call and why—national, state, or local. No matter which one is called, corporate management must also be prepared to help them for an extended period of time. Initially, the cyber security officer in concert with the Director of Security should:

- Prepare a briefing for investigators;
- Ensure that executive management and the Legal Staff Director attend;
- Be sure of the facts;
- Brief in clear, concise, and nontechnical terms;
- Identify the loss, the basis for the amount, and the process used to determine that amount;
- Gather all related evidence;
- Know the related laws;
- Describe action taken to date;
- Explain the real-world impact of the alleged crime;
- Identify and determine if any victims will cooperate;
- Explain what assistance they can provide.
  If the incident is to be handled internally:
- What is the objective?
- What is the plan to accomplish that objective?
- What expertise is available to help?
- What is the cost?
- What are the consequences?
- What can be done to be sure it doesn't happen again?

QUESTIONS TO CONSIDER

Based on what you have read, consider the following questions and how you would reply to them:

- Do you think the cyber security officer's responsibilities should include conducting any type of investigation or inquiry?
- If so, why?
- If not, why not?
- Do you think it is the job and professional responsibility of a cyber security officer and staff to support internal and external investigations by providing forensics support?
- If so, what limitations would you set on that support?
- As a cyber security officer, do you have a policy, plan, process, and procedure in place as to when and how you would support an internal or external investigation?
- If so, are they current?
- Have they been coordinated with applicable internal customers, such as auditors and Security staff?

SUMMARY

Usually, a security department's staff is not trained to conduct high-technology investigations, whereas the cyber security officer and staff are in the best position to support the security department or an outside law enforcement agency in conducting their investigations. An agreement should be worked out between the Director of Security and the cyber security officer as to who has what authority for investigations relevant to violations of corporate policies as well as those that would also be a criminal offense.

Corporations must have current policies detailing when an outside law enforcement agency should be called and when a matter identified as a violation of law, criminal or civil, should be investigated internally. It is absolutely mandatory that such decision not be made by the cyber security officer, but by the executive management supported by the Legal staff, Public Relations staff, and Human Resources staff. If a law enforcement agency is contacted, the corporation must be prepared for usually many months of support to the investigative agency as well as bad publicity.

High-technology crime investigations and NCIs are based on basic investigative techniques and answering the questions of who, how, where, when, why, and what.

High-technology criminals are beginning to install more sophisticated security systems, including encryption systems. Such devices will require very sophisticated devices and expertise to access them. Some have focused on methods of destroying evidence if law enforcement or investigators tamper with the system.

The challenges to high-technology crime investigators and computer forensics specialists are many and quickly increasing. Only through constant training will investigators and cyber security staff members have any hope at all of keeping up with these changes, including searching media for evidence.

Keys to successful searches include knowing the technology, having a plan, using common sense, and using a specialist who is an expert in the technology and accompanying software to be searched.

The Global, Professional, and Personal Challenges of a Cyber Security Officer

In the first two sections of this book, you were introduced to the internal and external world of the cyber security officer. The third and last section of this book discusses the major challenges for the cyber security officer, now and into the future. The most challenging threat to the cyber security officer—and a growing threat—is that of information warfare (IW), including terrorism. Although various types of IW have been around since someone first used the term *information,* because of high technology that threat is rapidly growing. Therefore, Section III begins with an introduction and overview of IW.

The IW chapter is followed by a chapter on the cyber security officer and his or her responsibilities related to ethical conduct, privacy, and liability issues. This chapter is considered important since such issues and being a cyber security officer professional go hand in hand.

The final chapter of this book looks into the future and discusses the challenges and risks the cyber security officer will face in the twenty-first century.

CHAPTER 13

Introduction to Global Information Warfare

War does not determine who is right—only who is left

Bertrand Russell

Contents

This chapter provides an introduction and discussion of global information warfare (IW). As a professional cyber security officer you may not know it as or call it information warfare on a global scale, but we certainly are in a cyber war. Furthermore, if you are to protect the government agency or corporate information, systems, and networks that are your part of the global or national information infrastructure, you better start thinking and acting as if you were in a war because, like it or not, you are.

It begins with a fictional scenario that soon can become all too real—some of it already has occurred. Some aspects of IW attacks have already been tested by government agencies, terrorists, hackers, organized crime members, and the general criminal out to get rich at our expense, through either theft or blackmail, or to deny their adversary the ability to function.

This fictional scenario is presented as part of an introduction to global IW so that the reader can see what devastation can be caused by global IW, global because it can happen from anywhere to anywhere. It is something that the global IW defender must consider when addressing global IW issues.

Let's look at the possibilities of a worst-case IW attack scenario on the United States.

THE POSSIBILITIES

At first, some thought it was a massive solar eruption worse than that of 1998, since communications, including microwave and cell phone towers, were made inoperable. Then it was theorized as a software glitch similar to the scare of the 2000 millennium bug years earlier. Then, all too soon, the real reason for the power loss and its domino effect became clear—a global IW attack on a massive scale.

It first started on Christmas Eve in the United States, for they knew only minimal staffing would be in place, many on vacation and out of the communication loop, those being vital to getting systems up and running again. They unleashed it late at night to cause the most havoc; it started in the Northwest, in the Seattle area, moved south to Portland, San Francisco, and Los Angeles, and at the same time moved East. The power went out, first on the western grids, shutting down power station after power station, blackening each neighborhood, each town, each city, from the Pacific Ocean moving slowly eastward like a swarm of locusts to the Atlantic Ocean, into parts of Canada and Mexico that were unfortunate enough to share America's power grids. They called the attack program "Locust Swarm."

America's energy grid slowly went down, and for those who had contingency plans that included generators, they bought them more time, but time was not on their side. Eventually, the gas-powered generators ran out of gas. Gas was not forthcoming as electrical power was out from gas stations to oil refineries and the oil pipes leading to them had no power to move the oil. Gas pumps were closed, panic ensued. The alarm systems in stores, banks, and everywhere else in the country ceased operation.

Local power companies found that some transformers had exploded, taking days to months to find replacements as so many were dead; some estimated it would take as long as six months to replace many of them, electricity being crucial to powering technology, and technology running everything. Whether they used solar cells, windmills, coal, natural gas, or diesel fuel, it didn't matter as all were controlled and run by computers. Even the monitoring systems were run by technology and when false readings were sent through them, they also helped cause the chaos and the overloads that ensued. Systems monitoring nuclear facilities to dams were affected.

Just before the rolling blackout hit an area, there were a number of Twitter broadcasts—"Power is out, bank alarms are out, store alarms are out, come take your share of the bounty." When the miscreants of each area where power failed got the message, they joined their friends and soon police and fire fighters were occupied with emergencies. Mobs broke into any place that offered them money, furniture, televisions, and other goods free for the taking, setting fire as they went. They acted with impunity as even CCTV cameras were out.

Fire departments were overwhelmed and fire trucks eventually ran out of gas and could not respond. The same thing applied to police departments, even the National Guard and other military facilities.

Medical equipment in hospitals vital to keeping people alive ceased to operate as generators failed, and thousands of patients across the country died, many on the operating tables.

Instead of aircraft losing communications with the towers, the Locusts that had infected the country did not shut down the control towers as rapidly. No one thought to ask why until it was too late. And it was too late when the Locusts were uploaded to aircraft and wormed their way into the computer systems changing the instrumentation settings on the aircraft without the knowledge of the flight crews, on both commercial and military aircraft.

Aircraft pilots had learned to fly using computers and their instruments. Long gone were the pilots who "flew by the seat of their pants," programming errors causing planes to crash and thousands to die. Some that were running out of fuel tried landing but relied on false instrument readings and burned up on runways, stopping other aircraft from trying to land. While some made it down safely, others crashed and burned in adjacent fields and taxiways. The skies glowed with the fires of crashed aircraft, bodies strewn everywhere. Some survived for a while but the emergency teams were overwhelmed and many died.

The Locusts program wormed its way into automated home systems. It was the middle of winter and heaters were turned off and air conditioners turned on. Many vulnerable people in the northern region of the nation froze to death. And those in nursing homes and animals in shelters could not be cared for.

Water pumping stations ceased operation, sewer systems failed. So when water was needed the most, bottled water started flying off store shelves until it ran out. People turning on their water faucets found nothing but stinking, brown water coming out, and then not even that.

All modern nations reliant on technology are vulnerable to such attacks. Of course there are those who say it can't happen. Really?

INTRODUCTION TO WARFARE

Wars have been fought ever since there were human beings around who did not agree with one another. These conflicts continue to this day, with no end in sight. The use of information in warfare is nothing new. Those who had the best information the fastest and were able to correctly act on it the soonest were usually the victors in battles.

Is it any wonder that since we are now in the Information Age we should also have information warfare? Because we now look at almost everything on a global scale, it should also not be surprising that information warfare is viewed on a global scale. Information warfare is today's much-talked-about type of warfare. A search of the Internet on the topic using Google.com disclosed that in 2002 there were 472,000 hits but in 2014 there were 27,700,000 hits. Information warfare is becoming an integral, digital part of warfare of all types in the modern era.

FOUR GENERATIONS OF WARFARE

Military historians and professionals over the years have discussed the various generations of warfare. Some believe there are four generations of warfare to date:[1]

- First-generation warfare started with the rise of the nation-state and included a top-down military structure, limited weapons, and armies made up of serfs. It ended in the early nineteenth century about the time of the Napoleonic Wars.

[1] Taken from a Gannett News Service article, September 27, 2001.

- Second-generation warfare began about 1860 in the United States with its Civil War. This generation of warfare included artillery, machine guns, mass weapons development, and logistics supported by trains. This generation of warfare ended sometime after World War I.
- The beginning of the third generation of warfare is attributed to the Germans in World War II, in which "shock-maneuver" tactics were used.
- In 1989, the U.S. *Marine Corps Gazette*[2] contained an article by several military personnel. The article, entitled "Changing the Face of War: Into the Fourth Generation," discussed the fourth-generation battlefield, where it is likely that it will include the *"whole of the enemy's society ....* The distinction between civilian and military may disappear .... Television news may become a more powerful operational weapon than armored divisions." If one were to have any doubts about the accuracy of that statement, one just has to remember the U.S. television news showing a dead American military man's body being dragged through the streets of Mogadishu. The loss of national will can be closely correlated with how quickly the United States departed that country. This, too, is part of the information warfare campaigns being waged on a worldwide scale.

One can argue that information warfare has existed in all generations of warfare and included spying, observation balloons, breaking enemy codes, and many other functions and activities. True, information warfare is as old as humans, but many aspects as to how it is being applied in our information-dependent, information-based world are new.

INTRODUCTION TO GLOBAL INFORMATION WARFARE

In the early 1990s, several people in the U.S. Department of Defense (DoD) articulated a unique form of warfare termed "Information Warfare." The Chinese say they were developing IW concepts in the late 1980s. Who is correct? Does it matter? The areas embraced by IW have been developed over the centuries and millennia and have been a normal part of human activities from humankind's beginning. What is unique about IW is that it is the first instantiation of trying to tie together all the areas that make up the information environment (IE). The IE runs through every part of your country, organization, and personal life. At the present time, there is no cookbook recipe to do the extremely complex task of bringing together all the areas.

---

[2] Network World, August 10, 1998.

What is IW? The general working definition of IW employed in this book is as follows: IW is a coherent and synchronized blending of physical and virtual actions to have countries, organizations, and individuals perform, or not perform, actions so that your goals and objectives are attained and maintained, while simultaneously preventing competitors from doing the same to you. Clearly, this embraces much more than attacking computers with malicious code. The litmus test is this: if information is used to perpetrate an act that was done to influence another to take or not take actions beneficial to the attacker, then it can be considered IW.

The definition is intentionally broad, embracing organizational levels, people, and capabilities. It allows room for governments, cartels, corporations, hacktivists, terrorists, other groups, and individuals to have a part. It is up to each enlightened enterprise to tailor the definition to fit its needs. This should not be a definition of convenience, to "check the box."

You are asked, and many times forced by government and businesses, to depend on the Internet; the Internet that is home to hackers, crackers, phreakers, hacktivists, script kiddies, Net espionage (network-enabled espionage), and information warriors; the Internet that is home to worms, Trojan horses, software bugs, hardware glitches, distributed denial-of-service (DDoS) attacks, viruses, and various forms of malware. All this, and the Internet is only a portion of the areas that IW addresses. Although the Internet touches many critical infrastructures, and these in turn affect the many IEs with which you interface, most of the IW areas were around before the Internet.

As "competition" is analogous to "enemy" or "adversary," other business–military analogies can be made with profit, shareholder value, competitive edge, and industry rank to achieve brand recognition, customer loyalty, exertion of power, influence, and market share. A business leader or military leader must train and equip forces; gather intelligence; assemble, deploy, and employ forces at decisive places and times; sustain them; form coalitions with other businesses and nation-states; and be successful. There are many physical and virtual world parallels, as can be seen in the following headline: *"Cisco to use SNA as weapon against competition …. Cisco believes its experience in melding SNA and IP internet works can be used as a weapon in the company's battle with Lucent and Nortel for leadership in converging voice, video, and data over IP networks."*[2]

Purists will focus on warfare as a state of affairs that must be declared by a government and can be conducted only by a government. But consider guerrilla warfare, economic warfare (one country "forcing" another country to spend itself into bankruptcy, as allegedly the United States did to the

Soviet Union), or a company adjusting prices to damage its competition (e.g., taking a long time horizon to use volume and time to adjust prices downward). "Conflict" or "that's business" does not carry the same sound of ultimate struggle as referring to business as "war." Clausewitz stated, "*War is an extension of politics.*" By analogy, because business is the implementation of a country's laws, economic policy, and values, business is also an extension of politics.

In a free market economy, competition is central to business strategy to win customers and market share. Competition, like war, is a struggle for a winning position. The marketplace can then be referred to analogously as a battlefield with winners and losers. It follows that business is analogous to war. Therefore, using military phraseology in a business context is appropriate. In fact, one just has to remember September 11, 2001, and New York's World Trade Centers to see that in today's world, warfare is waged on many levels by various adversaries against various targets. These targets can be nation-states, their governments, groups, businesses, or individuals. The tools will be any that can be applied for attackers to successfully attain their goals.

The counterargument is that some insurance companies' contracts state that if a loss is due to an act of terrorism or war, they will not pay for damages. In the United States, attacks on computers by default are criminal acts and are thus in the purview of law enforcement. Often, after an investigation determines that the criminal act is a national security issue, the intelligence agencies and other government organizations will take the lead.

There are adversaries, winners, and losers. All the writing on IW focuses on weaknesses, defenses, and losses. Despite the gloomy forecasts by government officials and the media, IW is also about strengths, offenses, and gains. These positive features are within the grasp of any government or business organization with a desire to seize and maintain a competitive advantage— to be a winner on the IW battlefield. Importantly, unlike some of today's physical wars and those of the past, without a great deal of resources, a small nation, for example, North Korea, has the power to successfully attack global and a nation's business, as well as governments.

What possible application can IW have outside specialized military circles? From a practical viewpoint, how does IW shorten decision cycle times, raise revenue, lower or avoid costs, and improve performance? If IW cannot improve effectiveness or efficiency, or bring about innovation, why do it? IW does do these things and ought to be the approach used rather than the top management fads that come and go, leaving businesses worse off for trying them. The purpose of IW is to gain power and influence over others.

Power and influence are at the heart of all such relationships. Because IW requires effort, the effort needs to resolve into some aspect of power, such as profit or economic or military domination on the battlefield or in the marketplace.

INFORMATION WARFARE WILL HIT YOU IN YOUR POCKETBOOK

There have been some events that were not expected. Hannibal crossed the Alps. Clay defeated Liston for the heavyweight boxing title. CD Universe did not think crackers would break into its systems. Buy.com did not expect a DDoS attack, nor did Sony, Target, or victims too numerous to mention. It seems new websites are discovered and hacked within minutes of being on the Internet. One honey pot project was attacked within 5 min. It will happen: one day your IE defenses are going to be beaten. When they go down, your revenues and profits will go down. The Internet Age has again proven the adage that "time is money." Suppose a company has US$1 billion in electronic and mobile-commerce revenue. That equates to $2,739,726 per day, $114,155 per hour, $1903 per minute, and $32 per second.[3] How long can your business afford to be adversely affected by an attack? In other words, what are the risks and consequences you are willing to accept?

In a portent of crippling events to come, since early 2000 there have been thousands of automated computer-based distributed attacks, extortion attempts for tens and hundreds of millions of dollars, and posting on the Internet of millions of supposedly protected credit card details and other private information. Apparently, the laws and court sentences for computer crimes lack deterrent value. Of course, if hardware and software products, communications systems, e-commerce sites, and other information technology (IT) components were designed with security in mind, we would not have this predicament—something that even Bill Gates of Microsoft finally realized.

In many cases, the dollar loss is secondary to the loss of trust. Banks and insurance companies especially feel customers' wrath. When customers believe their trust has been compromised, they vote with their pocketbooks and take their business elsewhere. That is when revenues and profits decline,

---

[3] "If Most of Your Revenue Is from E-Commerce, then Cyber Insurance Makes Sense," Perry Luzwick, "Surviving Information Warfare" column, *Computer Fraud and Security*, a Reed-Elsevier publication, March 2001.

which leads to a decline in the stock price, which in the not too distant future will lead to shareholder lawsuits for negligence and other claims.

IW conjures up many images: computers, networks, and telecommunications-savvy experts in the military and intelligence communities, corporate espionage, and pale 14-year-old looking like they could be the next door neighbor's kids—or yours. Dire prognostications about how an "electronic Pearl Harbor" threatens national security and the daily media coverage of viruses and denial-of-service attacks interchangeably using phrases such as information warfare, cyber warfare, and cyber terrorism may make IW seem distant and surreal.

Some of the attacks, premeditated or unintentional, resulted in billions of dollars in damages. Computer emergency response teams and law enforcement agencies stress protection and defense of information, information infrastructure, and information-based processes to ward off malicious attacks. What do these and many other aspects of operating in the IE have to do with managing a government organization or running a business? For businesses, this may mean new business generation, cost avoidance, profit, customer retention, market leadership, and positive power public perception. For nation-states, this may be economic, political, or military power, influence, or defeat.

The once high-profile events such as the Morris worm and Citibank's $400,000 loss ($10 million was stolen, and all but $400,000 allegedly recovered) should have been sufficient warning shots across the bow that a different approach was needed. However, such attacks of "long ago," in technology terms, pale in comparison to the number, sophistication, and scale of losses of today's attacks.

Note: Many of us since the late 1980s and into the 1990s forward have been warning of the potential for IW attacks and what should be done to prepare for them. Of course, as usual when it comes to security, management in businesses and in government agencies ignored our warnings and are now reaping the results. We predict the worse is yet to come.

The much-needed security fixes are years away as defenses continue to lag behind the attackers in sophistication. However, there are pockets of government-sponsored sophisticated attacks; some may even be called "defensive attacks" or preemptive strikes against an adversary. Demand is low because the general public appears to be uninterested in cracker exploits, made indifferent by the almost daily news stories. Said differently, the public has come to expect identify thefts, theft of their credit cards, and such. However, since corporations are held liable in most cases, and credit card corporations absorb the losses of their customers, the general public remains complacent in general but personally outraged only when it is their own identity or financial instruments that have been compromised.

BUSINESS IS WAR

An advertising campaign can be considered a subset of an IW campaign. Here is a perhaps not so hypothetical example. Taking grocery store shelf space, owing to product or packaging redesign, from a competitor is notionally no different from denying use of a radar or a seaport to the enemy. Instead of cereal boxes that stood and poured vertically, what if they stood horizontally and had spouts for pouring (besides, vertical boxes are prone to tipping)? This would result in more shelf space needed for the same amount of cereal boxes. The packaging will carry a message that conveys "new" and "improved." The boxes will be at eye level—easy for the consumer to spot. In-store advertising will attempt to vector shoppers to the cereal aisle. Newspaper and magazine advertising will attempt to convince customers to try the "new" and "improved" product, and coupons will be used as further enticement. There may even be an in-store demonstration. Because there is limited shelf space and if the cereal company has bargaining power, other cereals have to lose space. Lost space, it is hoped, then translates to lost product sales, which in turn leads to reduced revenue and profits as well as a lower stock price.

In business, the IW target can be the customer, the competition, or another entity. The purpose of the IW campaign is to have the competitor take action that will result in increased profits for your company. In the best of all outcomes, your revenues go up and the competitors' revenues decline. Even if your sales were constant, just having less space to sell should make competitors' sales decline, so your industry ranking will improve. What will the competition do? Redesign packaging? Alter ingredients? Lower the product's price? Counter with coupons? Have a television campaign employing a doctor to extol the health benefits of their cereal? Play hardball with the supermarket chain? A combination? Nothing, taking a wait-and-see approach? This is physical and virtual IW at the corporate level. It embraces the media, perception management, physical operations, intelligence collection, and more.

This is no different from one country observing another and bringing to bear economic, diplomatic, and military means. These means may include very advanced open source searches and analyses and covert means involving manipulation of the radio frequency (RF) spectrum. From a business perspective, operations, marketing, public relations, manufacturing, finance, transportation, and other parts of the company must operate in a synchronized and coherent fashion. The competition must be monitored, intelligence collected so the company can be in position to agilely and effectively respond to any countermoves.

IW BROADLY ENCOMPASSES MANY LEVELS AND FUNCTIONS

IW is not the sole purview of a modern, technology-based, and dependent government; otherwise, only the wealthy countries could practice it. A narrow interpretation of IW flies in the face of reality. Other than a unique set of capabilities that are based on unlimited deep pockets and specialized espionage capabilities, more brainpower and, perhaps, more capabilities reside external to a government. Any organization, and even individuals, can conduct offensive and defensive IW. It is about seizing control of perceptions, physical structures, and virtual assets. Seizing control can be done from both offensive and defensive positions. That puts any organization squarely in control of its destiny. Those that are unenlightened will never perform at or near the top of the pack and may well go out of existence. Those that embrace IW have a much better chance of surviving and reaping the rewards.

The military, intelligence community, and law enforcement generally do not embrace this perspective. Why? They have capabilities that are highly classified. If used by industry, then "all hell would break loose." Certainly, there are unique offensive and defensive capabilities that can be developed only by the government because of their high risk of failure and the necessary funding. However, there has been an explosion of brainpower with regard to physical and virtual capabilities. The majority of brainpower in genetics, robotics, nanotechnology, microelectromagnetic systems, and hydrogen technologies resides outside the military, intelligence community, and law enforcement. What is to prevent these capabilities from falling into the hands of nation-states, individuals, businesses, and organizations that wish to perpetrate some form of hostile behavior? Absolutely nothing.

WHAT IW IS ... AND IS NOT

Information warfare is not about a one-time silver bullet for a quick fix and looking good on a quarterly financial report. IW is not restricted to using computers to attack other computers. It is not confined to the cyber realm. "Virtual" means electronic, RF, and photonic manipulation. Organizations need to use the capabilities within the virtual and physical domains in a manner that optimizes what they wish to do. The best approach for IW, as it should be with a business or government organization, is to conduct physical and virtual operations in a synchronized and coherent fashion. Easier said than done. Goddard's experiments contributed to manned space flight—four decades later. As virtual capabilities become more practical for the government, military, and business, the greater their importance becomes in operations. Fifteen years ago, laptops, mobile phones, and personal digital assistants—remember them?—were bulky, seldom more capable than their traditional counterparts, and much more expensive. For some people, the time-saving and cost-reducing capabilities of the gadgets borders on technological cocaine, and these people almost cannot function without their gadgets. Some business and government organizations have bought into technology so much so that their operations can truly be termed "network-centric business." What better way to counter this than with IW? Not many years from now, IW will be mainstream, and those who do not participate will fail.

Much hype surrounds hacker exploits and computer-based viruses. Most hacker, cracker, and phreaker exploits and viruses qualify as falling within IW, albeit at the low end of the spectrum, because there is an attempt to influence, either directly or indirectly, others to take an action. Approaches range from altruistic ("I found a hole in the software. Develop a patch for it.") to anger ("I will make them miserable for firing me.") to social awareness ("Stop drug research on animals.") to criminal ("Here is how to defeat the fraud control and computer security systems of fill-in-the-blank corporation as all are vulnerable, more or less."). Almost all of the events and attacks fall into the realm of theft, extortion, fraud, and related criminal behavior. Measures must be employed to protect and defend corporate and government systems because individual losses have already been in the tens and hundreds of millions of dollars.

Even if you have taken all the appropriate measures to protect and secure your physical and virtual assets, much falls outside your span of control: protected and secured power, finance, communications, transportation, water, and continuity of government infrastructures; security-rich and bug-free commercial off-the-shelf (COTS) software; and the creativity of crackers and phreakers to find new vulnerabilities in technology to exploit. Also, you probably cannot control your business partners', customers', financial stakeholders', and suppliers' IEs that are connected to yours. If you are an Internet-based company, then electronic and mobile-commerce accounts for the majority of your revenue. Any disruption and your customers will go to your competitors. If you are a traditional bricks-and-mortar company expanding into the Internet to enhance your customers' ability to do business with you, business interruptions and disclosure of customer data will taint your reputation and credibility. Business interruption can be costly on many levels.[4]

When properly employed, IW is an agile capability that can be tailored to any situation. It can bring a multitude of functions to bear. It can be implemented in both the physical and the virtual worlds. Central to IW is how it is used to influence decision-makers. Magazines, radio, television, newspapers, leaflets, e-mail, web pages, social media, and other forms of media can all be used as a vehicle to deliver IW.

IW should not be restricted to a small cadre. Certainly only a few people should know about the sensitive details that will make or break the execution of the IW plan. All parts of an enterprise, not just an organization, need to be linked for the most effective implementation of IW. Any organization has a finite portion of resources. Partnerships, alliances, consortia, and other relationships can serve to expand an organization's capabilities.

Proper use of information is central to profitable business and successful military operations. IW is used to provide your organization a competitive advantage while limiting the competition's capability to reduce your advantage and increase their own. Effective IW is not possible without control of your information environment.

An IE is an interrelated set of information, information infrastructure, and information-based processes. Data include the measurements used as a basis for reasoning, discussion, or calculation. Data are raw input. Information applies to facts told, read, or communicated that may be unorganized and even unrelated. Information is the meaning assigned to data. Knowledge is an organized body of information. It is the comprehension and understanding consequent to having acquired and organized a body of facts. Information as used here means data, information, and knowledge. No doubt horrific to purists, there is no one good word in the English language that embraces all three concepts together. All three processes exist within any organization. At any given time, one of the processes will be of greater value than the others. Your competition wants your information, so do not believe that "gentlemen don't read other gentlemen's mail."

---

[4] See footnote 3.

Information moves across information infrastructures in support of information-based processes. The information infrastructure is the media within which we display, store, process, and transmit information. Examples are people, computers, fiber-optic cable, lasers, telephones, and satellites. Examples of information-based processes are the established ways to obtain and exchange information. This includes people to people (e.g., telephone conversations and office meetings), electronic commerce/electronic data interchange, data mining, batch processing, and surfing the web. Attacking (i.e., denying, altering, or destroying) one or more IE components can result in the loss of tens of millions of dollars in profit or in degraded national security and can be more effective than physical destruction. Degrade or destroy any one of the components and, like a three-legged stool, the IE will eventually collapse.[5]

BEING PREPARED-BAD THINGS WILL HAPPEN

Bad things happen, such as floods, hurricanes, and earthquakes; power surges and sags; and fires. Disgruntled employees can steal, manipulate, or destroy information. Crackers work their way through the electronic sieve of protection mechanisms (e.g., firewalls and intrusion detection devices) into information assets.

Sound disaster recovery, business continuity, and contingency operating plans are essential. For every minute information systems are not up and fully running, revenues, profits, and shareholder value are being lost. The last thing a general counsel needs is a lawsuit from unhappy shareholders who are suing for millions because the corporation did not follow best practices to protect information. One problem is that COTS hardware and software are very difficult to protect. Another concern is that firewalls, intrusion detection devices, and passwords are not enough. The state-of-the-art in information assurance is against script kiddies and moderately skilled hackers. What about the competition, drug cartels, and hostile nation-states that are significantly better funded? There is no firewall or intrusion detection device on the market that cannot be penetrated or bypassed. Password dictionaries can cover almost any entire language, and there are very specific dictionaries (e.g., sports, Star Trek, or historic dates and events).

[5] "What's a Pound of Your Information Worth? Constructs for Collaboration and Consistency," Perry Luzwick, American Bar Association, Standing Committee on Law and National Security, *National Security Law Report*, August 1999.

THE POSSIBLE BREAKDOWNS IN AN INFORMATION ENVIRONMENT

IEs exist internal and external to an organization. An IE is tailorable so it can support many actors. An IE can consist of a corporation, its customers, and the government. Another IE can be a military, its allies and coalition partners, and the government. Whatever comprises a specific IE, the important fact remains: if its elements are not protected and secured, the consequences can range from irritants to catastrophes.

An organization has employees. These employees deliver products, services, and processes to the organization and its customers. To keep the organization running, suppliers deliver products, services, and processes. Financial stakeholders—venture capitalists, banks, stockholders, and others—provide capital. The public has a positive, neutral, or negative view of the organization. Strategic teaming partners provide physical, financial, cerebral, and other capabilities. Every entity with which the organization is linked has its own IE. IEs are connected to, and are interdependent on, other IEs.

GOING BEYOND THREE BLIND MEN DESCRIBING AN ELEPHANT: INFORMATION WARFARE TERMS OF REFERENCE

IW cuts across national borders, educational background, and cultural views. To ensure a consistent understanding during this discussion, working definitions of IW and many supporting terms are offered. This does not preclude national interpretations and certainly does not attempt to rationalize, harmonize, and normalize definitions. Common terms of reference (TOR) permit a shared understanding, as well as a point of departure for applying the TOR within specific organizations.

George Santayana said, "*Those who ignore the lessons of history are condemned to repeat them.*"

Here is an example of how parochialism caused a disaster.

In August and October of 1943, the Allies launched air raids against Schweinfurt with disastrous consequences—for the Allies. In the August raid, of 600 planes, 60 were lost along with 600 crewmen. Why? There was no long-range fighter escort. Why? In the 1920s and 1930s, resources were allocated for strategic bombardment over pursuit. Why? General Emilio Douhet and others postulated that air power alone could win wars by striking the enemy's strategic centers. Lesson learned: The decisions made in the 1920s and 1930s led to the wrong tactical employment a decade later. We must not make the same mistake with IW. If we do, national security, economic viability, and corporate capabilities will be lost.

It seems that there are as many definitions of IW and related topics as there are people. It is reminiscent of three blind men describing an elephant by touching the animal's various parts. One blind man said, "An elephant is a reptile and is thin and long," as he was touching the tail. Touching the tusks, another blind man said, "An elephant is like a big fish with its smooth and pointed body." The third blind man said, "An elephant resembles a large leaf with a hole in the middle" because he was touching the ears. None of them could extrapolate their interpretations to a real elephant. Similarly, what one sees is not necessarily what one gets. "Ques-que c'est?" will be mispronounced if one does not have a basic understanding of French diction. So, too, is it with terms used to describe various practices in the information realm.

Although the names are initially obtuse to those who do not work in those areas, these information practices have been a normal evolution in communications and computers and also the dark-side move/counter-move/counter-countermove "cool war." There are many other variations. Little wonder the terms are understood by few people and erroneously used interchangeably. Few understand the difference between a hacker, a cracker, and a phreaker, much less a white-hat hacker.

In some cases, more terminology only detracts. "Cyber" is too limiting. It is as if, rather than pushing through difficult points to achieve philosophical insights and technical understanding, people create terms to differentiate themselves without knowing what they are doing.

Information and knowledge are now in vogue. We are in the Information Age and rapidly transitioning into the Knowledge Age. Acquiring the right data, deriving good information, and applying it to make sound decisions to positively affect the bottom line are essential. Search engines have made finding information on the Internet very simple. Witness, during the past at least 40 years, the explosion of terminology related to the protection of information and using information for national security purposes. The most important point is to understand the meaning of these terms and what the different functions can—and cannot—do to make an informed decision whether to commit resources (i.e., people, money, and time).

Many countries have developed definitions. IW, information assurance, information operations, information superiority, information dominance, and other constructs popular in the U.S. military are part of the revolution in military affairs and in security affairs. Government organizations and businesses have developed additional terms, and some do not agree with the national version. So there can be a point of departure for this discussion, definitions accepted by many are put forth. In some cases, working definitions will be used. The following definitions are from the U.S. DoD *Dictionary of Military and Associated Terms*:[6]

Command and control warfare (C2W): The integrated use of operations security, military deception, psychological operations, electronic warfare, and physical destruction, mutually supported by intelligence, to deny information to, influence, degrade, or destroy adversary command and control capabilities, while protecting friendly command and control capabilities against such actions. C2W is an application of information warfare in military operations and is a subset of information warfare. C2W applies across the range of military operations and all levels of conflict. C2W is both offensive and defensive.

Defense in depth: The siting of mutually supporting defense positions designed to absorb and progressively weaken attack, to prevent initial observations of the whole position by the enemy, and to allow the commander to maneuver the reserve.

Information: Facts, data, or instructions in any medium or form. The meaning that a human assigns to data by means of the known conventions used in their representation. Here are some "oldies but goodies" terms that are still valid today as they describe the IW-related environment:

- *Information assurance*: Information operations that protect and defend information and information systems by ensuring their availability, integrity, authenticity, confidentiality, and nonrepudiation. This includes providing for restoration of information systems by incorporating protection, detection, and reaction capabilities.
- *Information-based processes*: Processes that collect, analyze, and disseminate information using any medium or form. These processes may be stand-alone processes or subprocesses that, taken together, comprise a larger system or systems of processes.
- *Information environment*: The aggregate of individuals, organizations, or systems that collect, process, or disseminate information; also included is the information itself.
- *Information security*: The protection of information and information systems against unauthorized access or modification of information, whether in storage, processing, or transit, and against denial-of-service to

---

[6] Department of Defense *Dictionary of Military and Associated Terms*, April 12, 2001.

authorized users. Information security includes those measures necessary to detect, document, and counter such threats. Information security is composed of computer security and communications security. Also called INFOSEC or cyber security.

An older definition focused on only physical protections: locks, alarms, safes, marking of documents, and similar physical world capabilities.

• *Information system:* The entire infrastructure, organization, personnel, and components that collect, process, store, transmit, process, display, disseminate, and act on information.

• *Information warfare:* Information operations conducted during time of crisis or conflict to achieve or promote specific objectives over a specific adversary or adversaries.

We can expand on this because of the definition of IW. What is IW? It is more than computer network attack and defense. That almost everyone agrees on. But what else is encompassed by IW? Heated debates go on today about what IW should embrace and accomplish. IW is an umbrella concept embracing many disciplines. IW is most effective when performed in a synchronized and coherent fashion. That is why knowledge management (KM) complements it so well. All components of an organization, as well as across the enterprise, need to be included in an IW action plan.

The good news is that IW embraces the marketing, public relations, counterintelligence, and other functions you now perform. IW is not these functions renamed. They continue to be run by the subject matter experts. IW is the coherent application and synchronized approach of these functions. What is needed are experts who, by analogy, are conductors of the orchestra. They know where the expertise resides within the organization, understand what the functions can and cannot do, and bring them to bear for optimum performance. At present, only the military in a few countries comes close to understanding the relationships and functions of linking the physical domain with the virtual realm and has begun policy development and allocation of resources. For the most part the equivalent does not exist in industry—yet.

The purpose of IW is to control or influence a decision-maker's actions. An area of control can be directly manipulated, whereas an area of influence can be only indirectly manipulated. Control and influence are the essence of power. From a business perspective, sector and industry-leading market share and profit are the results of proper IW execution.

What would make a decision-maker act or not act? Perhaps false or misleading information, an analysis of open source information, documents mysteriously acquired, or intelligence from an employee hired away from the competition. IW at the corporate level manifests itself in marketing, public relations, legal, research and development, manufacturing, and other functions. With the introduction of commercial high-resolution satellite photography, some companies have altered their delivery and shipment schedules, to include using empty rail cars and semitrailers to mask inventory, production capability, and customer quantities. IW is a full spectrum of capabilities. Ingredients are carefully selected and tailored to each case.

IW can be conducted without using physical destruction. Both military psychological operations and commercial advertising depend heavily on psychology and sociology, the study of individual and group behavior. The implications of this insight are enormous. Businesses engage in IW all the time, or is it that only the effective ones do?

IW enables direct and indirect attacks from anywhere in the world in a matter of seconds. Physical proximity to a target is not necessary. How is this possible? Because we have made conscious and unconscious decisions to have speed and connectivity without complementary security. In Sun Tzu's and Genghis Khan's eras, physical, personnel, and operational security were all that was needed for protection. Today we have fiber optics, satellites, smartphones and tablet computers, infrared and laser communications, interactive cable television, and a host of other technology marvels that allow us in a few seconds to reach anywhere. Now, in seconds, our information can be intercepted, modified, manipulated, and stolen.

No simple sentence or paragraph effectively describes IW. There are broad and narrow interpretations within national and international government, business, and academic communities, and some even totally reject the notion of IW. The overall view of IW must be expansive. Information is everywhere. We find information, for example, in mass media such as radio, television, and newspapers, at World Wide Web sites, in communications systems, and in computer networks and systems. Any and all may be subjected to attack via offensive IW. It follows that all these areas must be defended with defensive IW.

Offensive IW can make a government, society, nation, or business bend to the will of the attacker. Attacks can be very large, devastating, and noticed, such as economic or social disruption or breakdown and denial of critical infrastructure (e.g., power, transportation, communications, and finance) capabilities. They can also be small, low key, and unassuming, such as a request for publications and telephone calls (as the basis for social engineering). Businesses do not have the deep pockets of a government, but that does not restrict them from engaging in IW.

A business wants to deny the competition orders, customers, and information about its research and development. Industrial espionage has its share of illegal activities: theft, monitoring communications, and denying use of servers to conduct electronic commerce. Governments engage in psychological operations (with the subsets of mis/disinformation and propaganda using leaflets, television, and radio broadcasts). Businesses must identify when disinformation is being used to lure customers away and have the means to counter it. Of course, that is starting from a position of weakness. What is a proactive, defensive IW approach to counter the attack? Inoculate the customers, suppliers, business partners, and others in the IE.

Defensive IW is the ability to protect and defend the IE. Defense does not imply reactive.

Measures can be taken to forewarn of attacks and to preposition physical and virtual forces. Examples of virtual forces are software and brainpower. The acme of skill is to present a posture to prevent a competitor from attacking and to achieve victory without having to attack. Perception management is as important as demonstrable physical and virtual capabilities.

- *Information operations (IO)*: As stated above, for the purposes of this book, IW is not restricted to war, so IO as described below is included in IW. Actions taken to affect adversary information and information systems while defending one's own information and information systems.
- *Defensive IO*: The integration and coordination of policies and procedures, operations, personnel, and technology to protect and defend information and information systems. Defensive information operations are conducted through information assurance, physical security, operations security, counterdeception, counterpsychological operations, counterintelligence, electronic warfare, and special information operations. Defensive information operations ensure timely, accurate, and relevant information access while denying adversaries the opportunity to exploit friendly information and information systems for their own purposes.
- *Offensive IO*: The integrated use of assigned and supporting capabilities and activities, mutually supported by intelligence, to affect adversary decision-makers to achieve or promote specific objectives. These capabilities and activities include, but are not limited to, operations security, military deception, psychological operations, electronic warfare, physical attack or destruction, and special information operations and could also include computer network attack.

- *Information superiority*: The degree of dominance in the information domain that permits the conduct of operations without effective opposition. Information superiority is the relative state of influence and control of the IE between two or more actors. Some argue the opposite of "superiority" is "inferiority." This is not the case. All actors have equal access to open source information. Restricted, sensitive, and classified information can be acquired through overt or covert operations. Having the data, information, and knowledge is not the key to attaining and maintaining information superiority. What is done with the information and the speed at which it is done is the gold nugget. Information sharing, automation, cross-platform information sharing, and automating processes (such as air traffic control, sales–manufacturing/production–inventory–transportation, and military intelligence–platform maneuver–weapons selection and release–battle damage assessment) are essential to have execution cycles faster than those of the competition.
- *Operations security*: A process of identifying critical information and subsequently analyzing friendly actions attendant on military operations and other activities to: (1) identify those actions that can be observed by adversary intelligence systems; (2) determine indicators that hostile intelligence systems might obtain what could be interpreted or pieced together to derive critical information in time to be useful to adversaries; and (3) select and execute measures that eliminate or reduce to an acceptable level the vulnerabilities of friendly actions to adversary exploitation. Also called OPSEC.
- *Vulnerability*: In information operations, a weakness in information system security design, procedures, implementation, or internal controls that could be exploited to gain unauthorized access to information or information systems.

In addition to the above definitions, the U.S. National Security Telecommunications and Information Systems Security Committee (NSTISSC) 4009, National Information Systems Security (INFOSEC) Glossary 14 offers the following:

- *Attack*: Type of incident involving the intentional act of attempting to bypass one or more security controls.
- *Confidentiality*: Assurance that information is not disclosed to unauthorized persons, processes, or devices.
- *Critical infrastructure*: Those physical and cyber-based systems essential to the minimum operations of the economy and government.

- *Integrity*: Quality of an information system (IS) reflecting the logical correctness and reliability of the operating system; the logical completeness of the hardware and software implementing the protection mechanisms; and the consistency of data structures and occurrence of the stored data. Note that, in a formal security mode, integrity is interpreted more narrowly to mean protection of unauthorized modification or destruction of information.
- *Nonrepudiation*: Assurance that the sender of the data is provided with proof of delivery and the recipient is provided with proof of the sender's identity so that neither can later deny having processed the data.
- *OPSEC*: Process denying information to potential adversaries about capabilities or intentions by identifying, controlling, and protecting unclassified generic activities.
- *Probe*: Type of incident involving an attempt to gather information about an IS for the apparent purpose of circumventing its security controls.
- *Risk*: Possibility that a particular threat will adversely impact an IS by exploiting a particular vulnerability.
- *Risk management*: Process of identifying and applying countermeasures commensurate with the value of the assets protected based on a risk assessment.

Neither NSTISSC 4009 nor the U.S. DoD *Dictionary of Military and Associated Terms* defines consequence and consequence management. Risks are the intersection of threats and vulnerabilities. Residual risks are those that remain after mitigating actions. To plan effectively, decision-makers need to know the consequences of various courses of actions. The residual risks influence the outcomes. The outcomes are best represented via consequence management cascading effects. Third- and fourth-order effects, or further, need to be well estimated for the best course of action to be chosen.

INFORMATION WARFARE IS A POWERFUL APPROACH FOR ATTAINING AND MAINTAINING A COMPETITIVE ADVANTAGE

The purpose of a business is to create value for its shareholders, and the purpose of a government is to provide for the common good. From a business viewpoint, being effective and efficient in current markets and opening new lines of business are key to sustained revenue generation and profits. From a national security perspective, we should expect the military, intelligence community, and law enforcement to develop and use capabilities to maintain sovereignty, create and sustain peace and economic prosperity, and ensure public safety from criminals and monopolies. These entities cannot survive by insulating themselves. They must embrace, within their value system, whatever it takes to go beyond surviving to "thrive."

HOW TO USE IW TO ACHIEVE GOALS AND OBJECTIVES

Complexity interwoven across government, industry, and society presents a daunting challenge for IW. It is in the best interest of any government, business, and other organization to take prudent action to defend against information warfare attacks and to be able to launch them.

The advanced hacker breaks into online shopping exchanges, manipulates orders, steals merchandise, plunders credit card numbers—the modern-day pirate, highway robber, and Wild West outlaw. Those who would be part of the online shopping population come to expect this malicious behavior but are not dissuaded from shopping online.

Espionage, disinformation, physical destruction (normally permitted by law only for the military and law enforcement), and other actions are a means to an end. IW is a higher-level, cerebral activity. The target can be a population (the national will or a specific political, religious, or ethnic group), a despot, a general, or anyone in an organization. How, then, should IW be applied to industry? After all, is war not a declaration of Congress, Parliament, or other government entity? If a business is destroyed by an act of war or terrorism, it will not be remunerated by insurance. Is this a misnomer? By no means!

Because business is war, the principles of war normally associated with the military ought to be applied. These are not rigid, and their application is tailored to each use. Objective, offensive, mass, economy of force, unity of leadership, maneuver, security, surprise, and simplicity are generally recognized principles that will benefit any organization. Applying the principles to coherent and synchronized IW will produce a positive return on investment (ROI).

In the IT world, determining ROI is considered the Holy Grail. The problem for quantitative metrics for IW is that orders of magnitude are more difficult because of the many disciplines, many organizational levels, and sheer scope involved. Some prefer it that way because it allows them to hide behind classified information and black magic. If IW is to be successful, metrics are necessary. Existing traditional measures are a good start (e.g., how many probes did our intrusion detection system pick up?), but are not sufficiently expansive and precise. What is the value of a database? What is the value of that database after it has been successfully data mined? Because quantitative metrics need to be developed, qualitative ones will need to be used.

IW is an embracing approach, customizable to produce positive results in any organization and tailorable to meet the demands of the marketplace. By balancing tried and true capabilities with leading-edge technologies and concepts, IW remains a fresh and useful approach for achieving goals and objectives on the way to attaining and maintaining a competitive advantage.

COHERENT KNOWLEDGE-BASED OPERATIONS

IW for IW's sake is senseless. IW must help countries achieve their national security objectives and help businesses attain their goals. When IW is combined with KM and how business is done, the combination provides a powerful capability. Applying IW with KM results in information superiority. When KM is applied to how business is done, situational awareness will result. Combining IW with how business is done delivers tactics, techniques, and procedures to attain a competitive advantage. The intersection of IW with KM and how business is done is coherent knowledge-based operations (CKOs). CKO enables a country or a business to attain and maintain a competitive advantage through the synchronization and coherent application of all of its capabilities in the extended IE.

Organizations dabble in many pop management fads. Well-intentioned or not, these often are stovepipe solutions that divert finite resources—people, money, and time—from the organization's central interests and objectives. CKO brings together what appear to be several disparate components. Coherent means an orderly or logical relation of parts that affords comprehension or recognition. The parts are network-centric business (NCB) (how business is done), KM, and IW. When used in concert, their sum is far more powerful than the individual components, creating a powerful means of attaining and maintaining a competitive advantage. CKO can be used to execute and to survive IW attacks.

NETWORK-CENTRIC BUSINESS

We are told that we are in the Information Age, ride the information highway, and are part of the knowledge-based economy. We conduct electronic commerce, have electronic data interchange between computers, allow employees to telecommute and have remote access, and spend millions of dollars on websites to attract customers to buy products and services. Computers and robots are in the manufacturing plants, personnel and medical records are automated, and many of us participate in automated deposits and bill payments. If the computers stopped, not enough trained and skilled people could take over the functions in a manual system, and many businesses and government functions would quickly come to a halt. Computers, databases, and networks are as vital to a business as the circulatory and nervous systems are to your body. Computers and networks have become as ubiquitous as toasters, and network-centric appliances are in the works. The current generation of smartphones are the forerunners of tools with tremendous capability, limited only by human creativity. If you do not quickly gain control of your IE, doing so in the future will be exponentially more difficult—and expensive. The main advantage of controlling your IE is that your bottom line will improve.

There is no faster, more effective, or more efficient means to beat the competition than to use NCB. NCB allows an organization to take maximum advantage of its business processes: taking and placing orders, using the supply chain, conducting just-in-time production, and using distribution channels to field products and services. NCB leverages not only all the resources within an organization, but also its customers and business partners. They are all part of the solution set that drives the bottom line. The resources within the organization—people, money, and time—are finite, but can be effectively and efficiently allocated to provide optimal support to customers and to maximize the bottom line.[5]

KNOWLEDGE MANAGEMENT

KM integrates technologies, processes, and cultural changes to provide a means for well-informed, rapid decision-making via collaborative information and knowledge sharing by varied and dispersed organizations and individuals. KM tenets include support for organizational processes, tailored content delivery, information sharing and reuse, capturing tacit knowledge as part of the work process, situational awareness of information and knowledge assets, and valuation. KM enables an organization to be more agile, flexible, and proactive. The approach is ideal for integrating, for example, intelligence (e.g., economic and open source) and security (e.g., physical, personnel, and operations), sales and production, and research and development with business development.[5]

SUMMARY

Information warfare is an embracing concept that brings to bear all the resources of a nation-state or business organization in a coherent and synchronized manner to control the information environment and to attain and maintain a competitive advantage and gain power and influence. Judicious use of IW, when coupled with KM and NCB, leads to reduced or avoided costs, increased revenues, more satisfied customers, and larger profits and national security. Governments and businesses can use IW offensively and defensively in the physical and virtual domains. Counters to IW do not have to be in kind; they can be no, low, or high technology, and they can be asymmetric. Not conducting IW will result in a reduced market presence and lower national security. Although the name may change over the years, IW will evolve from its nascent stage and become mainstream in 20 years. We projected that in 2002. We are in fact there already.

IW occurs when, in the physical and virtual domains, you attack your competition or they attack you. IW is about synchronized and coherent relationships and capabilities. As previously discussed, central to IW are those physical and virtual capabilities to control the IE.

CKO couples IW in a useful approach with KM and how the organization does business. Not only is the corporation's IE engaged, the resources of its enterprise are brought to bear to use all its capabilities in a coherent and synchronized manner to seize as great a competitive advantage as possible. In this fashion, a country can call on its allies and coalition partners, and a business can call on its suppliers and business partners so as much knowledge and as many capabilities as possible can be brought to bear.

NOTE

The information presented this chapter was liberally quoted from the author's coauthored book with Dr. Andy Jones entitled *Global Information Warfare*, second edition, and used with the kind permission of CRC Press, who published the book.

CHAPTER 14

The Cyber Security Officer and Privacy, Ethical, and Liability Issues

Ethics is not a policing function. It's about creating the kind of climate in which people are encouraged to make the right decisions in the first place[1]

Kent Kresa

Contents

Chapter Objective

This chapter discusses the issues of ethics, privacy, and liability as they relate to the cyber security officer.

INTRODUCTION TO PRIVACY ISSUES

Much is made of the word "privacy" and the protection of privacy, privacy of an individual's personal information, for example. However, unless you have been hiding under a rock for the last, oh, 50 years or more, you know that only lip service is given to privacy as anything other than a concept, a "nice try, now let's move on" thing.

For example, when networks and databases are attacked and compromised, users'/customers' names, addresses, social security numbers, credit card numbers, and the like are stolen literally by the millions.

What do we mean by privacy anyway? Well, according to the Sharp electronic dictionary, privacy is "the state or condition of being free from being observed or disturbed by other people."

[1] Kent Kresa is Chairman of the Board and CEO of Northrop Grumman Corporation.

The U.S. government's Department of Justice website states the following:

The Privacy Act of 1974, 5 U.S.C. § 552a (2006), which has been in effect since September 27, 1975, can generally be characterized as an omnibus "code of fair information practices" that attempts to regulate the collection, maintenance, use, and dissemination of personal information by federal executive branch agencies. However, the Act's imprecise language, limited legislative history, and somewhat outdated regulatory guidelines have rendered it a difficult statute to decipher and apply. Moreover, even after more than thirty-five years of administrative and judicial analysis, numerous Privacy Act issues remain unresolved or unexplored. Adding to these interpretational difficulties is the fact that many earlier Privacy Act cases are unpublished district court decisions. A particular effort is made in this "Overview" to clarify the existing state of Privacy Act law while at the same time highlighting those controversial, unsettled areas where further litigation and case law development can be expected.

The interesting thing is that there seems to be more exceptions than not for government agencies and corporations. One just has to look at the massive collection of information being conducted 24/7 by U.S. agencies and the nation-states of pretty much the world. Of course, they cite their need to invade our privacy as being for our own good; you know, for our well-being and security. As a cyber security officer, you may be involved in this endeavor.

Corporations don't do it in the interest of national security but in the interest of getting that competitive edge, identifying and selling to targeted potential customers. Such techniques are getting more sophisticated it seems by the day. Of course, you volunteer to give up much of your private information just to be able to make a purchase or do anything with about anyone online.

Now, although we all abhor such invasion of privacy, as a corporate or government agency cyber security officer you may be involved in such invasion of privacy as a minimum by ensuring that the information collected is properly protected. We know from the numerous attacks, for example, on Target and Sony, that some aren't doing a very good job.

As a cyber security officer, you MUST find adequate ways to protect the information of the government agency or corporation. After all, that is what you are getting paid to do—protect the privacy of individuals and the corporation or government agency. So far, how's that working for you?

INTRODUCTION TO ETHICS ISSUES

We hear a lot about ethics these days, when it seems everyone is out for themselves, from the executives of major corporations to a secretary in a small company office who perpetrates a fraud. One thing that makes a professional a true professional is ethical conduct. That is especially a requirement for a cyber security officer.

When you think of ethics and ethical behavior, what comes to mind? For some it means "doing the right thing." But what is the "right" thing to do? For some, it is anything that they can get away with without violating any laws. In fact, some narrowly define being ethical as doing anything as long as it does not violate laws. However, ethics and morality go hand and hand, but what is moral? For example, communists believe that whatever furthers the advance of communism is moral and acting in a manner that does not further communism is immoral.

Remember that we talked earlier in this book about committing crimes, and committing crimes takes opportunity, motive, and rationalization. The same applies to ethical behavior. You can use opportunity, motive, and rationalization to do the "right" thing or to not do what is right.

eth·ics [éthiks] noun

1. study of morality's effect on conduct: the study of moral standards and how they affect conduct (takes a singular verb); also called moral philosophy;

2. code of morality: a system of moral principles governing the appropriate conduct for an individual or group (takes a plural verb).
    [15th century; via Old French ethiques from, ultimately, Greek ēthikē, from ēthikos "ethical" (see ethic).][2]

If you find someone's wallet, you have the opportunity to keep it. Suppose the motive is that you do not have a job and you have a family to support. You can rationalize it by saying that the money can buy much-needed food for the family, and besides, the person must be well off based on the number of gold and platinum credit cards in the wallet. Let's say that you just found the money and there is absolutely no evidence indicating to whom it belonged. Would it then be ok to keep it? The answer in both cases is no. Why? It does not belong to you. Therefore, even if it were not against the law to keep the money, it would be still unethical. However, sometimes the process is that you turn it over to the local police and if, after a set period of time, no one claims the money, it is yours. That would be ethical because you followed the locally established processes. What about illegally copying software in violation of copyright laws? Isn't that also unethical?

The interesting thing about ethics is that it may also depend on your culture. For example, the businessperson who gives gifts to a procurement officer in a corporation that he or she wants to do business with may be breaking the

---

[2] *Encarta World English Dictionary*, ©1999, Microsoft Corporation. All rights reserved. Developed for Microsoft by Bloomsbury Publishing Plc.

law in some countries, but such gifts are expected in others. Is it wrong to accept the gifts in those countries where that is a tradition? No. Of course, if it violated a law or company policy, it would be unethical because violating a law is in itself unethical. Add to all this the moral issues, knowing what is right and what is wrong, considering what you were taught growing up, and all this brought together and integrated in each of us with our culture, working environment, and the like. The philosophy of morals and ethics has been the subject of study and discussion for centuries. We surely will not provide the definitive answers here. However, we must understand the basics of ethics because it does have an impact on protecting corporate assets.

mor·al [máwrəl] adjective

1. involving right and wrong: relating to issues of right and wrong and to how individuals should behave;
2. derived from personal conscience: based on what somebody's conscience suggests is right or wrong, rather than on what the law says should be done;
3. in terms of natural justice: regarded in terms of what is known to be right or just, as opposed to what is officially or outwardly declared to be right or just; a moral victory;
4. encouraging goodness and respectability: giving guidance on how to behave decently and honorably;
5. good by accepted standards: good or right, when judged by the standards of the average person or society at large;
6. telling right from wrong: able to distinguish right from wrong and to make decisions based on that knowledge;
7. based on conviction: based on an inner conviction, in the absence of physical proof.

noun (plural mor·als)

1. valuable lesson in behavior: a conclusion about how to behave or proceed drawn from a story or event;
2. final sentence of story giving advice: a short, precise rule, usually written in a rather literary style as the conclusion to a story, used to help people remember the best or most sensible way to behave.

plural noun mor·als

standards of behavior: principles of right and wrong as they govern standards of general or sexual behavior.

[14th century; from Latin moralis, from mor-, stem of mos "custom," in plural "morals" (source of English morale and morose).][3]

---

[3] *Encarta World English Dictionary*, ©1999, Microsoft Corporation. All rights reserved. Developed for Microsoft by Bloomsbury Publishing Plc.

Ethical behavior is expected of everyone who works in a corporation. Few, if any, corporations or any type of business or government agency want to be seen as doing anything unethical.

Some people believe that if it is not against the law, it is ethical. Often it seems that corporations that walk a fine line between legal and illegal behavior use a great deal of rationalization to justify their actions. However, in most circumstances, the ethical question remains: Yes, it is legal, but is it the ethical thing to do?

If you see someone in your corporation doing something that violates corporate policy, should you report that person to management? This is probably an employee's most difficult ethical dilemma. In some nation-states, it is better to not report anyone, even someone committing a serious crime, because many children were brought up not to be a "squealer," a "fink," a "snitch." In some societies, that is almost as bad, if not worse, as committing the offense that is being reported.

Because of the amount of unethical behavior within some corporations and nation-states, there are processes by which one, sometimes called a *whistleblower*, can receive financial rewards for identifying illegal or unethical behavior. However, as much as corporations like to say that they have an ethics program within their corporation, when an employee comes forth and reports illegal activities, it seems that, more often than not, he or she is the subject of harassment, receives no promotions, and is made to feel unwanted in the corporation. Management looks upon that person as one who could not be trusted. Ironic, isn't it? A person reports someone's unethical behavior in accordance with the corporate policy. That person, instead of being considered an honest and loyal employee, is considered to be untrustworthy. There are many examples of such conduct within the corporations of the United States and other nation-states. Suffice it to say that corporate management can tout an ethics program, but one that truly works as stated in the brochures is another matter.

CODES OF ETHICS

Most, if not all, professional associations have a code of ethics. They are all about the same in that one must do what is right and report what is wrong. As a cyber security professional, you must behave in a professional manner at all times and, therefore, comply with the professional code of ethics.

It is quite possible that members of associations with a code of ethics have actually never read the code of ethics, even though as a cyber security professional and member of one or more security-related associations, you are required to comply with the association's code of ethics. In fact, it can even be considered unethical not to have ever read the code of ethics for the various associations to which you as a cyber security professional belong.

What does that say about you and your professionalism? One may counter by saying that he or she always acts in an ethical manner and doesn't have to read any code of ethics. This "know-it-all" attitude is a symptom of possibly a more serious matter: the idea that one has no more to learn about an information security–related topic. That not only is impossible but will end up costing the corporation in terms of effectiveness and efficiency. How? Because the cyber security officer who is not continuously learning and applying new and better techniques does not take advantage of new (and possibly better and cheaper) ways of protecting assets.

Now is a good time to take the opportunity to read some codes of ethics from security-related professional associations. Please take the time to search online, read, understand, and apply the codes of ethics as an integral part of your job and profession.

CORPORATE ETHICS, STANDARDS OF CONDUCT, BUSINESS PRACTICES, AND CORPORATE VALUES

Many corporations in many countries of the world today concern themselves with ethics, standards of conduct, business practices, and values. What does all that mean? Basically, it still means that one must know the difference between right and wrong, acceptable conduct and unacceptable conduct. In today's world, corporations are successfully sued because of the unethical conduct of their employees. Therefore, if for no other reason than loss of revenue, such matters are a serious concern of corporate management.

There are corporate policies and awareness training sessions given to employees and often special training given to management. This is because it seems that it is mostly management that is involved in unethical conduct. For example, management may direct their employees to act in an unethical manner by taking a shortcut in a manufacturing process such as a quality check to get the product out the door faster.

Cyber security professionals in corporations are often involved in following up on ethics matters that have been reported by managers or employees, either directly or through a corporate ethics hotline, for example, noncompliance with the cyber security program. The ethics hotline provides a communications medium to obtain reports of unethical behavior. It should never be used to try to identify the caller if that caller did not leave any information relative to his or her identity. In fact, to do so would be unethical in itself, and once word got out of such conduct by management, the chances of obtaining further information concerning unethical behavior would be almost zero. If that did occur, that manager seeking the identity of the caller should be the subject of an ethics inquiry. One should never dwell so much on the messenger as the message. After all, isn't that the objective of the ethics program and ethics hotline? It is amazing how many managers in corporations focus on identifying the caller instead of acting on the information the caller provided. That alone tells a great deal about the ethics of some managers.

One often hears about managers "shooting the messenger." Any manager who verbally or otherwise attacks the messenger is "not getting the message." So, what does this have to do with the ISSO and professionalism? As an employee of a corporation, you have probably been on one end or the other—or both—of such incidents. Think about it. No one likes to receive bad news, and finding out through some ethics channel that some assets were stolen, that someone was not complying with the assets protection policies, and that this person was a senior executive may cause management to "shoot the messenger."

As a cyber security professional, you have a professional responsibility not to allow the shooting of messengers. Instead, you must direct management efforts to the identified problem. If you are requested or directed to do all you can to identify the anonymous reporter of ethics violations, you should explain that such conduct is in violation of the corporate ethics policy and, therefore, the request or demand itself is unethical. Unfortunately, it may cost you your merit raise, a less than favorable performance review, and the like, but that is a price that you must be willing to pay. It is a matter of principle—your professional integrity—and that means a matter of ethical conduct.

LIABILITY ISSUES

One of the consequences of not providing adequate cyber security is the successful attacks that lead to violations of privacy and ethics. These result in often massive lawsuits in which the corporation that employs you must pay out. We are talking millions of dollars.

Your job is of course on the line because regardless of your telling management what needs to be done falling on deaf management ears, you will be held responsible. Saying "I told you so" and "I didn't have enough budget" or such will not help you. The best you can do is continually document all the "I told you so's" and requests for whatever you needed that you didn't get, for example, staff, security software, etc. It probably won't stop you from getting fired but maybe will help with a "wrongful discharge" lawsuit.

The other way to handle such issues is to convince your legal department, and then for both of you to advise management, of the need for insurance to cover such losses due to, for example, successful hacker attacks. In many cases, it is a prudent business decision.

Cyber attack risk requires $1 bn of insurance cover, companies warned[4]

[4] ft.com, April 20, 2015.

QUESTIONS TO CONSIDER

Based on what you have read, consider the following questions and how you would reply to them:
- Does your company have ethics and privacy programs?
- Are you and your staff actively involved in the programs?
- Do you support the programs by conducting inquiries into noncompliance with the cyber security program or company ethics policies?
- Does your corporation have an ethics hotline?
- Do you discuss proper behavior with your staff?
- If not, why not?
- If so, what do you discuss and how often?
- Do you use the corporate ethics and privacy programs to support following the cyber security program?
- If so, do you try to get management to view a cyber security noncompliance issue as also an ethics or privacy issue?
- Have you discussed liability insurance with your legal staff, maybe auditors and management?

SUMMARY

Cyber security professionals must be extremely honest people of high integrity. After all, they know the vulnerabilities of the corporate information and information systems assets as well as the protection mechanisms. That is very valuable information. Cyber security officers must conduct themselves in an ethical manner at all times. If they belong to a professional, security-related association, they must also adhere to the association's code of conduct.

Cyber security professionals must also do their best to encourage all corporate employees, led by executive management, to act in an ethical manner when doing their work at the corporation. The cyber security program will benefit through fewer information thefts, less damage, less unauthorized modification, and fewer cyber security violations and will provide for a corporate cyber security environment that is better overall.

As part of their job, they must also protect the privacy of the corporation, employees, associates, subcontractors, and of course customers. You may be personally liable if your cyber security program fails. Certainly your corporation will be.

CHAPTER 15

A Career as a Cyber Security Officer

A man must serve his time to every trade save censure—critics all are ready made[1]

Lord Byron

Contents

Chapter Objective

The cyber security officer professionals of the twenty-first century must possess many skills that differ from those possessed by some current and past cyber security officer professionals. In this chapter, the discussion will center on what are the necessary skills that a cyber security officer and professional cyber security staff should possess to be successful, as well as how to establish and maintain a cyber security career development program.[2]

---

[1] *Encarta Book of Quotations,* © & (P) 1999, Microsoft Corporation. All rights reserved. Developed for Microsoft by Bloomsbury Publishing Plc.; Lord Byron (1788–1824), English poet. "English Bards and Scotch Reviewers" (1809).

[2] Some of the information noted in this chapter was excerpted from another Butterworth–Heinemann book, *The Manager's Handbook for Corporate Security: How to Develop and Manage a Successful Assets Protection Program,* published in 2003, and coauthored by Gerald L. Kovacich and Edward P. Halibozek.

INTRODUCTION

Changes that have occurred over the years in the duties and responsibilities of the cyber security officer professional include a working environment that involves increasing:

- Complexity;
- Rapidity of change;
- Technology dependence;
- Technology drivenness;
- Sophistication of the workforce;
- Competitiveness in the business world;
- Instant communication;
- Information available to more people than ever before;
- Incidents of corporate fraud, waste, and abuse;
- Threats to, and vulnerabilities of, corporate information-related assets; and
- Competition for high-level cyber security positions.

Since this twenty-first century environment means more competition for cyber security positions, those who want to succeed in this career field must gain more experience and have more education than ever before—or at least more than the other cyber security professionals they are competing against.

The corporate culture, cyber security duties, responsibilities, and positions vary almost as much as the number of corporations. Many outsource much of their cyber security service and support functions, while others find it more cost-effective to use employees. No matter what type of corporation—or government agency for that matter—that you work for, the main goal is still to protect the information and information systems assets of the company (or government agency).

Corporations want to hire cyber security professionals who can do that successfully at least impact to cost and schedules.

---

pro·fes·sion·al [prō féshən'l, prōféshnəl, prə féshən'l] adjective
very competent: showing a high degree of skill or competence
noun (plural pro·fes·sion·als)
member of a profession: somebody whose occupation requires extensive education or specialized training
somebody very competent: somebody who shows a high degree of skill or competence[3]

[3] *Encarta® World English Dictionary* © & (P) 1999 Microsoft Corporation. All rights reserved. Developed for Microsoft by Bloomsbury Publishing Plc.

If you consider yourself a cyber security professional and want to be the world's best, then you need a career development program.

THE CYBER SECURITY OFFICER'S CAREER DEVELOPMENT PROGRAM

Some questions you may want to ask yourself about a cyber security officer career are:

- What cyber security-related career do I want to get into?
- Why?
- What are the qualifications (education and experience) for the entry level and other security positions?
- What are the positions (specializations) within that profession?
- Are there any that I would like to specialize in?
- Why?
- What are the other positions within the cyber security profession that I may want to specialize in?
- Can I list them in order of priority, including their education and experience requirements?

The cyber security officer profession should be researched to obtain the answers to the above questions by:

- Interviewing various cyber security officer professionals in different types of businesses, nonprofit entities, and government agencies;
- Researching the cyber security officer profession and its various specialties through the Internet;
- Discussing the profession with representatives from the American Society for Industrial Security, High Technology Crime Investigation Association, Association of Certified Fraud Examiners, Information Systems Security Association, and various training institutes and universities that teach cyber security-related courses; and
- Reading job descriptions for cyber security officer positions in the trade journals and newspapers and through interviews with recruiters.

Based on this research, you as a cyber security professional can establish a career development plan beginning at a high level with subsections for education and experience for each position.

The future cyber security officer might also set two limits:

- Experience and education must be relevant to eventually becoming a cyber security officer.
- Time learning through education, training, and gaining experience must be scheduled so that the intermediary milestones and ultimate goal can be met.

The cyber security officer should also include the goal of supervisory and management experience as well as experience in the worlds of finance, marketing, sales, accounting, investigations, communications, technology, international travel, and human resources. The cyber security officer should set a goal of gradually gaining increased responsibility, experience, and education in security jobs that would prepare the cyber security officer for a highly paid cyber security officer position in an international corporation.

Based on the research, you may come up with the idea of a "four parallel lines" approach to career development. These are items that should be integrated into the career development plan:

- Money—How much do I want, and by when, to meet my goals?
- Position—What cyber security positions pay me the money I want to meet my goals based on my timeline of goals?
- Education—What are the education requirements for each position I want to get?
- Experience—What are the experience requirements for each position I want to get?

The cyber security officer's goal should be to be the most qualified person for each position in the cyber security officer's profession.

Also during research, the cyber security officer may find that to be the best cyber security professional requires one to have knowledge, education, and experience in areas other than cyber security, including:

- Business
- Investigations
- Technology
- Dealing with people
- Communications skills
- Management
- Writing
- Project planning
- Public speaking
- Major foreign language or languages

EDUCATION

There are two different approaches that some cyber security officers have used:

- They began with a technical education such as a degree or degrees in computer science, mathematics, or telecommunications. Because of

their degree, or probably some related cyber security experience, they were chosen or volunteered to be the company's cyber security officer.
- They began with a general degree such as business, security, criminal justice, or liberal arts and eventually, somehow, found themselves in the cyber security officer position. And once in that position, they liked it and decided to stay in the cyber security officer profession.

In today's environment, a college degree with a major in computer science or telecommunications is one of the best ways to start a cyber security officer career. An alternative is to major in cyber security. As colleges and universities see the demand for such subjects, they will offer more cyber security courses and programs. As the need for cyber security grows, more universities and colleges will begin to offer majors in cyber security.

An alternative to a college or university is a technical school that offers cyber security-related specialized programs in various aspects of the computer and telecommunications functions. This training usually offers hands-on experience and may provide a faster avenue into the cyber security profession. Also, many colleges and universities offer certificates in a specialized cyber security officer-related field such as local area networks and telecommunications. These courses can also be applied to the degree program, but check the college or university to be sure. Those who choose the technical training path should still pursue a college degree that will enhance promotion opportunities in the cyber security officer profession.

Education, whether technical or academic, provides the future cyber security officer with an opportunity for more cyber security officer positions.

In today's marketplace, the need for experience coupled with advanced degrees and certifications has increased. It has increased to the point at which all your education, experience, and certifications only get you through the first resume filtering process. It is the interview that will get you the job.

What else can one do to prepare for such a position and also maintain a working knowledge of all that is associated with and needed to be a cyber security officer? These include knowledge gained through:
- Conferences and training classes;
- Networking with others in the profession;
- Using trade journals and magazines to learn more;
- Experience, which is always a good trainer;
- Certifications—knowledge gained studying for certifications; and
- Joining associations and attending their meetings, where information can be gained.

How to Market Yourself as a Cyber Security Officer

> Work is a responsibility most adults assume, a burden at times, a complication, but also a challenge that, like children, requires enormous energy and that holds the potential for qualitative, as well as quantitative, rewards.
>
> *Melinda M. Marshall*[4]

[4] *The Columbia World of Quotations.* 1996 (http://www.bartleby.com/66/2/38002.html); Melinda M. Marshall (20th century), U.S. writer and editor. *Good Enough Mothers,* introduction (1993).

Sometimes a cyber security officer will have some conflicts when it comes to seeking out a new position instead of staying a "loyal company employee." There should not be any such conflict, because in today's business world, it seems that it is seldom that the corporation is loyal to the employees, so why should the employees be loyal to the corporation?

If you are happy doing what you are doing and would like to do the same thing for the rest of your life in the same company, then do it. However, one word of caution—in today's corporate world, no position seems to last forever, and it appears that today's corporations do not want their employees to stay forever. So, it is always better to be prepared by having a backup plan in the event you are notified that your services are no longer wanted.

Also remember that it is easier to find a job if you already have a job. So, the best time to find out your worth as a cyber security officer is to look for advancement opportunities or lateral opportunities for other cyber security positions while you are still employed. If nothing else, the employment interviews will keep you in practice and help you fine-tune your interview skills and your personal portfolio.

Interviewing for the Cyber Security Officer Position

Congratulations! Your resume has finally made it through the filtering process and you are being asked to appear for an interview. You will probably find that cyber security officer positions are very competitive, with talented cyber security officer professionals competing against you for each of those positions. So, you must be prepared. As with most job interviews these days, you will probably be subjected to a series of interviews consisting of members of the human resources department, information systems organization, auditors, and security personnel.

Don't be nervous, but this interview is what will put you back on the road to cyber security officer job hunting or offer you the challenges of the new cyber security officer position. So, you must be prepared!

There are many books on the market telling you how to interview for a position. They offer advice on everything from how to dress to how to answer the "mother of all interview questions"—What are your salary expectations?

It is not the purpose of this book to help you answer those common interview questions. It is assumed that you will have read those books, and that you have prepared and practiced for the upcoming interview. The purpose of this section is to show you how you may be able to separate yourself from your cyber security officer competition.

You have probably already interviewed more times than you care to admit. In all those interviews, you probably, like your peers, walked in wearing dark, conservative business attire, neatly groomed, and prepared to answer any question thrown at you. The question is, what separated you from your competitors? What was it that would make the interviewers remember you and choose you above the rest?

You probably answered most questions in the most politically correct way, for example, "What is your major weakness?" Answer: "My major weakness is that I have very little patience for those who don't live up to their commitments. When someone agrees to complete a project by a specific date, I expect that date to be met unless the project leader comes to me in advance of the deadline and explains the reason that date can't be met. I believe in a team effort, and all of us, as vital members of that team, must work together to provide the service and support needed to assist the company in meeting its goals."

Will that answer to that question be considered a weakness or strength by the interviewers? Probably a strength, but that is how the game is played.

Many interviewees have "been there and done that" but still didn't get the position. Why? Maybe because our answers "float" in the interview room air. They hang there mingling with those of the other candidates before us and will be mingling again with the candidates that come after us.

The only real, lasting evidence of the interview is what was written down by the interviewers and what impressions you, the prospective cyber security officer, left in their minds! Many of the interviewers are "screeners," human resource people who have no clue as to what cyber security is all about. They are there because we do teaming today.

We operate by consensus. So, getting selected may be much more difficult.

So, you need one thing—one thing that will leave a lasting impression on the interviewers. One thing that will show them you have the talents, the applied education (that's education that you gained in college and other places and something that you can actually use in the business world!), the experience, and the game plan. You've done it! You've been successful in building a cyber security program before, and you will be successful again. You can prove that you can do it because you have your cyber security officer portfolio!

The next question that the reader may ask is, "What the heck is my cyber security officer portfolio?" You probably have seen movies in which the models show up at the model studio or movie studio and present a folder containing photographs of themselves in various poses. No, sorry—your photo will probably not help you get the cyber security officer position—but think about it. They took with them to their interview physical evidence in the form of photographs, meant to prove that he or she was the best person for the position.

What you must do is develop your own portfolio to take with you and leave with the interviewers—proof that you've been there, done that. You are the best person for the position. It's all there in the portfolio.

Your cyber security officer portfolio is something you should begin building as soon as you begin your first cyber security officer job or before. It should contain an index and identified sections that include letters of reference, letters of appreciation, copies of award certificates, project plans, metric charts you use for measuring the success of your cyber security programs, and, probably most important, your cyber security philosophy and cyber security plan outline that you will implement as soon as you are hired.

The cyber security plan is probably the most important document in your portfolio and should be the first page after your index. All the other documents are just proof that what you plan to do, you've done before.

In the case of someone who has never been a cyber security officer, the prospective cyber security officer can build his or her cyber security plan and cyber security portfolio from the information provided in this book. Build it for an imaginary corporation.

The next question that may arise is, "If I never worked there, how do I know what I should do if I get hired?" Again, go back to doing some research. Remember that if you really want this job, you have to work at least as hard to get it as you will once you do get it.

Your first stop should be the Internet. Find out about the company. Some information that you should know is:

- When was it started?
- What are its products?

- How is the company stock doing?
- Where are their offices located, etc.?

You should also stop by the company and pick up an application, any company brochures available, their benefits pamphlets, etc.

You should study the information, complete the application, and place it in your portfolio. After all, if they decide to hire you, you'd have to fill one out anyway. You should go into the interview knowing as much if not more about the company as the people interviewing you. This is invaluable, especially if you are interviewing for a senior-level position. These interviews will undoubtedly include members of the executive management. Your ability to talk about their company in business terms with an understanding of the company will undoubtedly impress them and indicate that you are business-oriented.

All your answers to the interviewers' questions should be directed to something in your portfolio. For example, if they ask you how you would deal with downsizing in your department and what impact that would have on your ability to adequately protect the company's information and its related systems, how would you answer?

You should be able to direct them to a process chart, a metric, something that indicates that you have done it before, or that you have a business-oriented approach to dealing with the issue.

If you have not done it before, write down how you could, and would, perform these functions, assess the cyber security program, etc.

The portfolio can work for any new cyber security officer in any company. The following is a sample portfolio outline, which can be used as a guide by a new or experienced cyber security officer. In this case, it is the cyber security officer applying for the cyber security officer position. It's up to you to fill in the details. Many of the ideas of what to put in your cyber security portfolio will be found in this book.

You will note that the prospective cyber security officer applying for the corporate position has done the research necessary to tailor a cyber security program for the corporation. The beauty of building this type of portfolio is that it seems specific, and yet it's generic.

The cyber security officer should also practice interviewing skills. The resume or personal contacts may get you the interview, but the interview will get you the job. Before any interviews, and during the interview, you must do the following:

- Learn all you can about the potential employer;
- Read and learn from books, magazines, and the like about interviews and proper clothing to wear;

- Prepare answers to typical questions that will be asked, and practice answering them without seeming as though the answers were rehearsed;
- Develop and maintain an updated work portfolio;
- During the interview always refer to "we" or "us" instead of "I" and "you" as much as possible, so it seems as if you already have the job and are just briefing fellow employees; and
- Refer interviewers to your portfolio in answering their questions.

The following is a fictional scenario of one individual's cyber security job hunt:

The cyber security officer established a career development plan as a formal project plan with an objective, goals, milestones, and tasks. The project plan helped the cyber security officer focus on career progression, and also that focus made it easier not to get sidetracked and waste time on matters that did not lend themselves to meeting the project plan milestones. The cyber security officer continually updated the plan. At the end of each calendar year, the cyber security officer would analyze the progress in meeting the plan goals and objective. Regardless of whether the plan progressed ahead of schedule or behind schedule, the reasons for the change were noted and lessons learned. Then the updated plan would be used for the next year.

Over the years, the cyber security officer developed a portfolio. In the portfolio, the cyber security officer maintained a plan that would be continually updated and used during all interviews, with extra copies available for the interviewers, and the cyber security officer successfully used it for the corporation.

When others went through the interview process answering the interviewers' questions, their responses were lost in the air like smoke; however, this cyber security officer's thoughts, experience, education, plan for a cyber security program, and other information relevant to meeting the corporation's needs were down on paper and could be referred to by the interviewers.

This portfolio also indicated a person who was organized and came in with an action plan. Furthermore, since this cyber security officer researched the corporation prior to being interviewed, the cyber security officer was intimately familiar with the corporation and even offered some information about the corporation that was new to some of the interviewers.

Becoming a Cyber Security Consultant

If you wish to succeed, consult three old people.

Chinese Proverb

To be in any type of profession working for oneself takes a special type of personality to succeed. After all, there is no one to continue to pay you when you are on vacation, no benefits that you don't have to pay for, and if you decide to just hang around the office and not work, you won't get paid for that, either. There is no safety net, no paid time off when sick. No work—no pay. For the independent consultant, the old saying "time is money" is certainly true. In addition, there is a constant need to maintain contacts (potential customers) and keep up with high technology, and of course there is the almost constant travel.

Some cyber security officers and managers may have the connections and believe that they are well thought of as cyber security professionals, called upon to lecture at conferences, assist clients with their cyber security needs, and the like. However, those that do so as a member of a large firm, such as a large accounting–consulting firm, believe that it is they who are the ones that draw clients to them for help, when in fact it is usually not that at all. It is usually the large corporate name that brings these clients to the cyber security person.

Some cyber security managers and technicians don't realize this fact. Then when they decide to go out on their own as cyber security consultants, they find that what they thought was a great client base on which to build their business trade turns out to be the client base of their former employer, and they aren't switching to your firm. Furthermore, there are legal and ethical matters relating to "stealing" clients away from a former employer. When the shock of this fact hits them, they find themselves scrambling for clients.

Some advice for those who may be ready to take the cyber security consulting plunge: Be sure that you objectively inventory your skills and potential client base, and also have at least two years of your current salary (including funds for equivalent benefits) safely in the bank. That emergency fund will provide a year or more of income as you grow your business. If nothing else, it will provide a good emergency fund for some lean times or for the times when you will want to take a break for a week or two and go on vacation. After all, you have to pay for your own days off now. Oh, and don't forget insurances such as "errors and omissions," also known as professional liability insurance, general liability, and worker's compensation.

Some clients require proof of some or all of these policies before you set foot in the door. With all that said, if you have the education, experience, business sense, and personality to handle being out on your own, it does offer its own rewards.

These rewards include setting your own schedule and hours, being your own boss, vacationing whenever you like, doing it your way—but wait a minute, that's not completely true.

Your hours will be set by your workload and your clients. You will be able to do the work pretty much your way, but doing only the work that meets the clients' needs. And vacations can be cut short by an urgent client need. You really can't afford to postpone an urgent client request, as you risk losing the client to a competitor. Payments from clients may be slow in coming and they may be shocked by their bill for services rendered, causing you to negotiate or get your lawyer to negotiate for you. That means additional costs if you can't get your lawyer's costs ported over to the clients. However, one thing is certain: When such issues arise, you may eventually get your money, but you will probably never do business with that client again. How many clients can you afford to lose?

Being a cyber security consultant looks great on paper and it may do your ego good, but after a while the real world takes over. It's a tough life and not for the faint at heart. So, before you think about it, be sure you have a good business plan and one that is done objectively. Also, be sure you can support yourself and your family without work for extended periods of time. Yes, it sounds great, but maybe that salary, those working conditions, and that boss weren't all that bad?

However, you have successfully worked your career plan and have developed the education and experience over the years that have given you the confidence to think about going out on your own as a cyber security consultant. You have had articles published in magazines, have lectured internationally, and have developed a reputation as a professional cyber security officer. So, you think you are about ready for this career move. If so, you need a plan.

If you decide to become an independent cyber security consultant, the first thing you should do is develop a business plan—before you resign from your current job. Developing the plan may ultimately make you decide that you don't want to or can't make it as an independent cyber security consultant. There are many sample business plans available in books and as software programs that can help you get started.

Regardless of how you proceed to develop your cyber security business consulting plan, you must be objective. If you are to assume anything, assume the worst. That way, you will be prepared for the worst-case scenario and will be able to successfully deal with it. Your plan should be looked at as a project plan and, as a minimum, should address the following:

- Your business goals and objectives;
- Why you want to start this business;
- Your education and experience skills and whether they will fit your consulting business—be realistic;
- How much money you will need to begin;

- How much money you have;
- How you will get the money you don't have but need;
- How you will financially survive when business is slow;
- If you have a family or significant other, whether they will support you;
- If not, whether you might have to decide your relationship–business priorities;
- Whether you are willing to travel the majority of your time—after all, you must go to clients and not them to you;
- What steps you will take to begin the business and the cost for each line item or task;
- Whether you will incorporate your business;
- Whether you know the marketplace—your competitors;
- Whether you offer better services at lower prices;
- Your competitors' strengths and weaknesses;
- Your strengths and weaknesses;
- A complete competitive analysis;
- A complete market scope;
- Whether you should have a logo and business motto, and if so, what they will be and why;
- Whether you should get a lawyer to assist you;
- Whether you will have copyrighted material, trademarks, and/or trade secrets and, if so, how you will handle those processes;
- Whether you have standard invoices, proposals, confidentiality agreements, contracts, and billing and general business processes and forms in place and ready for use;
- Whether you have trusted cyber security specialists available to support your contracts as subcontractors (after all, you can't be experienced in everything);
- How you will obtain business;
- How much you will charge for what work; and
- Whether you are aware of the laws and regulations that affect you doing business.

These are but a few of the many questions that you should answer before making the plunge into the cyber security consulting services business. Remember also the guiding principles that you should employ:

- Confidentiality;
- Objectivity;
- Professionalism;
- Respect;
- Integrity;

- Honesty;
- Quality;
- Efficiency; and
- Client focus ("we").

Once you have your business plan in place and have decided to become an independent cyber security consultant, your plan should provide you with a step-by-step approach to getting started.[5] Let's break down the cyber security consulting business into sections:

- Engagement setup
- Engagement process
- Assessment services
- Advisory services
- Security implementation
- Augmentation
- Legal issues
- International aspects

Engagement Setup

To begin, you need an "entry into the business" strategy. You must have established and continue to refine your information network (trusted contacts within your business arena who can tell you what is going on where, etc.). You must also use other sources to find your potential customers—or clients, as some like to call them. Such other sources include referrals and marketing through brochures, pamphlets, lectures, books, articles, and your business website. It also includes "cold calling" potential customers and explaining to them what services you offer.

Once you have made contact with a potential client, you must clearly and precisely communicate your services; you must "find their pain" and explain how you can help solve their problems. Try to make this a question-and-answer session in which a dialog takes place. You should also use the opportunity to explain your experience by citing examples of your past services to clients, without providing specific names, of course.

Assuming the meeting went well and they ask you for a proposal, you should provide one in the most expeditious manner possible and be sure that you understand: Each client requires a different approach depending on the size of the client—small, medium, or large organization—as the scale, tactics, and strategy will vary with each. In the proposal you should be

---

[5] Some of the information provided in this chapter was provided by Steve Lutz, President, WaySecure, a very successful international security consultant and Cyber security specialist for decades.

precise; include a project schedule with logistics requirements, roles, and responsibilities (for both you and your client); and address liability issues. Other matters to consider are:

- Understand who you are dealing with and be sure to get to the right level of authority to make decisions that affect your work;
- Identify their needs as specifically as possible;
- Understand their budget (size and cycle);
- Get the "big picture";
- Be sure you have a clear understanding of their expectations and your deliverables, before leaving the potential client;
- Determine any time factors that they want to consider; and
- If needed, exchange encryption keys so correspondence can be done in private.

As part of your engagement setup, you should have a specific written proposal prepared, as well as one in the standard format you have developed. Both should be on your notebook computer so that they can be modified immediately to fit the situation. If you believe your specific written proposal is just right for your potential client, be sure to have several hard copies available to present to the potential client. The proposal, as a minimum, should include:

- Proposal structure,
- Work to be performed,
- Project schedule,
- Timing and fees,
- Roles and responsibilities,
- Assumptions and caveats,
- Legal issues.

Engagement Process

Once you begin, remember to document everything to include:

- Time and dates,
- Whom you spoke to,
- What was said,
- Any action items resulting from the conversations,
- Tasks you completed and their time and date,
- Notable events that occurred, and
- All other matters that can be used to support your activities, position, time spent, and the like.

More than one consultant has found that they performed work based on conversations with a client's employee and then found that the client balked in making payments for that work, since they considered it unauthorized—the person had no authority to direct a consultant to perform that function. It is imperative that you and the client both have a clear understanding of what is agreed to, when it will be accomplished, proof that it was accomplished, and the fees relative to completing the work.

Notes help when discussing the work performed and especially in dealing with the billing process. An excellent technique to use during the engagement management process is to monitor the progress of the engagement on a daily basis. Constantly communicate with the client the progress (or lack of it) and delineate why there are delays. If there are delays due to a fault on the part of the client, inform the client of the impact to the engagement and give choices such as:

- Ask for additional funding,
- Abbreviate certain tasks, or
- Eliminate certain tasks.

This technique helps avoid unpleasant surprises and misunderstandings. It's a "we" mentality. You approach your counterpart project manager and say "Joe, we've got a problem. The project is behind because of this, this, and this. How do you think we can fix this?" If the project is screwed up, Joe has just as much to lose politically as you do monetarily. If there is a debate as to why things aren't going well, the events are fresh in everyone's minds and it's easy to sort out and correct or compensate. A common mistake is to wait until near the end of the engagement when things are way behind schedule and inform the client, thinking that somehow everything might work out.

This will end up in a best-case scenario as souring the client relationship and worst case, in court arguing over who did what when.

If there are delays due to your own performance or lack of planning, work extra hours and accept the loss. Do whatever you have to do to meet the objectives of the proposal, and don't complain about it. Make careful notes as to why you miscalculated or undermanaged the engagement, and use that knowledge when writing your next proposal.

Assessment Services

You may want to break your services into various groups. One group may be "assessment services." This should have been decided as part of your business plan. These services include such things as penetration testing and security tests and evaluations of software and systems and it may include supporting documentation analyses. Also included may be technical security countermeasures, audits, and risk assessments.

Advisory Services

Advisory services, also previously considered as part of your business plan, include the following:
- Technical design review;
- Policies, procedures, and guidelines;
- Security change management;
- Systems and network security; and
- Security architecture.

Security Implementation

The services to be considered, based on your expertise, of course, include ensuring that products to be installed on systems don't make the systems and networks more vulnerable and any security software meets the needs of the business and operates as advertised. Again, be sure to document everything.

Augmentation

Augmentation services may include such things as termination surveillance and assisting in client investigations of employees, such as computer forensic services. You may also be requested to respond to incidents. If so, this should be addressed in your contract and also the billing for such responses—which often seem to happen after midnight.

Legal Issues

Legal issues may arise as to your authority in conducting or assisting in high technology crime investigations; as well as issues related to your contract. It is imperative, to avoid legal problems later, that all matters be clearly and concisely stated in the contract. The worst thing you would want is conflicts in contract interpretations, delayed payments, or refusal to pay what you billed the client, not to mention the problem of your reputation, which will follow you (good and bad) from client to client.

Above all, never begin an engagement without a signed contract. Make certain that the person signing it has the legal right to do so for the organization (usually an officer or director).

International Aspects

More and more cyber security consultants are working all over the world and with foreign clients. In dealing with such clients, it is important to:
- Avoid slang and colloquial terms,

- Learn as much of the foreign language and culture as possible,
- Make positive comments on the food and architecture,
- Use local hand gestures and volume of speech,
- Understand the foreign governments where you will be working,
- Understand the latest terrorist threats in the region,
- Explain cyber security terms in local context,
- Don't complain about their country or culture or brag about yours, and
- Avoid political discussions or, if you are dragged into a conversation, remain neutral.

QUESTIONS

- Do you have a career development plan?
- Do you keep it current?
- Do you document all your experiences and education?
- Do you keep your resume current?
- Do you have your interview techniques down so your answers seem natural?
- Do you keep a general list of questions to ask during the interview so that you come across as interested in that job and that corporation?
- Do you have a plan to continue to keep up with changes in your profession?
- Do you want to eventually be a consultant?
- If so, are you preparing for that time?
- Do you have a business plan?
- Are you prepared for "feast or famine" times?
- Do you have what it takes to be a consultant?

SUMMARY

Having and keeping current a career development plan, keeping up with changes in the profession, and always being prepared for that next job so that you can compete at the highest possible level take planning and hard work. However, if done right, it is worth the effort as it can lead to your success.

CHAPTER 16

A Look at the Possible Future

If you consciously try to thwart opponents, you are already late
Miyamoto Musashi, Japanese philosopher and samurai (1645)

The future is disorder. A door like this has cracked open five or six times since we got up on our hind legs. It is the best possible time to be alive, when almost everything you thought you knew is wrong
Tom Stoppard, Arcadia

Contents

In this final chapter,[1] we look to the future and some of its possibilities as they relate to our global, more interconnected than ever society; governments, businesses, groups, and individuals' actions and reactions; technology; and the impact that all these topics have on cyber security.

When the first edition of this book was published in 1998, we discussed the future based on the impact of topics like those identified above. Much

---

[1] Much of the information presented is taken from the author's book, coauthored with Dr. Andy Jones, *Global Information Warfare*, second edition, published by CRC Press and quoted with their permission.

of what is required for cyber security and its program is based on proven cyber security techniques that have been around for decades, albeit under various names such as computer security, network security, and information systems security.

Although you will find much of the following redundant with this book's first two editions, it is not being repeated because we are too lazy to start anew. It is because the same issues and same basic methods to solve them have not changed any more than the threats that the future holds. So, let's take out our crystal ball and see what the future continues to hold for all of us.

Unfortunately, even the basics of computer security standards that have been around for decades have often not been meet. In fact, even U.S. federal government computer security standards, required to be followed by government agencies, often are not followed.

> U.S. Secret Service refused to provide data on its computer security systems to the Department of Homeland Security ... preventing it from being able to verify if it was complying with security policies, ... The service ... "refused to comply with mandated computer security policies," according to the report by the DHS inspector general.[2]

> [2] http://news.yahoo.com/secret-needs-beef-security-report-193616952.html.

Will this change in the future? Maybe, but probably not, if history is any indication; and if so, probably not to the extent needed.

In the business world, the same applies under the guise that it is not cost-effective. However, now and into the future, as lack of security influences the bottom line, we hope that that will change.

One of the problems is that we base our security requirements, including cyber security requirements, on "risk," and business is fundamentally based on risk taking. When you base your security requirements on the concept of managing risk, you are accepting that you are only buying time and that, at some point, an incident will happen.

However, as constant successful attacks show, the costs to patch systems, to pay out money in lawsuits, and of the adverse public relations issues that follow and the losses in stock values as they plummet based on all that are higher than to "do it right the first time" and continuously update and improve over time. Corporate management just doesn't get it, maybe never will. Governments, groups, and individuals have declared war. Will that increase or decrease in the future? All indications point to an increase.

Although not officially confirmed, at least one major business was successfully attacked because the default passwords that came with the software were never changed. That was identified as an issue at least as far back as the 1980s, if not before. That first hacker attack based on that vulnerability can be traced to at least the first 300-baud external modem based on a hacker software program using the BASIC program language. For those of you who don't know what we are talking about because you weren't even born at that time, it proves my point.

Why won't these leaders in businesses, industries, and governments change? Some of the "blame" rests in democratic nations where people enjoy at least some semblance of freedom, and being told what to do and how to do it is something that they don't like and try to avoid. Security and law enforcement people, and auditors, are always telling people what to do and what not to do. In the future, a way must be found to make them willing to do it or make security totally invisible to them, so that not even a password or biometric access control will be needed, unless error-free, and the user does not have to take any action. An "avatar" that is secure, maybe? Not an easy task.

SURVIVING INTO THE FUTURE

Senior corporate and government leadership support continues to be missing and is necessary to develop the appropriate planning, guidance, strategy, skilled workforce, plant, and equipment. Corporations and nation-states need to boldly accept the new reality lest they wish to lose and not be able to reattain the competitive edge. Bureaucracy has no place in a cyber security-protected environment with nanosecond attack weapons requiring nanosecond responses. As the past and present have shown, they have not changed, and personally I do not hold out much hope for that to change in the future.

Senior leadership is essential for security to be meaningful to the bottom line or national security of nation-states. Corporate espionage will continue to be as big a threat as government espionage—maybe more so. Netspionage[3] has become a valuable tactic in support of a corporation or government agency's overall espionage and competitive business strategy.

Information warfare attacks against global corporations have dramatically increased since that topic and term was coined more than a decade

---

[3] For a basic overview on that topic, see the classic *Netspionage* published by Butterworth–Heinemann.

ago. Let's face it, we certainly are in a global information war whose agents are all those who attack our systems and networks for fun, profit, and power.

They have grown in sophistication and are expected to do so, from governments to individuals around the world. Sadly, it has also never been easier. Financial losses due to attacks have been caused by successful security breaches, from financial fraud and theft of proprietary information to identity theft to sabotage and blackmail. A new term has come into usage over the past few years—"advanced persistent threat," or APT for short. APT is used to describe an ongoing set of stealthy computer hacking attacks, often targeting a specific business sector, organization, or system.

The motivation for an APT can be for business or political gain. As the name implies, APT consists of three elements: the attack is of an advanced type, it is persistent, and it poses a threat. The term was first used to describe an ongoing series of attacks that originated in China, but is now more widely used. What is clear is that we can expect these types of attack not only to continue, but also to increase. Why wouldn't they? We aren't very good at detecting and responding to them, and as long as the benefits outweigh the cost, it is worthwhile for the nation-state or group that is doing them. There have not been any repercussions.

Attacks from a nation-state go on as we trade with them. There are no penalties for attacking our networks. So adversaries, and that includes general hackers, attack with impunity.

There is no silver bullet, no one-time expenditure of money to "fix the problem," and no means to put the genie back in the bottle. Enlightened and dedicated leadership willing to stay the course is necessary to guide governments and businesses into the future.

NEW OLD APPROACH TO SECURITY—DEFENSIVE APPROACH

The approach that responsible governments, businesses, and other entities must take in the future to ensure that we have the correct environment to endure is to at least get the basic security processes in place!

This will require a significant change in the attitude and approach that are taken at all levels of governance and management. We have been saying this since the 1980s and we say it here once again in 2016. We must get on a war footing. Good grief!

What will be required in order for the structures that we understand to survive is a large-scale adjustment in the attitudes taken on the whole subject. The truth of what we have said in the past, "... the threats are real;

and the adversaries are serious about it," must be realized. To a certain extent, that realization takes place generally only after a massive, successful attack. However, after it is over, and everyone has calmed down and begun to forget it, management goes back to business as usual and so do government agencies. We do not seem to be able to learn from either our own past or that of other organizations and seem to be doomed to continue to repeat it.

There has been fear (and still is) that a "pearlharbor.com," as Winn Schwartau puts it, is coming. We have already seen it in the physical world. Can the virtual world's Pearl Harbor be far behind? Mini ones are taking place globally and daily. However, as those of us in the profession have said this for so long, it is like the boy crying wolf, or like the Year 2000 "world will end as we know it" owing to the millennium bug crash that never happened; we must in the future choose our words more carefully and present the probable risks in a more objective way.

THE CHANGING ENVIRONMENT

To the present day, we have a history of understanding the issues that are related to attacks and cyber security that are imposed by physical, procedural, or personnel means. We also now understand the attacks' offensive and defensive worlds better than ever before and we hope we will get better at understanding the issues coming in the future, but understanding the issues and doing something about them are two different things.

THE NEED FOR ENLIGHTENED AND DEDICATED LEADERSHIP

If an environment in which organizations can feel safe from successful attacks is to be achieved, there need to be significant changes in the attitudes of both government and management at all levels of organization.

An infrastructure, at an international level, for collaboration between governments and law enforcement agencies already exists, but until ALL countries sign up to this and allocate sufficient resources to make it effective, there will continue to be issues.

There are currently countries that provide "safe harbor" to both organized criminals and terrorists that are using the Internet to carry out cyber attacks. Allegedly China is doing that relative to North Korea's information warriors operating in facilities on the Chinese mainland. There are also other countries that are, themselves, conducting cyber attack operations.

While this continues, our defenses need to be improved to meet every possibility.

Perhaps one of measures that can be put in place will be forums in which incidents can be reported in a suitable manner by individuals, companies, and governments and where best advice can be gained—without worrying about the political and power-play games.

While these exist in some countries and communities, they must be ubiquitous and easy to access. If attacks are taking place at nanosecond speeds over structures that do not recognize national borders, then any impediment that the current structures and organizations impose will encourage the perpetrator.

In government, in most of the democratic nations, an individual who will champion the cause of creating the correct environment for the protection of information systems is a conundrum. It would require a political nominee who is willing to put the cause that he or she is supporting not only above his or her own ambitions (cyber security is not an area that has a track record of producing new party or national leaders) but also above party loyalty. He or she would need to have seniority within his or her own party, cross-party support, and tenure in the post for a period of more than one term of office to have any significant effect.

Will that happen? I doubt it. When something happens, they will hold public hearings, look for scapegoats, get their faces on the news, pontificate from on high, but afterward go back to their old ways. If they want to find those partially responsible they have but to look in the mirror.

GLOBAL TRENDS[4]

It is imperative that when looking at cyber security, cyber attacks, and the like, one should begin by understanding the global trends because that is the environment that will dictate much of the offensive and defensive environments and tactics and help one understand the reason for such attacks, as well as helping to understand the defensive needs and solutions.

Every four years the U.S. National Intelligence Council (NIC) publishes an update of its "Global Trends" series that identifies key drivers and developments likely to shape world events a couple of decades into the future.

---

[4] See http://www.dni.gov/index.php/about/organization/national-intelligence-council-global-trends.

In the "Report of the National Intelligence Council's 2020 Project," the NIC included an executive summary, some of which is quoted below:

...At no time since the formation of the Western Alliance system in 1949 have the shape and nature of the international alignments been in such a state of flux ... The role of the United States will be an important variable in how the world is shaped, influencing the path that states and nonstate actors choose to choose ...

New Global Players: The likely emergence of China and India as well as others, as new major global players—similar to the advent of a united Germany in the 19th Century and a powerful United States in the early 20th Century—will transform the geopolitical landscape, with impacts potentially as dramatic as those in the previous two centuries ... how we mentally map the world in 2020 ...

New global players are not really that new; however, they have increased in power and impact on the world stage. Such shifts and changes are causing the status quo to fade away. Thus, there will be more nation fighting and with that the use of cyber tactics to assist nations in gaining dominance.

Impact of Globalization

...Globalization as an overreaching "mega-trend", a force so ubiquitous that it will substantially shape all other major trends in the world of 2020 ... the world economy is likely to continue to grow impressively: by 2020, it is projected to be about 80% larger than it was in 2000, and average per capita income will be roughly 50% higher ... Yet the benefits of globalization won't be global ... The greatest benefits of globalization will accrue to countries and groups that can access and adopt new technologies ... China and India are well positioned to become technology leaders, and even the poorest countries will be able to leverage prolific, cheap technologies to fuel—although at a slower rate—their own development ...

...More firms will become global, and those operating in a global arena will be more diverse, both in size and origin, more Asian and less Western in orientation. Such corporations, encompassing the current, large multinationals, will be increasingly outside the control of any one state and will be key agents of change in dispersing technology widely, further integrating the world economy, and promoting economic progress in the developing world ... Thus sharper demand driven competition for resources, perhaps accompanied by a major disruption of oil supplies, is among the key uncertainties.[5]

Today's economic wars have included offensive operations and these are expected to increase in volume and sophistication as the demand for economic power is supported and made more vulnerable by the world's dependency on technology.

[5] Report of the National Intelligence Council's 2020 Project.

New Challenges to Governance

The nation-state will continue to be the dominant unit of the global order, but economic globalization and the dispersion of technologies, especially information technologies, will place enormous new strains on governments ... political Islam will have a significant global impact leading to 2020, rallying disparate ethnic and national groups and perhaps even creating an authority that transcends national boundaries ... The so-called "third wave" of democratization may be partially reversed by 2020—particularly among the states of the former Soviet Union and in Southeast Asia, some of which never really embraced democracy ...

...With the international system itself undergoing profound flux, some of the institutions charged with managing global problems may be overwhelmed by them ...[6]

Technology can free us or help enslave us. We are even so much closer to George Orwell's predictions in his book, *1984*. It all depends who has dominant power over it in each nation, business, or group, including religious groups. One has to just look at the latest efforts by the NSA, CIA, and their counterparts in Russia, China, Iran, and the like to see that we citizens of the world are in danger of losing more of our freedoms, but maybe even our humanity. Of course, many agencies cite doing this in the name of security for us all. Many also would give up more freedom for security, but when is it enough?

> Like the Asian view of the world and life in Yin–Yang terms, we should look at our security versus our freedom in a similar fashion.
> When do we know when we are giving up too much of our freedom and how do we get it back, or will it already be too late?

Since the first edition of this book was written, there has been a dramatic increase in terrorism. Terrorists' offensive use of cyber war tactics, techniques, and cyber weapons has drastically increased and it is expected to do so into the future. Terrorists still prefer the propaganda effect or barbaric acts such as bombing, kidnappings, beheadings, and the like; however, they are ever increasingly relying on cyber weapons to exploit the vulnerabilities of their enemies—which are basically most of us.

In the past they have had to rely on the news media of the nations involved to propagate their messages, whereas now they have the means to get their messages to anyone who is willing to listen. Blogs and social media are great propaganda tools for spewing their hatred and are also great recruiting tools, as we have seen with "lone-wolf attacks." Physical attacks, yes, but recruited online.

[6] See footnote 5.

Pervasive Insecurity

Even as most of the world gets richer, globalization will profoundly shake up the status quo—generating enormous economic, cultural, and consequently political convulsions … The transition will not be painless and will hit the middle classes of the developed world in particular … Weak governments, lagging economy and extremism, and youth bulges will align to create a perfect storm for internal conflict in certain regions …

…The likelihood of great power conflict escalating into total war in the next 15 years is lower than at any time in the past century, unlike during previous centuries when local conflicts sparked world wars … Countries without nuclear weapons—especially in the Middle East and Northeast Asia—might decide to seek them as it becomes clear that their neighbors and regional rivals are doing so …[7]

We must also remember the power that individuals now have to exploit those that they feel are against them, whether they be governments, businesses, groups, or other individuals, for example, even school bullying causing some to commit suicide—and on a global war front. The worse the economy gets, the more hostile and dissatisfied a nation's citizens become. So, we may not have a global World War III, but certainly we are having thousands of global cyber attack skirmishes 24/7 and this, too, is certain to increase into the future.

Transmuting International Terrorism

The key factors that spawned international terrorism that has no signs of abating over the next 15 years … We expect that by 2020 al-Qa'ida will be superseded by similarly inspired Islamic extremist groups … Our greatest concern is that terrorists might acquire biological agents or, less likely, a nuclear device, either of which could cause mass casualties …[8]

This has already taken place with the advent of ISIS, and surely more groups will follow and even look at other terrorist groups as their enemies as they all continue vying for global domination. Surely their use of cyber attacks will not be limited to only nonterrorist groups.

Policy Implications

…Although the challenges ahead will be daunting, the United States will retain enormous advantage, playing a pivotal role across the broad range of issues—economic, technological, political and military—that no other state will match by 2020 … While no single country looks within striking distance of rivaling US military power by 2020, more countries will be in a position to make the United States pay a heavy price for any military action they oppose. The possession of chemical, biological, and/or nuclear weapons … also increase the potential cost of any military action by the US …

[7] See footnote 5.
[8] See footnote 5.

...A counterterrorism strategy that approaches the problem on multiple fronts offers the greatest chance of containing—and ultimately reducing—the terrorist threat ... Over the next 15 years the increasing centrality of ethical issues, old and new, have the potential to divide worldwide publics and challenge US leadership ...[9]

While governments around the world continue to think in terms of twentieth century weapons in this twenty-first century world, we must remember how vulnerable our technology-dependent governments and businesses are to successful cyber attacks. The more "advanced" a nation is and the greater its dependency on technology, the greater the exposure to cyber attacks.

It is a sad commentary, but chances are the use of cyber-offensive operations will continue to increase and the lack of viable defensive operations will allow more and more attacks to be successful, causing greater scales of damage as these cyber weapons continue to increase in sophistication while defensive tools continue to lag behind.

OFFENSIVE-DEFENSIVE CYBER ATTACKS

When will we get to the point at which a person, group, business, or government is going to say: "I'm mad as hell and I'm not going to take it anymore!" We are fast approaching that time, if not already past it.

If an entity is attacked, it is about time that the victims, in self-defense, go after those attacking them and not rely on someone else to protect them. Obviously, agencies such as the FBI and local police investigators come in after the attacks, run their investigations, and may even identify the adversary. Then what? No jurisdiction, so no prosecution. So, basically, maybe time for a little "Wild West" independent action?

What we need in the future is a covert "mirror-image" software program that will not only deflect the attack but have that program turn on itself and bounce back to attack the attacker.

Yes, some government agencies are beginning to take covert, offensive-defensive actions. However, more is needed at all levels of victimization. The "reap what ye have sown," "eye for an eye," old-style philosophy and justice maybe need to come back in vogue?

Some will criticize "vigilante" justice, warning that we can't be like them; chaos will reign. The ones saying that are primarily those in law enforcement who fear that dependency on them will wane, politicians who fear losing power, and those who have no "skin in the game," among others.

[9] See footnote 5.

THE FUTURE OF THE INTERNET

Because of the power and influence of the Internet, some nations want to control it, others want to have the United Nations be responsible for its management. Governments don't like something they cannot control to their benefit. The day the Internet falls into political hands to control it, our freedom on the Internet as we now enjoy it, we as users, is doomed. I would hope that, as users, we will not allow that to happen.

That being said, some are optimistic that new technology will allow global users to reconnect on a global scale using another form of technology as it supersedes the "old-fashioned" Internet. In fact, global users may even be able to establish their own mini-Internets and connect to other mini-Internets through advanced communications, even embedded microprocessor technology as a form of cyber-telepathy. They become their own Internet service providers. One can only hope.

QUESTIONS

- Are you preparing now for the future of cyber security, information warfare, cyber-terrorist attacks, and the like?
- Do you keep up with technology and project what-if new technologies into your future cyber security plans and program?
- What do you think the future holds for all of us if the Internet freedom we now have is taken away?
- Will you be a freedom fighter or a cyber security officer that "just follows orders?"
- Do you maintain a database of defensive software and offensive software (that used by the cyber attackers) that you can use when needed and also compare your database of cyber attack software to incoming events to see if they are an attack?
- What are you, as a cyber security officer, going to do now to meet the future challenges of cyber security?

SUMMARY

The saying "the more things change, the more they stay the same" certainly seems to be holding true. Although we have and will continue to have advances in technology allowing for more sophisticated offensive cyber attacks and defenses, we are fighting more cyber battles and losing more of them than ever before.

In the future, we must reconsider our defensive approaches, fund them as a high priority in every entity, and go on the offensive as a defensive approach.

> The future is disorder. A door like this has cracked open five or six times since we got up on our hind legs. It is the best possible time to be alive, when almost everything you thought you knew is wrong.
>
> **Tom Stoppard, Arcadia**

INDEX

Note: Page numbers followed by "f" indicate figures, "t" indicate tables, and "b" indicate boxes.

HTCPP. *See* High-technology crime prevention program (HTCPP)
Human factor, 24–26
Human Resources (HR), 141

I

IAPPD 500–1. *See* Information Assets Protection Policy Document 500–1 (IAPPD 500–1)
IE. *See* Information environment (IE)
IMs. *See* Instant messages (IMs)
Industrial Age, 12
Info-warriors, 89
Information
  assurance, 263
  categories, 181–182
  Information Age, 12
  information-based processes, 263
  superiority, 267
  value, 180, 182
    business information types and examples, 183–184
    time factor, 183
Information Assets Protection Policy Document 500–1 (IAPPD 500–1), 142, 145–146
Information environment (IE), 132, 151, 251, 263
  breakdowns in, 261
  components, 260
Information operations (IO), 266
Information security (InfoSec), 36, 106, 263–264. *See also* Cyber security
Information system (IS), 264, 268
Information technology (IT), 104, 136–137, 202, 254
Information warfare (IW), 91, 95, 247, 252, 264
  for attaining and maintaining competitive advantage, 268–269
  business, 256–257
  CKO, 270
  COTS software, 258–259
  goals and objectives, 269–270
  government organization, 257–258
  information, 259–260
  KM, 271–272
  levels and functions, 257

NCB, 271
  in pocketbook, 254
    defensive attacks, 255–256
    high-profile events, 255
  possibilities, 248
    aircraft pilots, 249
    local power companies, 249
    "Locust Swarm" program, 248
    water pumping stations, 250
  TOR, 261
    C2W, 263
    cyber, 262
    decision-maker act, 264–265
    defensive IW, 266
    information superiority, 267
    IW-related environment, 263
    KM, 264
    military psychological operations, 265
    NSTISSC 4009, 268
  warfare, 250
    generations, 250–251
InfoSec. *See* Information security (InfoSec)
INFOSEC. *See* National Information Systems Security (INFOSEC)
Instant messages (IMs), 79
Intel's Pentium III, 83
Internal use only information types, 183
International Security in Cyberspace, 53
Internet, 17, 30, 52, 75
  annihilation of time and space, 77–78
  ARPA, 75–76
  communication technologies, 76
  cyberspace and GII, 77
  electronic commerce, 77
  future, 311
  global nervous system, 75
  handgun, 78
  impact, 17–19
  Internet-enabled communications, 15
  organizational impacts, 19–20
  protocols, 76
  to share information, 20–21
  society's struggles, 78
  World Wide Web, 77
Internet, Birth of, 13–15
Internet Governance Developments, 53
Internet service providers (ISPs), 29, 78

Printed in the United States
By Bookmasters